Contents

Introduction

The teaching of English to bilingual students is a field which has always been marked by rapid growth, a dynamic philosophy and an ever-increasing range of work. Even as we write, the on-going debate is being stimulated by the findings of the CRE Investigation into ESL teaching in Calderdale and the House of Commons Select Committee Report on the Bangladeshis in the London Borough of Tower Hamlets. Any collection of papers on ESL can therefore only represent a selection of current issues at one point in its history, in this case at a time when the debate is shifting away from a narrow concern with English language teaching towards the place of language in education and a positive recognition of linguistic and cultural diversity in modern Britain.

The book consists of a series of papers reflecting individual views which we as editors have grouped around a common area. Each section begins with a short introduction which pulls out the major themes but there is no attempt to present an agreed view within or between the sections. Not all authors will concur with the ideas expressed by other contributors.

The papers have been written by a wide range of people working in education with bilingual adults. They include teachers with extensive practical classroom experience and advisers with a national or regional overview of practice and curriculum development, those working in community and adult education and others whose context is vocational training and further education. A number of contributors bring a bilingual and bicultural perspective to their writing; all have wide professional experience both within language teaching and in education generally.

Authors have been free to write in their own style. This is reflected not simply in the way they have organized their contributions but also in the language they have chosen to use. Many of the terms used in ESL have political connotations, e.g. *black*. As editors we have not imposed any language on the contributors but readers may wish to refer to the glossary at the back of the book for definitions of terms with which they are not familiar.

The book has been written for all teachers who are interested in language and learning and particularly for those who teach bilingual students, whether as learners of English or as students or trainees studying in linguistically-mixed groups. It is not a practical handbook on how to teach but is intended to stimulate discussion of classroom teaching and related issues. To this end the book is organized so that readers may dip into it to read individual papers or sections.

Over the last decade we have seen the emergence of a range of publications on issues related to this field. We hope this volume will contribute to the literature but look forward in turn to those publications which must supersede it so that the debate can be carried forward into the 1990s.

Acknowledgements

The publisher would like to thank the following for their permission to use copyright material:
Modern English Publications and the British Council for 'ESL Provision in the Post-school Sector: Developments and Dilemmas' by Sandra Nicholls published in *ELT Documents 121, English as a Second Language in the United Kingdom;* Writers' and Readers' Publishing Cooperative for 'Dress Factory' by Mahbubar Rahman published in *Classrooms of Resistance* edited by C. Searle; The Institute of Education, University of London for the use of the pie charts and table (pp 16–18) taken from *Languages in London* by Reid, Smith and Morawska; Associated Book Publishers UK Ltd for the use of the pie charts (page 13) and table on page 15 published in *The Other Languages of England* by the Linguistic Minorities Project, © Routledge & Kegan Paul; ILEA Learning Materials Service for the use of worksheet 8 taken from *World in a City; a teaching pack* produced by the ILEA Learning Materials Service.

Section 1 Influences and Developments

ESL provision in the post-school sector — a historical perspective

Sandra Nicholls

Twenty years ago there was virtually no ESL provision in the post-school education sector. There were, of course, some language classes for foreign students visiting Britain, and there were a substantial number of English and general Education courses for native speakers — and, no doubt, these courses were attended by adult immigrants.[1] However, the notion of a need for specific and specialized provision did not really exist. By the mid seventies the majority of ESL provision was still *ad hoc* and taught either by volunteers or part-time teachers. There was very little professional training available and those working in the field certainly had no professional voice. Today the picture is dramatically different. ESL provision is firmly established in the post-school sector. There are two nationally recognized in-service training qualifications and a national professional organization. There is a high level of political consciousness and concern within the field which is expressed through anti-racist initiatives and the positive validation of bilingualism in the educational process.

From the sixties to the eighties

What, then, has happened across the intervening years to bring about such change? To answer this question it is necessary to delve back into the conscious beginnings of ESL in the post-school sector. I use the word 'conscious' advisedly and in a national sense because, although Britain has always had non-indigenous second language speakers, it was not until forced migration started to cause large numbers of East African Asians to arrive in the 1960s that the need for language provision for adults was officially recognized and ESL schemes came into existence.

The late sixties

The general belief in the late sixties was that once the immigrants had acquired English they would be quickly assimilated into British society at large. It was also presumed that the men would pick up the language at work, that the children would absorb it at school, and that it was only the women, isolated in the home, who might require formal English language tuition — and even then, it would probably only be a temporary need, for six months or so.

The organization and content of tuition was, of necessity, extremely pragmatic. Volunteers and part-time teachers taught women (and some men) English for day-to-day interactions. The lessons took place either in the students' homes or in locally convenient centres, such as primary schools, community centres and clinics. There was little, if any, specialist training for the teachers, and apart from home-produced materials the only materials available for adults were those commercially devised for the newly burgeoning EFL market — the contents of which had little relevance to the lives of bilingual British citizens working and bringing up their families in the UK.

The early seventies

By the first half of the seventies the assimilationist 'melting pot' theory had been replaced by the longer-term view of integration. It was recognized that acquiring English for the workplace, the school curriculum and day-to-day needs was both more complex and required greater time than had at first been thought. ESL was obviously not the temporary band-aid that had initially been envisaged. Nor was it only the women who had need of English language tuition.

In 1974, money was made available to establish a national industrial language training scheme which was to concentrate on providing English language tuition and management training in the workplace. At the same time, the post-school sector, particularly adult education, began to make a more structured offer to second-language speakers of English. This was done both through 'graded' classes at adult education centres and through a more complex network of classes in the community. Diversification was beginning to take place — although the concern at that time was more to do with the extent than with the nature of ESL provision. ESL literacy classes were becoming more commonplace and there was a growth in specific-purpose classes for groups such as those seeking employment or attending ante-natal clinics. This additional provision did not replace the volunteer home-tuition schemes; indeed, they were still seen as an essential link between the community and the educational establishments. The new provision complemented and extended what already existed. A national training scheme, specifically designed for teachers of ESL to adults, began in 1975 when the Inner London Education Authority piloted the Royal Society of Arts' Certificate in the Teaching of English to Adult Immigrants. Before then, the little training that had existed had been mainly for volunteers — a situation reflected by the publication of a home-tutor kit in the early seventies by the Community Relations Commission. A second publication appeared in 1978.

The late seventies

During the second half of the seventies, ESL received a new impetus largely through statistics revealed in the 1977 *PEP Report* (Smith, 1977) — stark figures like those shown in Table 1, about the amount of English spoken by Asian adults.

Table 1 *Speaking English only slightly or not at all*

	%
African Asian men	19
Indian men	26
Pakistani men	43
African Asian women	41
Indian women	60
Pakistani women	77

These revelations prompted the BBC to produce its first series aimed at the 'non English-speaking' community. *Parosi*, a soap opera, actively encouraged Asian women to learn English, either through home-tuition or by joining an ESL class. Many local education authorities, anticipating the same flood of requests for tuition that had followed the BBC Adult Literacy series *On the move*, looked seriously at their local ad hoc provision, and began to make contingency plans.

Unfortunately, central government did not set aside the one million pounds which had been made available for staffing during the Adult Literacy Campaign — although some money was earmarked for new equipment and materials in the Urban Aid Programme. In the event, the *Parosi* campaign did not bring forth the number of requests that had been anticipated. What it did do, however, was put the language needs of adults firmly on local and national education agendas, and by bringing ESL teachers and organizers across the country into a network for the first time, it sowed the seeds of what was to become the national professional organization, The National Association for Teaching English as a Second Language to Adults (NATESLA).

People in this field were still very much concerned with the availability and accessibility of ESL provision for all who needed it and desired it. Among other ventures, a caravan was used to provide mobile ESL in Bradford and a double-decker bus was fitted out as both classroom space and crèche in South London. Information leaflets were produced in as many local languages as possible and libraries displayed the national logo to signal the availability of ESL tuition in their area.

As far as the curriculum was concerned, the cornerstones were still the day-to-day language and literacy needs of adult migrants 'adjusting' to life in Britain, although there was emerging a concern about the relevance of what was being taught. This concern was, of course, to grow, but meanwhile the overwhelming belief held by most ESL providers was that a greater command of the English language would inevitably lead to better education and employment prospects which in their turn would, again inevitably, enhance the quality of life of the migrant communities. Looking back, we can shudder at the naïvety of this view and realize that it was based on an extreme deficit model of the ethnic minority communities. Despite the approach to ESL teaching being grounded in the best traditions of adult education, we had neither thrown off its monocultural yoke nor come to terms with the wider and more far-reaching issues affecting Britain's ethnic communities.

Meanwhile, the seventies closed with the second BBC series designed for bilingual adults, *Speak for Yourself*, and the accompanying radio programmes for teachers of ESL. This series not only focused on the language and access information required for day-to-day situations, but also explored the issues of cross-cultural awareness, underlining the fact that communication is a two-way process with the onus for effective communication lying with both non-native and native speaker of English alike. This refinement reflected the changing focus of the ESL curriculum at the time.

Into the eighties

By the late seventies and the beginning of the eighties, the belief in integration had been replaced by the reality of cultural pluralism. Britain was having to recognize and try to accept that it was now a multilingual, multicultural, multiracial and multifaith society and that this diversity was not temporary — it was here to stay. Statements made at the time about the aims of ESL provision reflected this new climate of opinion (Nicholls and Naish, 1981):

> English as a second language provision is designed for people living, working and bringing up families in this country. Like all adults, second language speakers need to:
> — make informed choices about their own lives and the lives of their children
> — be able to take advantage of the opportunities for further education and training
> — understand the institutions and structures of the society in which they live so that they can play an active part if they so wish.

This was the period when local education authorities began producing multicultural policy statements, and when school curricula were called into question over their cultural bias. It was also the time when major changes began to take place in ESL — changes which were brought about by a combination of three sets of factors — content and pedagogy, the changing economic situation, and racism.

Content and teaching methods

Firstly, the earlier battles to establish ESL provision for adults had to a great extent been won. No one now questioned that ESL should be made available as part of the post-school education offer for bilingual adults. This situation was reinforced by the arrival of the Vietnamese 'boat people' and by the subsequent government funding of English language tuition in the reception centres and, later, as part of the resettlement programme. The recognition I have already mentioned released ESL organizers from their earlier preoccupations with the funding and quantity of provision, and enabled them instead to focus more on the quality and relevance of what was on offer. Questions were raised about the linear progression of ESL provision. Did such a step-by-step model help or hinder adult bilinguals? Was the implied goal of 'native-speaker competence' either realistic or even desirable? How could ESL teachers best establish realistic goals — goals which would include not only language and literacy, but also access, study skills etc. — and how could they demonstrate the transferability of these skills and thereby increase the students' confidence and autonomy? Other questions were raised concerning the adult nature of the ESL offer. How far were the life experiences of students attending ESL classes really being taken into account? To what extent were their skills and interests being tapped in the language learning process? How could the ESL classroom acquire a more democratic base, and how could the ESL teacher create a more equal learning partnership?

These, and other questions like them, led to various developments, the most influential of which was the creation of linked-skill courses where the acquisition of communication skills is integrated with the learning or expression of practical skills (e.g. dressmaking, car maintenance, computer programming). This form of provision proved extremely successful, providing students with a realistic and stimulating language learning environment in which their confidence increased. Such classes continue to play an important part in provision for bilingual adults. However, a significant development has been the extension of this notion of language support into the main curriculum where it is applied to a wide range of academic and vocational courses at all levels.

Another area that ESL organizers focused on was that most challenging of teaching situations — the mixed level community class. Despite all the difficulties that these classes presented, they were for logistical and very good community reasons, the mainstay of provision in many areas. In this situation how could the isolation of the lone teacher be overcome? What was the most appropriate and most possible form of syllabus design for groups which might include a newly arrived graduate bride learning alongside a recently widowed woman who had no experience of formal education but who had lived in Britain for many years? There were no ready answers then, and there are still few today, but the use of more team teaching was explored, and greater effort was put into the development of suitable resource materials.

The changing economic situation   Another major factor that affected ESL at the time was the dramatically changing economic situation. The recession was now deepening and in its wake came the high growth of unemployment — a situation which often hit ethnic minority communities earliest and hardest. The government response to growing unemployment overall was to use the Manpower Services Commission to fund 'up-skilling' and retraining courses for adults, and vocational preparation courses for young people. The majority of these courses were based in colleges of further education, and although initially the particular needs of bilingual adults and young people were overlooked, eventually some special programmes were evolved. These included ESL preparation courses for adults, skills training for particular minority groups and work experience courses for bilingual school-leavers. These courses had an important, if indirect, effect on the development and growth of ESL provision and language support for bilingual students in the further education sector. However, at this time energies were mainly focused on obtaining a greater number of preparatory courses for bilingual adults, on establishing study skill courses for those wishing to gain access to academic programmes, and on providing more foundation courses for those school-leavers who had not had sufficient time within the school system to acquire the language and the general education that would enable them to enter further education 'mainstream' provision.

Growing awareness of racism

The third factor, one which caused a shift in our perspective in ESL, was the increasing national awareness and concern among teachers about the growth of racism, particularly in the urban areas. In ESL we began to question our provision in terms of racism. We asked what we were actually achieving through what were, by now, our traditional language programmes. Were we contributing to the educational offer to bilingual adults, or were we, in fact, by not challenging the monolingual entry requirements of both mainstream education and the market place, hindering people's chances? Questions like these also caused us to look at our own steadily increasing ranks of language teachers and to note the very obvious lack of ethnic minority teachers in our own area of work. Were we as guilty of institutional racism as those establishments which we were so quick to criticize? It was, however, not until we were well into the eighties that practical steps began to be taken on these matters (FEU, 1987).

With the eighties came an expansion in specialist in-service training which signalled the increasing professionalism in the field. The original RSA Certificate, Teaching English to Adult Immigrants, since renamed the Diploma in the Teaching of English as a Second Language in Further, Adult and Community Education, continues to be offered in various parts of the country. Materials developed by teachers as part of their course work make an important contribution to local ESL resource banks, as well as sometimes being published more widely. In 1981 the RSA launched a new certificate — the Initial Certificate in the Teaching of English as a Second Language to Adults[2] — which has had far-reaching effects, one of the most important being the increased recruitment and training of ethnic minority teachers. This in turn has led those responsible for leading courses to re-examine the ethnocentric bias of much of the training and methods of assessment (NATESLA, 1986).

Continuing concerns

In the past decade the debate on ESL has diversified, and it is now taking place at a variety of levels within a wide range of educational provision. However, two overriding matters of concern remain for everyone involved in the teaching of bilingual adults:

Cultural and linguistic diversity

The first of these is the importance of recognizing and utilizing the linguistic and cultural resources that bilingual and multilingual adults bring with them to both language acquisition and other areas of learning. The ILEA (1983) discussion document *Mother Tongue and ESL* has led to some important developments. In the classroom, teachers are using their students' knowledge of other languages within their lessons; in some local teacher-training programmes, bilingual method-ologies are being developed as an alternative approach to language teaching and learning; the recruitment of more teachers from ethnic minority groups is making it possible to extend the scope and nature of provision and to provide more appropriate counselling services. ESL organizers have also been turning their attention to the world outside the educational establishments, and following the example set by Industrial Language Training, have been working with professional agencies on language and cross-cultural awareness programmes for groups such as health visitors and staff at job centres. Similar work is also taking place within the adult education service, though at present it is still on a small scale (Shackman, 1988).

Equality of opportunity

The second concern is more complex and relates to the problems teachers face in confidently discussing the need for equality of oppor-tunity for all, while operating in a climate which seems to do little to combat institutionalized racism and in an education system in which it is difficult to bring about the changes necessary actively to encourage and support bilingual adults within mainstream provision. Here we are facing two dilemmas. On the one hand we recognize that no real progress can be made until fundamental structural and attitudinal changes take place, both within the educational service and outside. On the other hand, we are aware of the needs of bilingual adults who at present are having to function in a system which equates less than total native-speaker fluency in English (just *one* of the languages used by bilingual or multilingual adults in this country) with a general deficiency in all other areas of learning (Robson, 1988).

Various steps have been taken to try and minimize the disadvantages facing bilingual students, including the development of a variety of forms of language support, specific targeting of vocational courses and the creation of alternative access routes for those who do not possess the traditional entry qualifications, but who wish to enrol in professional training programmes. These developments obviously represent an important shift away from the view that it is merely language which impedes the bilingual adult from participating fully in the education system. However, such provision must be perceived as only an interim measure, and continuing efforts must be made to bring about funda-mental changes within the education service and society as a whole (FEU, 1987).

As teachers we have a particular responsibility to help bring about these changes. In the classroom, we must be certain that value is always given to the students' linguistic and cultural diversity, and that all our teaching is built on the knowledge and skills that they already possess. In the institutional context we must continue to challenge the deficit image of the bilingual adult and to work towards a provision where equality of opportunity is secured for all students. Most important of all, within the education service we must work with others to achieve a post-school provision where no bilingual adults are impeded in their progress through the system because of racial, cultural or linguistic bias.

Notes

1. Students who do not speak English as their first language have been variously characterized in the education service as immigrants, second-language speakers, ESL students and bilingual students. These terms are used throughout this article in order to reflect the particular perspective of the period under discussion. Currently the term 'bilingual' is used because it most accurately describes an adult who has to operate in two or more languages. Its use, however, does not denote any specific level of attainment or fluency.

2. This part-time course was designed to meet the growing need for an introductory level qualification which could be taken by experienced volunteers, trained language teachers wishing to move into ESL from other areas, and less experienced ESL teachers.

Acknowledgement

This paper is based on an article which originally appeared in *English as a Second Language in the United Kingdom*, ELT Document 121, Modern English Publications in association with The British Council.

References

FEU (1987) *FE in Black and White*, Longman for FEU

ILEA (1983) *Mother Tongue and ESL*, National Extension College, Cambridge

NATESLA (1986) *Training of Teachers of English as a Second Language in the Post-16 Sector*, National Extension College, Cambridge

NICHOLLS, S. AND NAISH, J. (1981) *Teaching English as a Second Language*, BBC, London

ROBSON, M. (1988) *Language, Learning and Race*, Longman for FEU

SHACKMAN, J. (1988) *The Right to be Understood*, NEC

SMITH, D. J. (1977) *Racial Disadvantage in Britain*, Penguin

Minority languages in England — a neglected resource?

Euan Reid

Languages and speakers

For many centuries refugees and migrants have settled in England from all parts of Europe. There have, for example, been speakers of Flemish from the Low Countries, French-speaking Huguenots, Spanish-speaking and Portuguese-speaking Sephardic Jews, Italians from both the North and the South, Polish-speaking, Yiddish-speaking and German-speaking Ashkenazy Jews. By now these older migrations have been almost entirely assimilated, at least in terms of language use in daily life.

However, since the Second World War, urban England has been linguistically transformed. In the first place, many refugees and 'displaced persons' from Eastern and Central Europe had settled here by the late 1940s, resulting in important communities of speakers of languages such as Polish and Ukrainian in various parts of the country, (Linguistic Minorities Project, 1985). Later, like other industrialized countries in Western Europe, Britain attracted a large immigrant workforce to feed the expanding economy of the 1950s and 1960s. In Britain's case, workers came in particular from the Caribbean, India and Pakistan, Cyprus and Hong Kong. Families followed from all these countries, and are still following when they can meet the now much more stringent immigration control mechanisms.

In the 1970s and 1980s, refugees and settlers have continued to arrive from, among other places, East Africa (after the expulsions during the Amin regime), Vietnam (in the wake of the settlement of the war there), Iran, Ethiopia and Chile (as a result of civil strife in these countries), and from Bangladesh — the main source of current 'secondary' immigration.

From 'ESL learner' to 'bilingual student'

It is probably above all the arrival in British schools and colleges of so many students from South Asia and the Caribbean that has made it impossible to continue with the *de facto* assimilationist policies that have typified the mainstream educational response to immigration over the centuries. As long as the migrants had white skins, they had the option of more or less complete anglicization, and nearly all took that option — at least as far as language was concerned.

However, comparative economic decline, the growth of racism among the indigenous white population, and the response of many minorities to that racism is closing off the option of complete cultural assimilation. We find in this context increasing interest in alternative linguistic and cultural values.

The expression of this in terms of the education system is, at least in part, an extension to a more comprehensive approach of the formerly exclusively ESL-focused language education. In this teachers look at all aspects of what the language learner brings to the classroom and take as their target the development of a full linguistic repertoire, appropriate to the multiple roles which language users may adopt in the course of living in a multilingual society.

The role of 'teacher of ESL' has therefore been extended, and needs to be extended further, to embrace skills which will facilitate the development of other components in the bilingual or multilingual repertoires of their students. Hence the inclusion in this collection of a contribution about minority languages.

Facts and figures?   No one at the moment is in a position to say with confidence how many speakers of different languages there are in England, or how these languages are distributed. This is because even this most basic linguistic–demographic information is not collected through the ten-yearly National Censuses as conducted in England. (The otherwise identical Census forms for Wales, Scotland and Northern Ireland do have such questions — but only about the indigenous Celtic minority languages.)

Language surveys of their school-age populations conducted by local education authorities do, however, provide a reasonably reliable indication of the current distribution of languages other than English in selected areas. These were first carried out by the Inner London Education Authority, beginning in 1978 (ILEA, 1979), and from 1981 onwards on a two-yearly basis (ILEA, 1981, 1983, 1985, 1987).

In 1980 and 1981 the Linguistic Minorities Project (LMP) collaborated with five LEAs in other parts of the country, to conduct Schools Language Surveys in their areas. Fig. 1 represents a summary of the findings of these surveys, and more detail is available in the Working Papers from the project (Reid, Morawska and Couillaud, 1984).

A word of caution is necessary when interpreting the data in Fig. 1. Although these schools language surveys were very carefully planned and conducted so as to minimize the risk of serious distortion, what is represented there is the total numbers of school pupils who answered positively a teacher's question about languages other than English used at home. It is very likely that some pupils chose not to reveal their use of other languages, where, for example, they believed that the teacher or the school did not value or even approve of such use. It is also possible that other pupils exaggerated their linguistic skills.

Since these studies were completed, further surveys using the same instrument have been undertaken in the Outer London Boroughs of Brent (1982 and 1985), Hounslow (1983), and Ealing (1985), as well as in Newcastle-upon-Tyne (1984). Bradford undertook further surveys based partly on the LMP model (1983 and 1985), and Barnet has used the ILEA approach. In most cases details of these surveys are available direct from the LEAs, even where they have not been more widely published.

The situation represented in Fig. 1 is at the moment the nearest approximation available to a partial linguistic demography of urban England. Since the school population surveyed represented in each case approximately ten year-cohorts, multiplication of the individual language figures by five or six gives an indication of the probable total numbers of speakers of a particular language in the place surveyed.

Unfortunately, it is not possible to extrapolate from these figures to totals for numbers of speakers of particular minority languages in the country as a whole. Nevertheless, even incomplete information is helpful to local educational administrators and planners. It ought also to be useful to local minority organizations, as they attempt to negotiate equitable and rationally-based decisions about local provision and distribution of educational resources.

What is common to all areas so far surveyed is that everywhere a very wide range of languages is represented — Inner London schools in 1987 had more than 170. Nevertheless, outside Inner London some three or

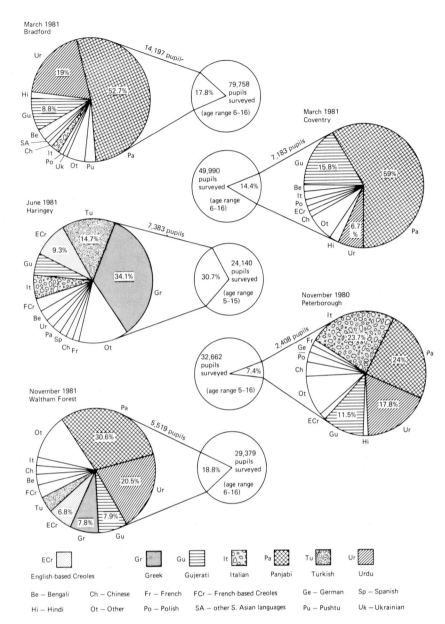

Fig. 1: *Proportions of bilingual school students and main languages spoken in five areas of England, 1980–81. (Source: Linguistic Minorities Project, 1985.)*

four languages together account for perhaps three-quarters of the bilinguals in an area. Outside Greater London the dominant minority languages are clearly Panjabi, Urdu and Gujerati, and in the London area the most frequently spoken languages other than English are Bengali, Turkish and Greek.

The significance of these recurrent patterns is that they undermine a still commonly used excuse for not doing anything in the schools and colleges to give support to or make use of community languages: the idea that there are simply far too many different languages for educational institutions to cope with the logistics.

In spite of the Swann Report's (DES, 1985) dismissive attitude towards the role of the mainstream school in supporting minority languages, many education authorities continue to develop language education policies which are much more supportive. For example, they encourage the continuing use of home languages after initial school entry, they make it possible for children to develop literacy in the minority language alongside literacy in English, and they extend the traditional range of modern languages taught in secondary schools to include some of the major community languages in their localities. (Reid, 1984; Houlton, 1985.) The European Commission Directive which came into force in 1981 (EC, 1977) has given some 'external' support to those who can overcome their ideological objections to using such support.

Language skills and language uses

The levels of skills in various languages, and their use by bilingual speakers in different contexts and for different purposes, has only begun to be studied in England. The major source of easily available data on this is from the *Adult Language Use Survey* (ALUS), conducted by the Linguistic Minorities Project in Coventry, Bradford and London in 1980–81 (LMP, 1983, 1985), and studied further in follow-up research by the Community Languages & Education Project (Smith, Morawska and Reid, 1984; Morawska, Reid and Smith, 1985; Reid, Smith and Morawska, 1985).

The ALUS involved a total of some 2,500 interviews conducted by bilingual interviewers among eleven linguistic minorities in the three places mentioned. The languages included were Sylheti–Bengali, Chinese, Greek, Gujerati, Italian, Panjabi–Urdu, Panjabi–Gurmukhi, Polish, Portuguese, Turkish and Ukrainian. ('Panjabi–Urdu' refers to Muslim speakers who use spoken Panjabi, but whose language of literacy is usually Urdu; 'Panjabi–Gurmukhi' refers to mostly Sikh speakers of Panjabi who when they write use the Gurmukhi script.)

The data available from the ALUS include information about speakers' linguistic repertoires, language-learning histories, language use in domestic, work and leisure contexts, and respondents' attitudes to minority language maintenance. We concentrate here on two aspects which may be of particular interest to teachers of English as a Second Language to Adults: level of linguistic skills, and language use in the domestic and work contexts.

Table 1 summarizes for all the ALUS respondents their own assessments of their language skills, in both the minority language and English. Spoken skills in the minority languages are reported as being pretty uniformly high, with the possible exceptions of the Italian and Chinese samples in Coventry. In these cases the researchers had reason to believe that the relevant question may have been interpreted as referring to standard Italian and Cantonese respectively, whereas many of the respondents were speakers of other varieties.

The proportions claiming at least moderate literacy skills in the minority language were much more variable, ranging from around half

Table 1 *Summary of language skills for ALUS respondents*

% of respondents who:

(A) understand and speak the minority language 'fairly well' or 'very well'
(B) read and write the minority language 'fairly well' or 'very well'
(C) understand and speak English 'fairly well' or 'very well'
(D) read and write English 'fairly well' or 'very well'

		A	B	C	D
Bengali					
Coventry	N = 79	98	70	52	37
London	N = 185	94	70	47	40
Chinese					
Coventry	N = 43	79	51	44	30
Bradford	N = 50	88	28	10	6
London	N = 137	96	65	47	42
Greek					
London	N = 193	94	66	72	57
Gujerati					
Coventry	N = 203	98	84	74	64
London	N = 99	98	79	76	72
Italian					
Coventry	N = 108	73	63	83	39
London	N = 94	81	69	65	34
Panjabi (G)					
Coventry	N = 200	99	61	67	60
Bradford	N = 96	99	54	54	45
Panjabi (U)					
Coventry	N = 86	98	57	61	44
Bradford	N = 177	99	47	36	28
Polish					
Coventry	N = 168	92	82	91	64
Bradford	N = 155	92	83	84	55
Portuguese					
London	N = 196	88	74	50	27
Turkish					
London	N = 197	98	80	75	46
Ukrainian					
Coventry	N = 48	92	83	50	31

Source: Linguistic Minorities Project, 1985: 188

to more than four-fifths of the different local linguistic minorities —
leaving aside the Bradford Chinese sample, where there were again
special factors at play.

Skills in spoken English are, with the one exception of the Italian
speakers in Coventry, rated markedly lower than the equivalent skills in

the minority languages. However, they are by now substantial in most groups, and it is above all in English literacy skills that the existing needs are perceived to be. In nearly two-thirds of the local linguistic minorities represented in our survey, under half the respondents claimed even moderate skills, pointing to a very clear need for resources to be deployed to develop English literacy among adult bilingual students.

Two key contexts for the future of minority language use in England are clearly the home and work. Fig. 2 and Table 2 respectively set out the data from ALUS on language use in these two settings.

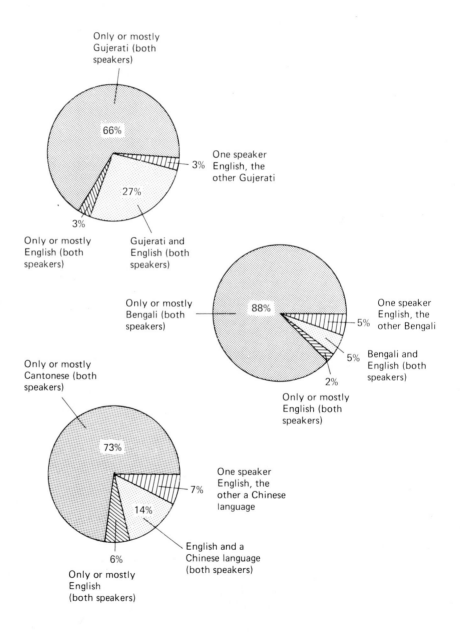

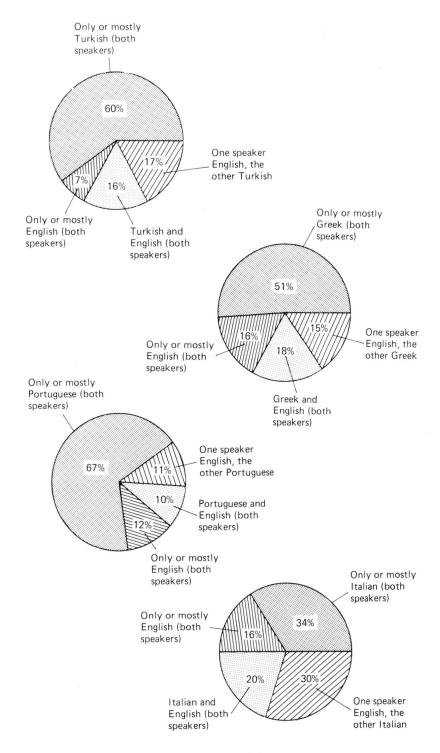

Fig. 2: *Household language use among London ALUS respondents in 1981. (Source: Reid, Smith and Morawska, 1985.)*

The data about household language use presented here relate to interactions between all the household members reported, not only to those between bilingual respondents and other bilingual people. So the possible permutations are complex, as the pie diagrams show. Nevertheless, the high proportion of Sylheti–Bengali-speaking and Cantonese-speaking minorities still making use of the minority language at home is striking, and contrasts markedly with the longer-established Italian-speaking and Greek-speaking communities.

As far as workplace language use is concerned, there is also a very wide range, as Table 2 demonstrates, not so much between proportions of respondents who have at least one colleague who speaks the same language, as between those where all other fellow workers can do so. The highest proportions are in both cases again among Sylheti–Bengali and Cantonese samples.

It is evident from the data presented in this section that there is a very rich resource in England now in terms of speakers of a huge range of languages from almost every corner of the world. At least the newer

Table 2 *Language use in the work setting among London ALUS respondents in 1981*

% of working respondents

(A) where at least one fellow worker can speak the minority language
(B) where all fellow workers can speak the minority language
(C) (who work for someone else) where the boss can speak the minority language
(D) who use only or mostly English to all the workmates they listed
(E) who said it was essential to read English for their job
(F) who said it was essential to speak the minority language for their job

	A	B	C	D	E	F
Bengali N = 87	79	39	32	18	37	38
Chinese N = 67	91	64	53	18	52	36
Greek N = 101	66	26	51	37	60	28
Gujerati N = 62	69	21	2	32	75	7
Italian N = 76	65	28	31	42	51	16
Portuguese N = 154	56	12	5	32	50	7
Turkish N = 103	58	22	31	40	58	20

Source: Reid, Smith and Morawska, 1985

arrivals among them still have a strong domestic base for these languages, and there is also more limited support in the workplace.

As has been mentioned earlier, educational institutions have tended until quite recently to think of the appropriate response to such diversity in terms almost exclusively of the teaching of English. Even the modern languages curriculum has been highly Eurocentric, more or less totally dominated by the five 'traditional' school languages — French, German, Spanish, Italian and Russian.

The design of GCE 'O' and 'A' level examinations in the 'smaller' languages has also until recently been a serious discouragement to bilingual students wanting to add to their examination pass total, although moves are afoot to improve this situation (Broadbent *et al*, 1983). The teacher supply situation, however, remains a crucial block (Craft and Atkins, 1983), although again the establishment of the RSA Diploma in the Teaching of Community Languages scheme is helping in this respect, at least at the in-service level.

The consequences of not attempting more vigorously to break out of our present parochial language in education policies (DES, 1983) will almost certainly be to lose within a generation or so the opportunities now on offer.

The presence at the moment in our schools, colleges and adult institutes of so many speakers of languages from every part of the world gives us the chance to refresh and invigorate our dangerously inward-looking education system. There is the possibility, if we act now, of real intercultural exchange, to the benefit of all.

Acknowledgements

It would not have been possible to produce this paper without the work of former colleagues on the Linguistic Minorities and Community Languages & Education Projects. Thanks, therefore, to all of them, and in particular to Xavier Couillaud, Marilyn Martin Jones, Anna Morawska, Greg Smith and Verity Saifullah Khan. The opinions and assertions are of course my own.

References

BROADBENT, J. *et al* (1983) *Community Languages at 16+*, York, Longman, for Schools Council

CRAFT, M. AND ATKINS, M. (1983) *Training Teachers of Ethnic Minority Community Languages*, Nottingham, School of Education

DEPARTMENT OF EDUCATION AND SCIENCE (1983) *Foreign Languages in the School Curriculum. A Consultative Paper*, London, DES

DEPARTMENT OF EDUCATION AND SCIENCE (1985) *Education for All*, London, HMSO (Chapter 7: Language and Language Education)

EUROPEAN COMMISSION (1977) *Council Directive on the Education of Children of Migrant Workers*: 77/486, Brussels, Commission of the European Communities

HOULTON, D. (1985) *All Our Languages*, London, Edward Arnold

ILEA (INNER LONDON EDUCATION AUTHORITY) (1982) *Bilingualism in the ILEA: the educational implications of the 1981 Language Census*, London, ILEA

ILEA (INNER LONDON EDUCATION AUTHORITY) (1979, 1981, 1983, 1985, 1987) *Reports on the Biennial Language Censuses of ILEA pupils*, London, ILEA — Research and Statistics Branch

LINGUISTIC MINORITIES PROJECT (LMP) (1983) *Linguistic Minorities in England —* Report for the Department of Education and Science, London, Tinga Tinga for Heinemann Educational

LINGUISTIC MINORITIES PROJECT (LMP) (1985) *The Other Languages of England*, London, Routledge and Kegan Paul

MORAWSKA, A., REID, E. AND SMITH, G. (1985) *Languages in Bradford*, London, University of London Institute of Education (LMP/CLE Working Paper No 11)

REID, E. (ed.) (1984) *Minority Community Languages in School*, London, CILT

REID, E., MORAWSKA, A. AND COUILLAUD, X. (1984) *The Schools Language Survey of the Linguistic Minorities Project: the Data in Context*, London, University of London Institute of Education (LMP/CLE Working Paper No 7)

REID, E., SMITH, G. AND MORAWSKA, A. (1985) *Languages in London*, London, University of London Institute of Education (LMP/CLE Working Paper No 12)

SMITH, G. P., MORAWSKA, A. AND REID, E. (1984) *Languages in Coventry*, London, University of London Institute of Education (LMP/CLE Working Paper No 10)

Maps of interaction for the language traveller

Celia Roberts

Three major trends over the last decade have affected our view of language teaching. Firstly, the small-scale, and often *ad hoc* work of the early and mid-1970s, shining with pioneer spirit, has turned into a complex network of provision and issues which can empower but often perplex. Secondly, the professionalizing of second-language teaching has exposed large numbers of teachers to current practice and ideas. Thirdly, theoretical and applied studies of language have staked out whole new territories of understanding to give us new maps of language.

In order for these three trends to work together effectively, there is an urgent need for a principled and expanded view of language. This view must include an understanding of the relationship between culture and communication, the learners' role in analysing language and in deciding on the learning process, the social and political issues of language and the kind of learning required to tackle these issues. We do not, as yet, have a principled and expanded view of language available to teachers and learners, but we have many, if not all, the elements to make up such a view. By reviewing the changes and developments over the last ten years, we can identify what these elements are and how they have informed our thinking and practice.

In the early 1970s it was obvious that the traditional approaches to teaching English as a foreign language were in no way adequate to provide the support for and access to equal opportunities that minority ethnic groups, learning English as a Second Language, needed (see, for example, Jupp and Hodlin, 1975). At the same time as there was a new situation in Britain, there were also new developments in applied linguistics and in the disciplines of linguistics, sociology, anthropology and psychology. Of course, it would be naïve to assume that there could be a beautiful symbiotic relationship between the practitioners and those working on theory. This kind of relationship rarely develops. But there has been quite considerable leaking of ideas and practice and it is these leaks which have been so productive in developing a view of language relevant to the issues of contact and access in a multi-ethnic society.

The most important theoretical influence on language teaching for adult learners came from four different sources. The first was the linguistic philosophers John Austin and John Searle who formulated and developed the Speech Act Theory. Their great contribution to our understanding of language was to show that language performs social acts. When we say, 'I warn you' or 'I promise you' or 'I apologize', those words themselves are the warning, the promise or the apology. Words don't just say things, they do things. And often what words do is not what is contained in the surface message but is in the conventional meaning associated with the words — for example, as in all the typical polite request forms like 'Can you shut the window?', where the surface message is a question but the intended meaning is a request. By focusing attention on what people do with words, Austin and Searle helped language teachers to look at language from the point of view of speakers' intentions. It was an easy step from here for language teachers to develop a functional approach which accorded with their intuitions about how language is used. After all, labels such as 'greet', 'request' and 'report' are part of our everyday repertoire and do not require an elaborate theory to be understood or rationalized.

The second important influence was the work of anthropologists such as Dell Hymes. In both his methodology and his findings he brought new insights to the language teacher. He introduced the concept of ethnography to language teaching at a time when, in a limited and rather *ad hoc* way, work was beginning on ethnography in the multi-ethnic workplace. Ethnography is the study of groups and events in their own terms. It requires detailed observation. As an anthropologist, Hymes was interested in the 'speech events' of different cultural and ethnic groups, in what made up these events and in what the rules were for participating in them. As a result of his work on the ethnography of communication, he established seven components which made up the speech event: sender, receiver, message, channel, code, topic and setting. This analysis has been very helpful in establishing how we account for the variety of language in interactions and so in the design of syllabus and materials. It has helped to alert the language teacher and learner to the effect of different roles, settings and topics in any particular interaction. And this has provided a more systematic way of practising language in useful contexts, while encouraging the learners to see language as a system of options.

Example:

	Role	Locale	Context	Personality
1. Greeting on arrival at work	Fellow worker	Cloakroom	After the weekend	Awkward person
2. Complaint from a customer	Server and customer unknown to each other	Works canteen	Complaints procedure	Unknown

(from *Post Elementary Language Communication Skills in the Workplace*, NCILT 1976)

From his analysis of speech events, Hymes concluded that there were rules of use 'without which the rules of grammar would be useless'. Much of the language teaching in the 1970s was concerned with trying to establish and teach what these rules of communicative use were. Here, the influence of sociolinguists such as Ervin-Tripp was significant in trying to specify some of these rules — for example, rules of social appropriateness, deciding what to call somebody; sequencing rules, for example, the need to greet and make contact before making a request; and co-occurrence rules which regulate how formal or informal to be.

The descriptive work of anthropologists and sociolinguists was transformed by language teachers into the search for teachable language rules of behaviour. The major concern at the time was to help marginalized minority ethnic learners to interact socially with the white majority group. In retrospect, this concern appears limited and conformist but at the time it provided a framework for the systematic development of effective and appropriate language for the post-elementary learner.

The third major influence on this developing framework came from the work of Michael Halliday. In one way, his work has been useful in helping us to understand what is regular and patterned in particular transactions:

Much speech does take place in fairly restricted contexts where the options are limited and the meaning potential rather closely specifiable . . . Many of the routines of the working day represent situation types in which the language is by no means restricted as a whole, the transactional meanings are not closed, but nevertheless there are certain definable patterns, certain options which typically come into play. (1973)

But his work has also had a much more wide-ranging and challenging influence on language teaching for adult learners. He has helped us to understand the powerful social role of language. Language not only reflects and transmits the values, relationships and structures of a society, it actively creates and maintains them. This notion puts enormous responsibility on the language teacher in a multi-ethnic society. It raises serious questions about the values and assumptions embedded in the language taught and about whether there are norms of language behaviour in such a society.

Finally, the work of the applied linguist, David Wilkins, in the mid-1970s was influential in drawing together many of these theoretical issues into what he called 'Notional Syllabuses'. Wilkins showed that it was possible to design a syllabus which was not grammatical or situational — a syllabus which acknowledged that language was to do with communication, but which did not trap language into rigid set pieces determined by the situation. Wilkins' work was particularly helpful in two ways. Firstly, he identified the categories for a comprehensive syllabus: the semantic and grammatical, the functional and the modal (concerned with the speakers' perspective, such as how certain or personal or committed they wished to appear). Secondly, he put great emphasis on the importance of needs analysis and specification based on observable behaviour. The needs analysis approach has been fundamental to the Council of Europe's attempts to define a threshold level for modern languages in Europe and it encouraged a great deal of work on needs analysis in specific industries and the public services, both in Britain and on the Continent. This approach was particularly influential because it gave a framework to what had begun as a grassroots movement in both community education and Industrial Language Training.

By the late 1970s, the influence of linguists and other social scientists on language training could be summarized as follows. There was much greater understanding of what constituted communicative behaviour and useful labels had been borrowed to help analyse typical situations into meaningful patterns of language use. The emphasis was on what could be observed, analysed and converted into useful teaching materials. There was also some debate about the wider social and political issues related to language in an ethnically diverse and divisive society. The approach of language teachers at this time is well illustrated in the National Centre for Industrial Language Training's publications on *Role Play* (Gubbay, 1978) and on *Discourse Skills* (NCILT, 1978) and in *At Home in Britain* (1980).

However, there were many issues which had not been addressed. Again, as practitioners, we found that linguists, anthropologists and sociologists using a multidisciplinary approach were tackling a number of the issues that were becoming increasingly important to us. These were, notably, the relationship between communication and disadvantage in society; the relationship between language and culture; the increasing concern with understanding the internal processes of interaction and learning; and a growing awareness of the need to shift the power base from L1 teacher to a contractual relationship between learners and teachers in a multilingual classroom. The work of anthropologists and ethnographers studying communication in multi-ethnic societies was particularly relevant to our concerns. The major influence was John Gumperz.

As a linguist and anthropologist, he related Hymes' work on the ethnography of communication to the specific issues of language and linguistic diversity. He has made a major contribution to our understanding of these wider issues and has worked closely with the Industrial Language Training Service for many years. His fundamental arguments are:

1. There is a communicative dimension to discrimination which is rarely perceived as such.
2. Different ethnic and cultural groups may differ systematically in the way they convey information and attitudes in talk and this can lead to communication breakdowns and negative stereotyping.
3. By analysing communication breakdowns, it is possible to isolate what these differences are; to help both native and non-native English speakers to look out for and try to repair these breakdowns; and to help those in positions of power and responsibility to appreciate the consequences of not taking action.

Gumperz is primarily interested in the processes of inferencing and interpreting that go on in people's heads and the way in which people use language to signal their meaning. The basic linguistic tools for signalling and interpreting meaning seem 'natural' to speakers, but in fact they are culturally relative. In other words, these tools are developed as a person grows up and interacts with a group whose members share the same ways of communicating. Linguistic features such as intonation, pausing, pitch or ways of organizing talk may seem unimportant items when considering issues such as access to equal opportunities and equal treatment. However, when the speaker's meaning and intent are consistently misunderstood because these features of talk are misinterpreted, the cumulative effect is that not just individuals but the whole group is mistrusted and misjudged.

Studies of inter-ethnic communication, therefore, bring together different cultural assumptions, different linguistic features and different ways of managing and organizing interactions. In a multi-ethnic society such as Britain, where the power structures reflect and transmit the views and ways of operating of the white majority, ethnically specific ways of communicating are regularly judged as odd and inadequate.

Misjudgements of individuals are most damaging in 'gatekeeping' encounters. These are encounters where decisions are made about people's chances of getting a job, housing, advice on health or education or any of the other matters crucial to people's lives. Studies of inter-ethnic gatekeeping encounters include job and counselling interviews and courtroom interaction in the United States (see Gumperz, 1982, and Erickson and Shultz, 1982) and job interviews in Britain (see Roberts and Sayers, 1987). These studies show that the way, typically, a white native-speaking 'gatekeeper' makes decisions about a minority ethnic applicant or client will not depend on any objective criteria. Ultimately, decisions about suitability and worth depend upon how the client or applicant comes across.

Even gatekeepers with goodwill are unlikely to appreciate that they are judging someone on the basis of their own assumptions about appropriate behaviour. For example, in a job interview, the interviewer will normally expect the candidates to 'sell themselves' but to do it modestly; to talk about their experience when asked about their personal qualities; to understand the hidden message behind questions like 'What is it that attracts you about this job?' And there are also likely to be even more subtle assumptions affecting how well the interaction goes. Frederick Erickson, for example, has shown how, when people share the same communicative style, a rhythm is established between the speakers as they listen and respond. This makes the interaction smooth and comfortable and affects the outcome of the encounter — such as the quality of advice given in a college counselling session.

Gumperz's work with sociologists has also helped to show how communication forms part of a negative cycle:

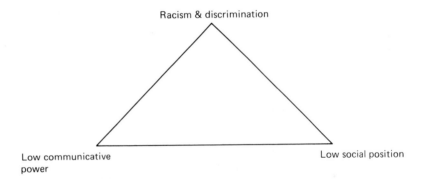

The way in which communication feeds into and reinforces this negative cycle is largely a hidden process (see Jupp, Roberts and Cook-Gumperz, 1982). As such, it is often overlooked or dismissed as trivial or missing the point. But since institutions and workplaces largely carry out their affairs through interaction, what takes place in face-to-face communication is bound to affect the life chances of those involved. People talk their way through to getting help, to getting things done and to making decisions. By locating issues of communication within this negative cycle it is possible to relate the bald facts of institutionalized discrimination to individual gatekeepers' attitudes and behaviour.

The close co-operation between ILT and John Gumperz created change in four main ways:
1. The ethnographic approach. In any interaction, all the participants are invited to interpret what they perceived as happening. This approach has put the perceptions of minority ethnic learners at the centre of the learning process. These perceptions can then be used to challenge what is taken for granted as normal and natural by the majority.
2. The focus on stressful situations and in particular 'gatekeeping' encounters. The demands of a gatekeeping encounter amplify those features of communication which are often most difficult for both

language learners and native English speakers: how to present yourself, how to give bad news, how to convey and sort out complicated narrative sequences. The need to train white people in decision-making jobs had long been acknowledged. It was now clear that one way of tackling institutional discrimination was to train gatekeepers at the point of interaction with black clients. Here the aim has been to develop sensitivity and communicative flexibility in inter-ethnic communication, to help white gatekeepers to challenge the way they make judgements of others, to help them develop a respect for different ways of communicating and to prevent them from jumping to conclusions about people, either because they have exaggerated the language difficulties of minority ethnic applicants or because they have interpreted communication differences in terms of personality or ability.
3. The fact that language and culture are inseparable in interaction. Culture is not something that can be separated off from communication: assumptions about the purpose of an encounter and the way it can best be accomplished, ideas about how to present oneself, what to talk about, when to speak and when to be silent — these may all be culture-bound, as are the precise ways in which emphasis, contrast and important information are conveyed through word order, intonation, pausing etc. The assumptions about talk and the ways we talk are intimately associated with our identity as a person and as a member of a group. So, any language teaching must be sensitive to these issues of identity and must help students to see language as a series of choices. Students will want to have access to the standard variety of English and will want to be familiar with the typical assumptions and styles of interacting of standard variety speakers. However, they will also want to decide to what extent they wish to maintain their ethnic identity through the way they communicate.

Some of the most influential work on communication, which assumes that language and culture cannot be separated, has been undertaken by Penny Brown and Stephen Levinson (1978). Their work on politeness strategies is based on the fundamental assumption that in all conversation we have two needs. We need to make contact, show that we share things in common, make the other person feel interested or sympathetic and show interest and sympathy in them — what they call 'positive face'. We also need to respect the other person, not impose or make assumptions, recognize their autonomy and for them to do the same with us. This is called 'negative face'. These are universal politeness strategies but different ethnic and social groups will have different notions about how the balance between these two should be maintained. When different notions of 'face' are in conflict it can have a devastating effect on people's lives as Ron Scollon and Susanne Scollon have shown (1983). They have examined why, in Alaska, native American Indians were getting much stiffer sentences than whites who had been found guilty of the same crime. They found that pre-sentence reports on native Americans commented on their pessimism and their unwillingness to express any intention about the future. In other words, native Americans were anxious to use the 'negative' politeness strategies which they considered appropriate for the kind of interviews on which these reports were based, but which may well have been held against them when sentence was passed. Brown and Levinson's work is equally useful in analysing inter-ethnic interviews in Britain, particularly the job or training interview.

4. Comparative analysis of North Indian languages and English. The contrastive analysis of different languages is a well established exercise but it has tended to focus on phonology and certain aspects of syntax. However, Gumperz and his associates (see Gumperz (ed.) 1982) have examined how some of the features of discourse of North Indian languages, and of English which is influenced by these languages, contrast with the standard variety of English. The most interesting aspect of this work for language teachers is the way in which syntax and intonation, pitch etc. are used together in quite different ways to convey meaning. So, for example, in English, emphasis is frequently conveyed through intonation and pitch whereas in North Indian languages word order (which is much freer than in English) and emphatic particles are used. Non-native speakers of English may be irritated or confused by what they perceive as the exaggeratedly stressed or emphatic use of English by native speakers. This type of contrastive work, undertaken by learners and teachers together, helps the learners to analyse and compare their own and the second language, to work out which discourse principles are common to both languages and what skills they need to develop, in order to acquire or compensate for those features in the second language which are different from their own.

As we understand more about the nature of interaction, so we are able to extend the type of provision and to address, more explicitly, the nature of the learning process. We have moved from a preoccupation with needs analysis, with teaching the language behaviour of the white majority, and from provision that separated the issue of language and disadvantage. There is now more emphasis on developing the pragmatic ability of individuals, on the analysis and perception of the learners and their experience, and on providing training for both whites and bilinguals which examines the relationship between language and discrimination through analysis and role-play, using videos of naturally occurring interactions. In many ways, the detailed analysis of real videoed interviews draws together many of the issues described in this paper. Through the close analysis of the texture of talk, of both intra-ethnic and inter-ethnic encounters, both bilinguals and white gatekeepers can be helped to identify certain underlying patterns that tend to occur. For example, in counselling interviews, both Asian–Asian and English–English interviews can be very effective but the way in which these interviews are conducted seem quite different. From these interviews we can make different inferences about how a client's problem is introduced and categorized, about what is a satisfactory advice interview and about the different ways of managing the interaction in terms of style of questioning, degrees of directness and pacing. Understanding these differences can help both sides to be more aware of what is involved in such encounters, to develop skills in, for example, being more explicit, to gain new insight into bureaucracy and issues which are culturally sensitive and to relate these features of interaction to the wider social and political issues of discrimination.

It has and always will be the business of practitioners to get on and do what is realistic and relevant. The task of developing language in all its different aspects is such a tremendous one that, as language teachers, we have often acted with a very restricted and compartmentalized view of language – a teachable view. But the issues of language and disadvantage are so important that we cannot afford to do that. Nor can we feel satisfied if any learners and decision-makers communicating in a multi-ethnic society are left with such a restricted and compartmentalized view. Language is power and we all need to recognize what that means. Those working in theories of interaction – linguists, sociolinguists, anthropologists, sociologists and social psychologists – are helping to deepen our understanding of language and its power. One of the Grand Old Men of linguistics, Sapir, once likened language to a generator capable of generating enough power to run an elevator but, in fact, operated almost exclusively to feed an electric doorbell (1921). When practitioners and scholars of language work together informing, and perhaps even sometimes reforming, each other, then a view of language can be generated which can power a lift, and not just a doorbell.

References

BROWN, P. AND LEVINSON, S. (1978) 'Universals in Language Usage: Politeness Phenomena' in Goody, E. (ed) *Questions and Politeness Strategies in Social Interaction*, Cambridge University Press

ERICKSON, F. AND SHULTZ, J. (1982) *The Counselor as Gatekeeper: Social Interaction in Interviews*, New York, Academic Press

GUBBAY, DENISE (1978) *Role Play*, NCILT

GUMPERZ, J. J. (ed) (1982) *Language and Social Identity*, Cambridge University Press

HALLIDAY, M. A. K. (1973) *Explorations in the Functions of Language*, London, Edward Arnold

JUPP, T. C. AND HODLIN, SUSAN (1975) *Industrial English*, Heinemann Educational Books

JUPP, T. C., ROBERTS, CELIA AND COOK-GUMPERZ, JENNY (1982) 'Language and Disadvantage: The Hidden Process' in Gumperz, J. J. (ed) *Language and Social Identity*, Cambridge University Press

NATIONAL CENTRE FOR INDUSTRIAL LANGUAGE TRAINING (1976) *Post Elementary Communication Skills in the Workplace*, NCILT

NATIONAL CENTRE FOR INDUSTRIAL LANGUAGE TRAINING (1978) *Discourse Skills*, NCILT

NICHOLLS, S. M. (ed) (1980) *At Home in Britain*, National Extension College

ROBERTS, C. AND SAYERS, P. (1987) 'Keeping the Gate: How Judgements are made in Inter-Ethnic Interviews', in Knapp (ed) *Analysing Inter-Cultural Communication*, Mouton de Gruyter

SAPIR, E. (1921) *Language: An Introduction to the Study of Speech*, New York, Harcourt, Brace & World

SCOLLON, R. AND SCOLLON, S. (1983) 'Face in Inter-Ethnic Communication' in Richards, J. C. and Schmidt, R. W. (eds) *Language & Communication*, Longman

WILKINS, D. A. (1976) *Notional Syllabuses*, Oxford University Press

Issues of anti-racism and equal opportunities in ESL

Rakesh Bhanot
and Yasmin Alibhai

> *Imagine a group of British people (in any kind of situation) and hold this picture in your mind for a few seconds.*
>
> *Now, imagine a group of people from the USA and do the same.*
>
> *Compare the two pictures and note any differences.*
>
> *Before reading on, visualize the two groups again.*

Ask yourself these questions:

1. How many black people were there in the British group?
2. How many black people were there in the American group?

If the answer to either or both of the above questions is none, stop and ask yourself why. This exercise has been conducted with a variety of groups (all white, all black, and mixed groups) and it is remarkable how often no black faces appear in either picture. Coincidentally, it is usually the case that the groups visualized consist mostly of men. We do not need to labour the point that nearly all the 'images' that confront us daily tend to be white — whether these are through the media, advertising, or the printed word. At the same time, black people still tend to be portrayed in certain well-defined, usually negative, roles. These range from traditional images such as slaves, servants, exotic princes and princesses, to contemporary images including manual workers, claimants, and law breakers. Where exceptions exist these tend to be primarily in the worlds of entertainment and sport.

Ethnic diversity in Britain

There is now substantial research evidence to indicate that, while Britain is clearly a multiracial society, the establishment, institutions and a large proportion of the population have not come to terms with the implications this has for us all. This failure is seen in such things as black youth unemployment rates, lack of upward economic mobility and access to housing and health services (PSI, 1984). In the educational sphere, a succession of parliamentary enquiries (e.g. The Chinese Community in Britain, 1985, and The Bangladeshi Community in Britain, 1986), as well as reports by the CRE, NFER and the EEC among others, have drawn attention to inequality of access, achievement and outcome.

Current responses to such findings range from the development of LEA and institutional policies concerning equal opportunity to national initiatives in the areas of curriculum and staff development coordinated by organizations such as the FEU and the MSC. While all this is laudable, there is a danger that it will have minimal effect in terms of challenging institutional and individual racism and, therefore, on curriculum design and classroom practice.

Images in ESL materials

ESL is located within this context. Many teachers have been concerned about issues of racial equality for some time. Yet the ethos of ESL teaching often seems to collude with the system and has not always challenged its inequalities.

An examination of some ESL materials in current use illustrates this clearly. Take a typical 'ESL family':

> The first thing that strikes the objective observer is that its members are appallingly accident-prone. They are constantly burning, scalding and cutting themselves or falling off ladders. In spite of strong warnings about throwing lighted matches into waste-paper baskets, they have managed to set their house on fire. This is probably a blessing in disguise, as the sink, basin, bath and loo were permanently blocked, the roof leaked and the kitchen ceiling had collapsed.
>
> They appear to be very unhealthy. They are always telephoning the doctor and collecting prescriptions, but to little purpose, as once they get the medicine bottles home, they cannot get the tops off. This, no doubt, is why they appreciate so much the therapeutic qualities of a nice cup of tea. Sometimes this is 'English' tea and sometimes it is 'Asian' tea, but it doesn't really matter anyway as they keep forgetting how to make it and have to be given the instructions again.
>
> Diet and dress give cause for concern as they rarely succeed in buying anything but mouldy tomatoes and sweaters that are too small. If they manage to buy clothes that are the right size, they shrink them by washing them at the wrong temperatures. Their conversation is limited to describing problems, complaining, apologizing and occasionally asking the way.
>
> There are some things they never do: argue, express opinions, go to meetings, study, laugh, tell stories, protest, run their own business. After unblocking all those loos, they don't have the energy.

Thus, not only are the characters shown to be leading narrow, restricted and boring lives, they are also shown to be completely powerless in a variety of situations. This may, of course, reflect reality but there is an underlying implication that the characters (and hence the students) are personally responsible for breakdowns in communication. In other words, it is alleged that their failure to adopt the 'British way of life' is a direct result of their inability to speak English.

As language teachers, we must constantly examine all materials for racist and sexist images and be alert to less overt stereotypes such as illustrations showing the passive black patient and the assertive white doctor.

However, it is not enough to say that certain books present a negative image of black people and that these should be condemned or banned. After all, it should be possible to use such materials given a sensitive, critical, anti-racist teacher. As Gillian Klein says:

> *Even a biased book can be used to some good purpose in the classroom, so long as the teacher has control over how it is used and is alert to the bias within it. Teachers need to recognise their responsibility as agents between their pupils and the books: they are automatically endorsing the materials with their own implicit approval unless they specifically say otherwise and indicate the passages with which they disagree.*

> *The elimination from the shelves of all books and materials that are biased is totally unrealistic, but would it even be desirable? A totally sanitised collection of resources would be so out of touch with reality as to be of little use to the pupils. Prejudice is a reality of their lives and cannot be wholly expunged from their literature.*

Gillian Klein ends her book with the following words:

> *But the racism that is embedded in the structure of our Society will have to be eradicated before we can expect the publications of that Society to be no longer racist. (Klein 1986).*

Developing an anti-racist perspective

Recently ESL teachers have been developing criteria for designing and selecting materials with an anti-racist and anti-sexist perspective. Such criteria are useful for raising awareness but they can deflect people from considering the much larger issue of institutional racism, the problem being perceived as confined to the materials and not related to their own attitudes and conditioning.

Racism can only be eradicated if people understand what it is, what part it plays in the lives of black people, and how it is woven into the very language and culture of 'British Society'. For example, linguistic theory recognizes that all words have connotative as well as conceptual meaning (Leech, 1974). Connotative meaning is volatile and words which, at one point in time, are perceived as having positive connotations, may quite rapidly acquire negative ones through their association with particular groups or points of view. A second type of connotative meaning is more permanent and is internalized to such an extent by the general population that they are unaware of how the connotations offend the people with whom they are associated. English is no different from many other languages in this respect. For example, synonyms for 'white' have positive associations, while those for 'black' have mostly negative ones. Many of the latter are directly related to race, e.g. nigger, blackamoor. Another feature of English is that the majority of similes and metaphors hold 'whiteness' in esteem, associating it with concepts such as purity, and belittle or denigrate (this word in itself is such an example) 'blackness'. In short, as Baldwin says:

> *For a black writer in this country (USA) to be born into the English language is to realise that the assumptions on which the language operates are his enemy. . . I was forced to reconsider similes: as black as sin, as black as night, blackhearted.*
> *(from an article entitled: 'On Language, Race and the Black Writer',* Los Angeles Times, *29 April 1979, part V, page 1)*

Implications for ESL teachers

What are the implications of all this for the classroom teacher? The attitudes and practices of the ESL teacher operating in a racist environment do, obviously, have an effect on the kind of teaching that takes place, particularly in terms of needs analysis and the resulting course content. For instance, *Housing*, a topic frequently chosen in response to expressed student interest, will be inappropriately treated if the teacher actually believes that council housing is available to all people on a fair and equal basis. If the reality is that discrimination takes place when black people apply for council accommodation (PSI 1986), then teaching students how to fill in application forms and how to perform at interviews with a friendly and sympathetic interviewer are not likely to be of much use to the student in the real situation. Even where tutors may think they share with their students the knowledge and experience of dealing with institutions such as the DHSS and the NHS, the fact is that black claimants are often treated very differently. Yet courses tend to deal with crisis situations of the eminently solvable kind — hence all those leaking pipes — rather than empowering students to challenge racist attitudes and discriminatory practices.

It is remarkably difficult, however, to find the language of assertion, confrontation, and self preservation in ESL materials. It would be illuminating to have units in textbooks which deal with discrimination and how to combat it. For instance, in terms of patient/doctor relationships, this may mean teaching students to question the lack of appropriate care, rather than simply make-believe that they would be treated equally if only they could get the English right. In practice, the opposite is true. It should be a matter of concern that real life hardly makes an appearance in the many materials still widely in use such as the CRE/NATESLA Home Tutor Kit. In fact tutors are often advised to shy away from those aspects of life which can encapsulate the real concerns of students. In the Home Tutor Kit would-be tutors are warned not to take over when a problem arises, because 'Parveen needs to be an independent adult'. Parveen *is* an independent adult; she just can't speak the Queen's English. There seems to be an underlying implication that no one can participate in real life unless they are fluent speakers of English. This is reinforced in the Home Tutor Kit by the reference to Carlo who, it is claimed, can 'find few opportunities to socialize' because he works 'alongside people who do not speak any English at all'. Socializing with people who don't speak English is not socializing? This is somewhat similar to referring to Asian women who don't speak English as 'silent women'.

It is clear therefore that we need to change our perceptions and that the problem is not simply one of whether books and materials are racist, but whether ESL tutors are aware of the issues involved (Bajpai, 1987).

The following categories attempt to provide a working check-list for teachers and may serve as a useful starting point.

> A racist book in some way demonstrates the superiority of one race, usually the white race, at the expense of other races and serves to perpetuate cultural and racial oppression.
>
> A non-racist book does not demonstrate white superiority but neither does it actively challenge it. It helps children to learn about other races and cultures but it does not seek to confront racism.
>
> An anti-racist book addresses the attitudes and practices that are racist in our society and projects positive images of black and ethnic minority people. An anti-racist book helps children to understand and confront racism.

Conclusion

This paper has drawn attention to issues of racism and equality in ESL and discussed ways in which they need to be tackled by teachers within the classroom. Three areas have been pinpointed: teaching materials, syllabus content and methodology. The paper has also highlighted how action within the classroom can only be fully effective when complemented by institutional change. Teachers of ESL have an important part to play in this process, both individually and as members of educational institutions. Later papers in this book consider ways in which change can be brought about in areas such as access and accreditation, curriculum and classroom practice, teacher recruitment and training. It is only by tackling the structural problems while simultaneously questioning personal attitudes and approaches that we can ensure that black and bilingual students have equality of opportunity in education and training.

References

BAJPAI, ANIL (1987) 'ESL: The Way Forward', *Language Issues* No 2, NATESLA

BALDWIN, JAMES (1979) 'On Language, Race and the Black Writer', *Los Angeles Times*, 29 April 1979, Part V, p1

The Bangladeshi Community in Britain (1986), Report of the Home Affairs Committee, HMSO

BROWN, C. (1984) *Black and White Britain*, Third Policy Studies Institute Survey

The Chinese Community in Britain (1985), Report of the Home Affairs Committee, HMSO

CRE/NATESLA (1978) Home Tutor Kit

KLEIN, G. (1986) *Reading into Racism*, Routledge & Kegan Paul

LEECH, GEOFFREY (1974) *Semantics*, Penguin

Section 2 Policy and Practice

Introduction

Since the 1970s ESL provision has developed in two sectors of post-school education: community (adult) education and vocationally-oriented contexts including Industrial Language Training and MSC-funded provision. Within both these settings there are wide regional variations which reflect the decentralized nature of the British education system. In some areas there is close integration of provision for students who wish to learn English for everyday life and those wishing to study skills-related language to further vocational or academic aims. In other LEAs there is a clear divide between the two types of provision, with students having to move from one type of institution to another (e.g. from adult education institute to further education college) if their aims change. A second influence on patterns of organization has been funding: the ESL schemes of many LEAs are largely dependent on central government funding, such as Section 11 or MSC-funded courses, either for all their provision or for vocationally-oriented courses, but a few have invested additional money or redirected resources, in order to ensure that educational opportunities are available to bilingual members of the population. The result is that, over the country as a whole, the range of educational opportunities for bilingual students varies widely.

The three papers in this section focus on further education colleges, adult and community education, and work funded through training agencies (the MSC). Each of these sectors has a distinct philosophical ethos and operates under different funding constraints, with the result that they interpret the common philosophy and concerns outlined in Section 1 in different ways. At the same time all recognize that simply securing resources and establishing a range of provision will not in itself ensure equal opportunity for bilingual adults. Responsibility for the education of bilingual adults must not be delegated to language specialists but recognized and acted upon at the LEA and institutional level. Changes must be made not simply to the taught curriculum but to

institutional practices such as enrolment policies, assessment procedures and staff development. The conclusion to be reached from this
section is, therefore, that while one sector may initiate new provision
and practice, e.g. language support for students studying alongside
other English speakers, there is an underlying shared philosophy which
enables ESL specialists to build on what has been developed by
colleagues working in other sectors. This is undoubtedly to the benefit
of the students as they progress through the system, frequently
studying on courses in more than one part of it.

Issues and developments in further education

Elizabeth Hoadley-Maidment

Introduction

This paper will deal with issues related to students whose aims are to
further their general academic or vocational education but who need
English language support in order to achieve their goals. The information given is based largely on practices in those LEAs which now have
well-established provision within further education colleges, at least
some of which is funded by the LEA itself and therefore not subject to
the constraints of courses funded by the central training agencies.

The students

Students in further education include both 16- to 19-year-olds and
mature students. The number of bilingual students entering FE is rising
in the late 1980s, both because bilingual children are moving through
the education system and because numbers of adults wish to take
courses which are certificated and which lead to academic success or
vocational qualifications. Adult students may have decided to enter
further education because of unemployment but the development of
schemes to accredit prior learning, such as the establishment of open
colleges, also encourages students to move from general community-

based courses into more structured provision. Both groups of students provide a challenge to FE because, as they regularly use more than one language and operate in more than one cultural context in their daily lives, they may have needs for English language support of a different type to that traditionally offered in colleges.

The requirements of students in the 16–19 age range vary. Those who were born in the UK or who have spent most of their lives here may not need any special help with English language. Others will succeed on general college courses provided they are given English language support which enables them to develop their written English, to cope with UK style examinations and to develop the study skills required to study within further and higher education in this country (see McAllister and Robson, Section 3). There are also smaller numbers of students who initially need much greater language support. These students are 'late arrivals' who have come to Britain as teenagers and, consequently, have had little or no contact with the school system. Many of them will need to spend time on a course in which ESL is a major component. Here they will be able to develop their self-confidence and learn to capitalize on knowledge they have acquired in another linguistic, cultural or educational context. They will then be in a position to progress on to courses alongside other English speakers, although they may continue to need English language support in the early stages of these. (See Faine and Knight, Section 3.)

A substantial number of students over the age of 19 also wish to study in FE. Because of patterns of migration and educational practice in other countries, the administrative categorization (important for deciding fees) of FE students into 16- to 19-year-olds and over 19 has long been recognized as invalid for bilingual students. There are many bilingual students aged 19–25 whose needs are identical to those of younger students. In addition, there are adult bilingual students who wish to study in FE on courses that lead to vocational or academic qualifications. Some of these people will already have studied in adult education, but others may enter FE directly, for example, refugees who have already had some higher education in their own countries and who wish to acquire the language and study skills to enable them to complete their studies in the UK, or people who have been made redundant and who wish to retrain or to increase their range of vocational skills.

Provision

Educational policy for bilingual students in FE aims to ensure that language support in both English and mother tongue is provided to suit the varying needs of these groups of students. Since in many LEAs language policy is developed as part of equal opportunity policy and the latter is still being written in many authorities and institutions, very few colleges are yet able to offer a full range of support. A few colleges have developed a pattern of provision that tries to ensure genuine equal opportunities for bilingual students, but at the other end of the spectrum are colleges who provide little or no support and who often appear to confuse the needs of bilingual students with those of overseas students.

On the whole, provision has developed in response to the needs of late arrivals, with a consequent emphasis on the establishment of courses at the foundation or access to FE level. These courses have a substantial ESL input as their core, with academic and/or vocational options which serve to introduce students to subjects available in the FE curriculum. The ILEA may be used as an example of an authority which, because of the large numbers of bilingual students enrolled in FE and the development of a coordinated approach to equal opportunity policy, has been able to develop a range of courses for students entering the system. In 1985–6 the following types of provision were available.

Table 1 *Courses for students needing substantial ESL support*

Type of course	No. of colleges
1. *Foundation courses*:	
(a) 16- to 19-year-olds	7
(b) adults (including 16+)	10
(c) school-link	3
2. *MSC funded*:	
(a) YTS	4
(b) Adult Preparatory	6
3. *Business studies*	
(a) Introductory (RSA Voc. Prep. etc.)	2
(b) Business 'O' level	3
(c) BTEC General	2

While it is important for a wide range of provision such as this to be on offer, there is also a need for authorities to rationalize their provision or course enrolments will not reach practicable levels. This obviously introduces difficulties for the smaller LEA which may have only one or two colleges and which may be forced to select subject options from a narrow range determined by, for example, staffing constraints or the expertise of the college. In some instances this has resulted in courses being offered to bilingual students in vocational areas such as engineering when the employment opportunities in the area have been greatly reduced as a result of the recession and consequently the traditional market of white students (often on day-release) has disappeared.

English language support for students on mainstream courses is also vitally important since students should be provided with a network of support for as long as they need it. Most colleges claim to provide support for a wide range of courses including GCSE and 'A' levels, BTEC and MSC-funded provision. In 1985–6 colleges in the ILEA offered support on the following courses:

Table 2 *Mainstream courses with language support 1985/86*
(provided as part of full-time or 21-hour provision)

Type of course	No. of colleges
1. *GCE*	
'O' level English	6
'O' level Science	7
'O' level unspecified	7
'A' level Science	6
JMB	8
'A' level unspecified	1
2. *MSC funded*	
YTS Mode A	2
3. *Business studies*	
BTEC General	8
BTEC National	11
Office Skills	7
4. *Technology*	
TEC Electronics	5
TEC other	2
Computers	2
5. *Craft*	
Hairdressing	1
Catering	1
Motor vehicle	1
6. *Drop-in-workshops*	10

A number of models exist for this work (see McAllister and Robson, Section 3) and there is a need for flexibility if the widely differing demands of both students and course requirements are to be met. Students in colleges with well thought-out provision may be offered substantial support through timetabled back-up lessons, double-staffing (in which a subject specialist and an ESL lecturer work in the subject classroom together), or in specially designed workshops, but in other places they may simply be offered access to a workshop outside their regular course programme. The quality of materials in workshops varies enormously and they may not have been designed with bilingual students in mind. The patchiness of English language support on mainstream courses means that at the present time in many areas little is done to acknowledge the positive role that bilingualism and multilingualism can play in the educational process.

Curriculum issues

Because of the earlier development of courses at the access to FE level, more attention has been paid to their curricula than to the way in which learning is organized in language support. However, both types of provision have certain underlying principles. These include the recognition that course aims and objectives need to be agreed by both subject and language specialists working together as a team, and the need for this team to be provided with time for coordination, planning and evaluation on a regular basis. Language and subject specialists bring two complementary sets of skills to this process: subject specialists bring ability to analyse in terms of skill objectives, subject content and examination demands; ESL specialists bring expertise in student needs analysis and language teaching methodology.

The language syllabus itself is a complex entity, the constituent parts of which will be balanced differently according to the overall aims and objectives of the course. The syllabus may be divided into a number of categories:

1. *Language of and for the subject(s)*. This category is subject-led because it is here that the subject-related language, including technical lexis and jargon, is taught. Subject staff are generally well aware of the need to teach this element to all students and, in itself, it tends to present few problems for bilingual students that do not also exist for other English speakers. The exception is where the bulk of the technical language is assumed to have been taught within the school system, for example in pure sciences, with the result that bilingual students who have not previously studied the subject in this country are seriously disadvantaged.

2. *Study skills*. Bilingual students studying in a British cultural context need to acquire an appropriate range of study skills. These will include language skills such as the ability to use references, skim-reading, extracting relevant information from verbal presentation, and a range of different writing skills. However, in addition to the language skills themselves, a strong element of cross-cultural learning is involved. This includes handling discursive essays, formal written examinations and tasks requiring students to 'analyse and interpret in your own words'. Another difficulty may arise because students are unable to relate to the context in which subjects are taught. Teachers constantly refer to a wide variety of Eurocentric concepts such as 'before the War', the climate, the Bible and Shakespeare. If teaching is to reflect our multi-ethnic society, references need to be more explicit and students should have opportunities to make comparisons with philosophical and cultural concepts from their own language.

These two categories of language work often form the basis of the programme for language support work, with actual content being chosen to reflect and develop the material presented in the subject class. However, in courses with a large ESL component they will be supplemented by, and in some cases, subservient to, two further areas of language work.

3. *Skills for classroom interaction and general language development*. This category is skills-led (i.e. listening, speaking, reading and writing). Students need to develop their general language skills both in order to participate in a wide range of learning activities in the classroom, such as taking part in discussions, answering questions, group work and a variety of written tasks, and in order to use English as and how they wish in their everyday lives. There is some overlap here with study skills and in some instances, staff may choose to help students develop

language within the context of study skills work. The actual parameters of the syllabus in this area will be based on individual and group needs as perceived both by the students themselves and by the ESL specialist.
4. *Formal language*. Each student will have learnt English in a unique way and may have acquired much of it informally. As a result any group of bilingual students will be 'mixed' in terms of formal language attainment and a linguistically-led syllabus will be required in order for students to work on areas such as tense control, spelling, punctuation and vocabulary development. Goals in this area will need to be chosen in relation to accuracy and fluency as individual learning styles mean that, while some students use a limited range of English accurately, others will use a wide range of structures and vocabulary with many errors. Students on special courses will need to develop skills in both oral and written English, whereas those on programmes of language support may already have a good command of spoken English but write it poorly. A variety of approaches is called for in this area. In addition to formal group instruction there is a need for individualized study through workshop methods, self-study and less formal learning such as reading. As it is also important that students feel a sense of progress, records should be kept and time taken for revision and testing.

Role of the college

Provision of courses with an ESL core, and of language support, are not in themselves enough to ensure equal educational opportunities for bilingual students. Responsibility for the development of this area of work has to be accepted at an institutional level and by all individual members of staff, including both academic and support staff. Provision is most effective in those colleges where there is a shared commitment to education for bilingual students, whereas in many places the issues are seen to be of relevance only to ESL specialists.

At an institutional level colleges need to ensure that their policies and practices include:
1. *A refined admissions procedure* which enables bilingual students to gain access to courses at appropriate levels, with suitable language support. Some colleges have already begun to examine their enrolment procedures and ensure that these provide for bilingual students (see Bagchi, Section 5). Those who appear to need language support should be seen by an ESL specialist. Colleges also need to examine their entrance tests, college English tests and enrolment forms, many of which confuse or penalize bilingual students. At present bilingual students frequently find themselves on unsuitable courses because staff lack information about what is available or lack the skills to help students assess their requirements.
2. *A range of provision* which enables bilingual students to progress through the college and the FE system. Students need to feel that they will be able to enrol on mainstream courses after completing foundation courses, i.e. that there is a system of intra-college enrolment. Since much of the provision for bilingual students is in inner-city colleges with accommodation problems, it is worrying to find that at present many courses are housed in annexes where students are cut off from the rest of the student body, have few opportunities to take part in student

activities and gain little impression of what the college can offer them when they have completed their initial course.

3. *An examination of procedures for educational counselling.* Bilingual students often lack confidence to use general college support services. Cultural concepts regarding education, careers and job opportunities differ greatly and many bilingual students and their families have little experience or knowledge of how the system operates. Students are also affected by racism, both personal and institutional, and often have social and personal difficulties with which they need help. They tend to look to ESL teachers for assistance, thereby increasing teachers' workloads in areas they may not feel qualified to handle.

4. *A recognition of the role played by cultural considerations* in the education of bilingual students. This should be built on in a positive way, for example, by encouraging multi-ethnic approaches in the classroom and in the life of the college, by recognizing the particular needs of groups such as Muslim girls and by consulting the communities when planning new provision for bilingual students.

Role of teaching staff

The implementation of policies and provision for bilingual students has implications for teaching practices and staff development. ESL specialists in FE are part of course teams and in this respect their role differs somewhat from that of teachers in adult education who may be working in considerable isolation. While ESL specialists provide direct support for bilingual students through the planning, teaching and evaluation of courses and language support sessions, at the same time they play an important role in staff development by working alongside subject specialists. Subject teachers, meanwhile, need to be aware of the role of language in all learning in order to organize their teaching so that bilingual students have the same opportunities to participate and progress as other English speakers. Finally, if the college is to provide the full range of support for bilingual students outlined above, then support staff, including librarians, counsellors and office staff, must also accept responsibility for the implementation of policy and be provided with appropriate staff development to enable them to carry out those elements that are relevant to their jobs.

New developments

Policies, approaches and practices in further education are changing rapidly and it is important that the needs of bilingual students are not lost sight of when large-scale change occurs. At the time of writing, ESL professionals are particularly concerned with the following developments:

1. *CPVE.* This major shift in curriculum for students entering FE has both benefits and disadvantages for bilingual students. The scheme has considerable flexibility built into it but may not provide sufficient opportunity for work on English language skills for students who are late arrivals. If bilingual students on CPVE programmes are to have as many opportunities for individualized programmes as other English speakers, there will be fewer groups of solely bilingual students and a greater need for language support for small groups of students studying

within groups of other English speakers. (For a more detailed study see Rosenberg, Section 5.)

2. *Opportunities for mature students including refugees.* As mentioned above, the barriers between community provision and further education are gradually being broken down and more students are moving from one kind of course to the other. Mature students require part-time provision which will enable them to receive benefits and they need courses with accreditation which is not geared to the needs of teenagers. The value of 'O' levels/GCSE, for example, declines sharply with the age at which they are gained. This has implications for course planning and resource allocation.

3. *Tertiary reorganization.* Many LEAs are currently rethinking their whole approach to the education of 16- to 19-year-olds. A number of different patterns are being used, including consortia of schools, sixth-form colleges and tertiary colleges. The emergence of tertiary colleges, in particular, has implications for bilingual students. Tertiary colleges are often perceived as institutions for this age-group alone, in which case the older bilingual student is in danger of losing educational opportunities. At present many bilingual girls stay at single-sex schools in the sixth form: where the only option is a coeducational college, parents may not allow them to continue their education. The educational philosophy underlying the planning of tertiary colleges is one based on British concepts of educational choice. For this age group these emphasize the development of autonomy and choice by the individual student, whereas in many of the cultures from which bilingual students are drawn, educational decisions are made by the family. There is a need for this to be recognized.

4. *Recruitment of bilingual teaching staff.* The numbers of ethnic minority staff working in FE are very small. Some authorities are now attempting to recruit more but this is still a slow process, especially as many bilingual teachers have qualifications which are not recognized in Britain. Bilingual teachers are needed both as subject specialists and as ESL teachers. Both groups provide role-models of successful language learners for bilingual students and can represent the students within the broader college and educational context in ways not open to other staff.

Conclusion

This paper has outlined the range of issues that currently concern people working in further education. They include the need not simply to provide a range of appropriate provision for a wide variety of bilingual students, but also to develop policies and practices that will provide genuine equal educational opportunities for these students and which recognize the positive contribution that multilingualism and multiculturalism can make to education in this sector.

Issues and developments in adult education

Julia Naish

Introduction

This paper focuses on ESL provision for adults. As there is enormous variation nationally in the organization and funding of provision for this group, the information presented here is based on those LEAs that have shown substantial commitment to this area of education.

Adult education in the UK is characterized by being generally for people over 19, non-vocational, with most courses organized on a part-time basis and not generally certificated. ESL is rooted in the best traditions of liberal education (see Nicholls, Section 1) and has adapted these to respond to the needs of a multi-ethnic, multilingual society. Consequently professional debate is now shifting away from discrete concerns towards a more broadly-based consideration of the part language plays in the general education of bilingual adults. This is beginning to be reflected in a number of areas: the range of provision available, the nature of the curriculum, and teaching approaches and methodology.

The students

The student population in adult education has always been extremely diverse and this is as true of bilingual students as of any other group. Traditionally students have been described under the same categories as those used by governmental agencies, i.e. as settlers or immigrants (often from the New Commonwealth), migrant workers, and refugees. The three categories relate to funding sources and government departments: for example, *immigrant* is used to define eligibility for funding under Section II or Urban Aid — central government funding for those groups. *Migrant worker* is an EEC category, *refugee* is a Home Office one. The categories imply definitions: immigrants are thought to be long-term or permanent settlers with an established community, refugees lack established networks, migrant workers are usually short-stay. These categories are simplistic and the edges may be blurred. For example, there are several categories of 'refugee' (Perrin and Monsah, 1986). From an educational perspective, teachers need to be aware of the effect this categorization has on students' ability to study and/or take paid employment. In addition, although students may come together as a group because of their individual need to learn English, this may be their only common need and there will probably be as many different motivations and aspirations as there are students in the class.

Provision   Considerable changes have taken place in provision over the years. The NATESLA survey of 1980 identified five class types: the 1985 report on teacher training showed a diversification to more than 20 class types. A number of factors have contributed to this change and diversification.

— *Growing unemployment*, which has led both to special classes for the unemployed being set up in adult education and to special funding for ESL work being channelled through the MSC.

— *Special funding*. For example, when the Vietnamese arrived, central government funding was used to establish provision and train teachers.

— *Growing criticism* by the linguistic minorities and others of ESL provision in terms of both its patronising blandness and the fact that it has been funded to the exclusion of mother-tongue or community language provision.

The other major contribution to change has come from education authority policies on anti-racism and equal opportunity. This has led to greater awareness and understanding of the context in which ESL work is done. We recognise '. . . the context in which the learning and teaching takes place in a society which rewards us as largely white, English mother-tongue teachers, in direct proportion to the way it penalizes our students. We are the providers in institutions that are for the most part inimical to their needs; we are paid to remedy deficiencies which underwrite their unemployment; and we move freely in streets where they meet a hostility that is frequent and overt'. (Rosenberg and Hallgarten, 1986.)

The rationale underlying provision has traditionally been that a student should be able to get to a class without too much difficulty, or be provided with a home tutor if for some reason a class is not appropriate. As a result much ESL provision has been determined by physical and geographical accessibility, with three main categories emerging.

Home tuition   Home tuition schemes vary enormously in size and in relation to the provision of classes. The idea is that volunteers are recruited, trained, matched with a student and supported. They usually teach for about an hour a week. In some parts of the country this service operates as a back-up to class provision and is only available to students who cannot take advantage of a class because of illness or handicap, childcare problems, or pressure from the family to stay at home. It is often an important first step in giving a student the confidence to join a class, although in areas where there are only a few bilingual students, or in unsupportive LEAs, this may be the only form of provision.

Community classes   Community classes are set up in a wide range of locations such as health clinics, temples, community centres and schools. They are held in places familiar to bilingual people, so that the student will feel more confident about attending. These community classes generally have an open enrolment policy and consequently attract a wide range of students with varying language needs and levels.

Institutionally-based provision

The offer at an adult education centre may be very diverse but will probably be based on a series of graded classes through which students can progress. There may be some special purpose classes, for example ESL-literacy or numeracy, study skills and grammar. In addition there may be classes based on subject or practical skills, often known as linked skills, and there may be some form of language support for bilingual students studying other courses in the institute/centre.

The above categories of ESL provision for adults have remained largely unchanged in the eighties. Where change has occurred, it is in the range of provision available both within ESL and adult education generally, and in the growing awareness of the place of language support for bilingual students in all areas of education and training. These have been brought about by a number of factors, the two most influential being:
1. the emerging recognition that students are partners in the learning process and that there is a need for greater consultation with them at all stages;
2. the changing employment situation which has brought numbers of new students into adult education, seeking courses that are relevant to a range of employment and training opportunities.

The result has been a wide range of experimental courses, e.g. *Introduction to work with the under 5s, Setting up your own business, Women in the community, Access to bilingual employment*, and various forms of language support in skills training centres.

In order for students to benefit from this increasingly wide range of provision, it has been necessary to provide educational counselling. Students need initial interviews to place them in the appropriate English class, to explain to them about other subjects on offer, sometimes to recommend another institution altogether. Counselling then needs to be done periodically to check how the student is progressing (see Lawson, Section 5). It is a time-consuming process but a crucial one. The ESL class is often the access point to the education system. It may well not be the desired destination.

Curriculum

One of the striking things about ESL until recently has been the lack of curriculum guidelines, often accompanied by a failure to consider issues related to the whole curriculum offer rather than the demands of the immediate course. The tendency has often been to respond to student needs in a very immediate way and to build a course outline from the teacher's perception of these. The result has been functionally-based syllabuses which have aimed to teach a range of skills for everyday use. Although this gave students language they could use straight away, it had two major shortcomings:
1. It focused on areas where they had problems and often where the situation was stressful, for example, dealing with the burst pipe, the robbery, the wrong change. There is nothing wrong with these as topics, but they are seized on in an often uncritical way and contribute to the 'students as needy' ideology. (See Bhanot and Alibhai, Section 1.)
2. By working on a functional basis without a strong structural/grammatical framework, student learning was often limited to

situationally-based language and they were given strategies for generating 'new' language appropriate to other contexts. Consequently, students had no sense of progress, a situation often aggravated by irregular attendance.

Work in the area of equal opportunity and anti-racism has caused teachers to re-examine the content of the curriculum and to move towards one in which students have greater control. This has resulted in the emergence of the following overall objectives:

1. for people to acquire and develop their English language skills;
2. to help students move towards further opportunities of their choice — work, training, further study;
3. for students to have a curriculum which values their various language skills and cultures, and which recognizes their experience of racism, sexism and other forms of discrimination.

Discussion of these objectives currently focuses on several specific issues:

1. *Bilingualism*. ESL has traditionally been a provider's model in which the teacher (who did not share the students' language) was the one who had the language and the information and decided how to structure the teaching and learning. Now there is a recognition that in order to work with students as adults and negotiate the curriculum with them, it helps to use their other languages. What is crucial is that the teacher, monolingual or not, uses all the language skills of the students and acknowledges the linguistic and cultural experience they bring to the class. (See Collingham and Piasecka, Section 4.)

2. *Independent learning*. The process of becoming a self-directed learner should be central to all syllabus and institutional planning in relation to bilingual students. These skills are particularly important for learners operating in an educational system which is unfamiliar to them, compounded by discrimination and institutionalized racism. Teachers therefore need to ensure that students have opportunities to participate in the development of the syllabus, the choice of assessment methods (see Lawson, Section 5) and the evaluation of the course. Both the syllabus and the language skills to be learnt should be made explicit to the students and independent learning should be fostered. (See Hallgarten, Section 4.)

3. *Literacy*. There is little homogeneity in this area. Within one class there may be students who are literate in their first language, those who are non/semi literate, those whose languages use the same script as English and others whose languages do not, as well as students with different types and degrees of motivation in relation to literacy skills. Because of this complex situation, a range of different types of class has emerged with a variety of teaching methods being used. At this point there is a need for teachers to re-examine both the content and method of these classes in relation to issues such as bilingualism and student negotiation. There has also been a tendency for adult literacy and ESL work to develop along parallel but separate paths, even where staff are members of the same department. Now there is an increasing recognition of the value to be gained by working together to pool ideas on approach and methodology. (See Baynham, Section 4.)

4. *Grammar*. The place of grammar in the ESL curriculum has now been reassessed. There is a recognition that in order to acquire and generate

language, students need to know what the building blocks are. This does not mean that the syllabus framework has become rigidly grammatical but that structures are made more explicit in the teaching and teachers recognize the value of enabling students to build up their formal language skills.

Evaluation

The flexibility of the curriculum in ESL has always posed problems of monitoring and evaluating student progress, and of measuring the effectiveness of provision. Evaluating this effectiveness is a difficult task. This is because there are few relevant objective tests, the take-up is uneven and there is no control group. It is also impossible to measure a student's confidence and increased access skills in the face of the unpredictable demands for English made in the world outside the classroom. Even the normal gross measure used to evaluate the effectiveness of adult education — continued student attendance — is not necessarily appropriate. Attendance by ESL students over a long period may indicate a high level of dependence and low level of confidence, with successful learning being marked by students moving on to other types of course after a reasonably short period.

The recent growth in profiling as an assessment tool, and in particular the introduction of the RSA ESL Profile Certificate (see Dunman, Section 5), has encouraged teachers to pay greater attention to this aspect of their work. At the same time this has been reinforced by the move towards autonomous learning and the desire of students to have more tangible evidence of their progress.

In the final analysis, the most important and valid forms of evaluation remain subjective assessments of increased confidence and competence expressed by the student and the teacher, personal feedback from outsiders such as neighbours, social workers and clinic receptionists, and the knowledge that students are successfully moving on to enrol on other adult education and further education courses (Council of Europe, 1983).

Conclusion

The issues discussed in this paper are an attempt to reflect the position that adult education has now reached in responding to the requirements of bilingual students. ESL is no longer seen as a subject of study for its own sake, but as a tool for people to use in order to achieve a diverse range of educational aims. In structural terms, enrolment in an ESL class often proves to be an access point to adult education and providers need to ensure that this is reflected in the provision that is available and the aims and objectives of this provision.

References

COUNCIL OF EUROPE (1983) *Case Study on Adult Education in the Inner London Education Authority*, Council for Cultural Co-operation, School Education Division, Strasbourg

NATESLA (1986) *Training of Teachers of English as a Second Language in the Post-16 Sector*, National Extension College, Cambridge

PERRIN AND MONSAH (1986) 'English Language Provision for Refugees in the UK', *Language Issues* Vol 1, Spring 1986

ROSENBERG, SHEILA AND HALLGARTEN, KATHERINE (1986) 'The National Association for Teaching English as a Second Language to Adults (NATESLA): its history and work', in *English as a Second Language in the United Kingdom*, ELT Document 121, Pergamon

Issues in working with training agencies and funding organizations

Brian Cheetham

Introduction

Training agencies and funding organizations, as well as education authorities, are involved in provision for people who use English as their second language. In Britain such organizations include the Manpower Services Commission (MSC), Industrial Training Boards, PICKUP (Professional, Industrial, Commercial Updating — of skills for adults in employment), REPLAN (educational opportunities for the adult unemployed), and the European Social Fund. The MSC in particular has had an enormous impact, with a wide range of programmes of in-service training, special provision for the unemployed — both for workers who have been made redundant and for school-leavers who have not entered employment — and special training for particular groups of people, including those who use English as their second language. For readers who want to find out more about the range of funding sources in Britain or to find help with the preparation of proposals for obtaining funds, the very accessible guide on the subject by Fey and Davey (1985) is recommended.

This paper looks at the main issues faced by the deliverers (teachers and organizers) of ESL provision when working with training and funding agencies. In particular it draws attention to factors — notably the content of training and the possible marginalization of provision — which can contribute either directly or indirectly to the discrimination faced by ESL-users as a disadvantaged group. In this discussion I have drawn on experience in Britain, and the examples refer to the situation there, but the issues presented are of general relevance to any similar partnership, however vaguely defined, between educational deliverers and a funding agency. This type of partnership tends to force teachers to become directly involved with aspects of curriculum, management and finance, which traditionally have been dealt with by educational managers and administrators, and if teachers have been involved in the past, this has most likely been on a voluntary basis. So what is new is the direct involvement of teachers with these aspects of provision. This paper will examine, in particular, significant issues in three areas: ideology, funding arrangements, roles in the partnership and its organization and management; and how each of these influences the curriculum.

Ideological and practical considerations

Underlying every aspect of the relationship between the partners are ideological factors. One is political, namely the beliefs and principles underlying policy-making. The second is the ideology of the institution itself as represented in the structure of the institution, its relationship to policy-makers, and the work ethos of employees. These factors are closely interrelated, and different permutations or emphases occur. For example, in Britain (in particular in England and Wales) the educational system favours decentralization and a high degree of local autonomy: educational institutions, with a few exceptions, come under the direct control of a local education authority and it is often the case that the local political ideology is completely at odds with that of central government. On the other hand, a funding agency such as the MSC is relatively centralized and is therefore likely to represent more directly the political ideology of central government. Of course, in both cases policies are interpreted by senior administrators, whose personal ideologies must also have some influence on implementation.

At a very practical day-to-day level teacher-organizers and agency officers will be influenced in different ways by the institution to which they belong. Teachers will expect to respond to local needs and assume a large degree of individual autonomy, whereas the officers of a national agency, especially if they are civil servants (teachers in Britain are not), are likely to see themselves as being ultimately accountable to central government for the interpretation of directives and the spending of funds. The implication for the partnership is that there is likely to be tension at some level between teachers and agency officers on account of these backgrounds. Any potential for tension is further increased by the different professional concerns and relative status of the two groups.

Education and training

Ideological factors obviously have implications for the curriculum. In Britain these are well demonstrated by the debate over 'training' versus 'education'. Training is represented as vocational skills development, described in terms of the achievement of performance objectives, whereas education is regarded as the more general development of the individual. Critics, however, have pointed out that it is virtually impossible to identify cognitive or mechanical criteria to distinguish training from education (FEU, 1978; Charnley and Jones, 1979; Central Policy Review Staff, 1980; cited in Roberts, 1984). Roberts suggests that it is the different images produced by the two terms that allow the distinction to persist; images, of course, are a reflection of ideology. The training agency's concept of acceptable provision is likely to impose constraints on the curriculum at all levels, including the nature of the course, the level of resourcing, and monitoring and evaluation. We will now look at each of these in turn.

In her survey of MSC-funded ESL provision, Roberts (1984) found that at the local level there were often doubts expressed as to whether it was appropriate for a training agency to fund ESL provision at all, because it was regarded as education, not training. This view was probably reinforced by the agency officers' contact with the type of ESL curriculum which operates on what can be termed a deficit model. This not only regards adult learners as deficient, and disregards the experience and knowledge which they bring to any learning situation, but is also based on an approach to second-language learning which treats language acquisition as something which can take place as a result of teaching language in isolation, rather than as an integral part of the learning of any new skills or ideas.

The example of the deficit model illustrates how decisions made about the curriculum for ESL-users may contribute to racial discrimination and also reinforce certain negative stereotypes. An explicitly anti-racist model therefore has to be put forward, which argues that all members of the community, regardless of differences, including linguistic and educational backgrounds, have an equal right to the provision of appropriate training. It may require considerable effort to convince the training agency of such a need, since it requires not only a new approach, but also a relatively high level of resourcing.

In Britain a move in this direction has been the development of skills-linked courses with paid training allowances for trainees. These attempt to integrate the learning of language and of vocational skills, and to provide trainees with general skills and information so that they can increase control of their life chances. Incidentally this kind of course generally brings ESL teachers into direct contact with one other ideology, that of the vocational skills trainer, which derives from the ethos of the industrial or commercial workplace, and the tradition of apprenticeship.

The difficulties faced in this situation, which may be in a college or in a special training centre, are similar to those met in the workplace itself. The experience of ILT (Industrial Language Training) is relevant here, not only because it operates in the workplace, but also because the development of ILT reflects some of the advantages that can accrue from having agency funding, as well as highlighting some of the difficulties faced by other providers operating with agency funding.

ILT is an organization directly funded by the MSC via the local education authorities. It provides training services in the workplace, focusing on communications practices as a vehicle for tackling racial discrimination and for implementing equal opportunities. At first, in the early 1970s, ILT concentrated on providing, in the workplace, functional language and communication training for bilingual workers, but it was soon realized that this type of training did very little to tackle the real problem of discrimination and negative attitudes from white supervisors, managers and others with whom the language trainees come into contact. Over a decade, an approach has been developed which emphasizes the need to tackle the structures which maintain disadvantage and discriminatory practices, and to provide training at all levels of the organization so that new practices will be adopted which will ensure outcomes that are fair to all employees. In other words there has been a shift in ILT's work from a deficit model to an anti-racist one, with major implications for the design of courses, content and methodology (Brooks and Roberts, 1985).

This illustrates that in the hands of innovative practitioners agency funding can provide the freedom to respond quickly to local needs and to break the old curricular mould. This may benefit not only the clients but also the teaching staff, who have the opportunity to develop new skills, and to gain managerial-type experience. ILT, however, is relatively privileged, because it operates in the workplace, and therefore has little difficulty in having its work accepted as 'training'; it has a national dimension, and is therefore protected to some degree from changes at local level; and it is funded directly from the agency headquarters. All these factors give ILT a comparatively high profile, and have enabled it to maintain a relatively high level of resourcing. Other types of provision for ESL-users do not have such advantages.

Resourcing is a particularly important issue because teachers traditionally take for granted resources that may have to be explicitly argued for when working with training agencies. While experience shows that there has been relatively little difficulty in maintaining adequate standards of accommodation and basic equipment, which is a familiar concept for agency officers used to industrial legislation, it has frequently been extremely difficult to argue for an adequate length of course for trainees. There is a major tension here between the established practice in adult education where, in general, courses are available for as long as needed, and the concern of the training agency to maximize throughput. Another aspect of resourcing which requires careful negotiation is the level of staffing required. Not only are there the special needs of the class, including mother-tongue and bilingual tuition, and counselling, but there are also the administrative pressures of working with an outside agency, which demand time and special skills.

Monitoring and evaluation are another aspect of work with agencies where differences are likely between teachers and agency officers. Whereas teachers measure achievement by the advances made by individuals, the training agency tends to expect statistically quantifiable results, a common approach being to count the number of trainees who enter employment. There are implications here both for the selection of trainees, and for the chances that trainees are given. There is the danger that only the most able and most easily employable people will be selected for courses. At the end of the course there is the additional danger that trainees will be encouraged to accept employment prospects below their potential because of pressure to get them immediately into work, rather than giving them high-quality grounding in new skills which will significantly improve their life chances. It is therefore very important to argue both that training provision should be available for all ability levels, and that courses be evaluated in terms of criteria based on the improved life chances of trainees.

Funding arrangements

I have already mentioned the importance of funding arrangements in connection with the work of ILT. Funding arrangements reflect the policies of the agency, and may in fact indicate them more clearly than written policy statements, since the structuring of funding reveals how the policies are actually interpreted.

It is therefore necessary to find out exactly how the funding operates, how funds can be obtained, what criteria are used for the allocation of funds for courses, whether there are pools of funds put aside to meet special needs (such as those of disadvantaged groups), and what are the priority categories in the allocation of general funds. It is also important to know what level of coordination exists between national, regional and local levels. To gain access to this information may require skills in public relations, so as to build up contacts, and research skills, in order to seek out information systematically and efficiently. It is also, of course, extremely time-consuming.

In Britain the main training agency funding of provision has been through outlets at local level (with the exception of ILT, as stated above). There has been no local pool of funds specially set aside for minority ethnic groups, but these are a high-priority category. Would-be providers of training put in bids for funds, which are assessed against the agency's criteria. This system has a number of drawbacks. It does not guarantee that any provision for ESL will be made, since it relies largely on would-be providers coming forward (although there is local variation here, and bids can be invited by the agency). Second, although the criteria set ensure minimum standards, there is nothing to encourage high-quality provision; theoretically, even if there were intense local competition among would-be providers, high-quality provision could be rejected in favour of a cheaper alternative. This system, therefore, cannot guarantee either high standards or the existence of particular types of provision. If the system operates at the local level with no national coordination, there is also likely to be inefficiency because of the duplication of the same work at each local base. These drawbacks must surely raise serious doubts as to whether the local tender system is efficient or cost-effective, even in the most crudely economic, let alone educational, terms.

Another feature of funding arrangements in Britain is that they often do not provide a guarantee of funding beyond a particular course, and courses may run for as little as six months or even less. Obviously morale, continuity and innovation are discouraged by this system, which can lead to high staff turnover, since many staff have to be employed on short-term contracts co-extensive with the length of the course. This also produces inefficiency, since new staff arriving need time to familiarize themselves with the course. This problem is further exacerbated because resources for materials development and the in-service training of staff are very limited in spite of the fact that such courses are extremely demanding on the teacher, and require competence in a range of skills not traditionally needed by teachers — a point we have made earlier and will return to below.

The combination of funding structure adopted by the training agency together with the decentralization of the education system has resulted in Britain in a situation where provision has been unevenly distributed. Fairly recent reports show that at the time of survey more than half the total national provision for ESL was concentrated in the London area (NATESLA, 1981), and there were other areas of high-density ethnic minority population without any MSC-funded provision (Roberts, 1984).

Another concern is that the criteria for the approval of courses have frequently changed, and there has been no consultation and prior agreement with providers of training. What is needed is some mechanism that will make it possible to consult with providers and interest groups and to channel funds rationally. In this way it should be possible to chart existing provision, to identify gaps and inadequacies and to overcome some of the previous inefficiency. It is to be hoped that in Britain the Work Related Non-Advanced Further Education (WRNAFE) initiative will have a chance of bringing this about.

The role of the teacher

The final major area of issues I shall examine focuses on the functions and roles demanded of teacher-organizers in the partnership with a funding agency. Teachers may be required to have extensive contact with funding agency officers in areas which include the approval of syllabuses, recruitment and selection of students, monitoring visits by the agency, coordination with the agency over skills-sampling placements and job rehearsals, employment counselling, and the short- and long-term evaluation of the course (Roberts, 1984). Teachers may also be involved in initiating new courses and ensuring the continuance of existing ones, in preparing and presenting submissions and reports, and in budgeting.

Additionally, some teachers have also undertaken the coordination of provision and of resources such as syllabus development and materials. This latter work is generally done on a voluntary basis and members of the National Association for Teachers of English as a Second Language to Adults (NATESLA), whose report was cited above, have been particularly active in this field and have encouraged the development of networks so that information and expertise can be exchanged.

While some direct contact between teachers and the agency officers is generally regarded as desirable and useful, there are certain areas which would place a teacher in a conflict of roles, reflecting the different ideologies discussed earlier in this paper. The main responsibility of the teacher is towards the learners whereas that of the agency officer is to ensure that the funds available are used to maximum effect within the brief laid down. In many situations compromise is inevitable, and this often places the teacher in a moral dilemma: to agree to compromise is to let down individual students and so endanger the relationship of trust between teacher and students. Such emotional pressures can lead to feelings of frustration, depression or even guilt in the teacher, which can adversely affect work in the classroom.

Two examples will illustrate this point. In the first the teacher may wish to push for additional funding to meet the needs of a certain group of students who, in the professional judgement of the teacher, need an extension of the course by a number of weeks in order to achieve the set objectives. The agency officer, on the other hand, has to weigh this demand against a large number of similar and apparently equally urgent cases, and to deal with all of these within the limitations of a tight budget.

Another example would be the negotiation of a new course. In this the experience of the teacher who is directly in touch with the intended target population, and feels strongly about the need to establish special provision for them, is very important. The teacher, however, may not be the best person to present all the arguments. Negotiation requires special skills, and it is important to have at least one person involved who is experienced in this. There is also the danger that someone who is directly engaged emotionally in an issue may fail to present arguments appropriately, and may not succeed in achieving the best outcomes, which can directly lead to feelings of inadequacy and guilt.

Such examples demonstrate that the partnership with a training agency not only increases the workload of the teacher, but can also lead to very considerable psychological stress. There is therefore a strong case for ensuring that more than one person be involved in the courses, both to spread the pressure and to ensure that the roles of teacher and negotiator can be taken by different people in order to minimize the conflict implicit in them.

Discussion of the issue of fair conditions and treatment of the teacher or organizer is relevant here. Increasingly those working with funding agencies are being required to take on many additional responsibilities with no recognition or reward, and it is important to examine why this is happening and what might be done about it. In some cases the constraints on the budget may be such that there is no obvious alternative, as is the case in many small adult education institutions, community centres, and new self-funding enterprises set up specifically to operate with agency funds, especially small YTS and Community Programme projects. This, however, should not apply in larger institutions and colleges, but frequently does, because we find that ESL work is accorded low status, which is reflected in the grades and employment conditions of people involved in it.

In many cases relatively junior staff become involved in a whole range of dealings with agencies, including negotiation at a high level, because of lack of management support. Another problem is tokenism, when an educational establishment takes a precipitate decision that in negotiations concerning people from minority ethnic groups, the institution should be represented by a person from that group. The establishment puts forward a junior member of staff who fulfils this requirement, regardless of suitability otherwise to do the job or of standing with other members of that group, and without giving the necessary training and support. In short, it is not uncommon for senior management to distance itself from the politics of disadvantage and race, thus contributing to the discrimination faced by the groups concerned.

Concluding remarks

In this paper I have examined three major dimensions of work with training agencies. In each case I have identified factors which determine whether or not provision is marginalized and, if it is, to what extent. First, at the ideological level there is the potential tension between political philosophies and between institutions which have a different ethos; in Britain this tension is characterized by the training–education dichotomy. Second, funding arrangements help to determine to what extent provision is *ad hoc* and piecemeal, or planned and coordinated; they also influence the level of efficiency in delivery of provision. Third, the position of teachers and organizers is also significant. There is a danger that they will find themselves pushed into situations where they are required to take on greatly increased responsibilities, and receive inadequate management support or recognition for the work they are doing. Their terms and conditions may also be adversely affected.

These interrelated factors all have an influence on the curriculum and therefore, of course, most importantly on the people for whom the provision is intended. In this paper we have seen examples of how response to local needs can be adversely affected, the constraints on the nature and length of courses, and inconsistencies in the availability and quality of provision. We have also seen examples of some advantages associated with external funding and ways in which disadvantages may be overcome.

The following are suggestions as to how the effectiveness of provision can be improved further. I assume here that issues fundamental to all provision in this field, especially the need to tackle racial disadvantage and to ensure the authentic representation of the communities concerned, discussed elsewhere in this volume, have been fully taken into account.

In order to avoid the isolation which can be faced by both teachers and organizers, and in order to give them support, it is important that existing focal points are strong. Such focal points include national institutions (e.g. NATESLA in Britain), teacher-training establishments, and the relevant examination bodies (e.g. Royal Society of Arts, City and Guilds). These can all raise awareness and ensure that basic information is available. Professional journals are also very important in this regard.

Those involved with agency funding need to have a good theoretical understanding of relevant issues and the personal skills to carry out action. This includes the ability to activate management support where appropriate. Research and public relations work is necessary to understand how structures and funding arrangements operate, and to get to know the culture of the agency and to be able to communicate in its language. When bidding for funds, the ability to prepare submissions and reports, and the ability to negotiate, are needed. Access to policy-making levels is also important, and at higher levels this requires considerable political skill. Coordination at local, regional and national levels needs to go on. In all these areas a strong national organization can be invaluable.

Finally, teachers need to have the confidence not only to use resources creatively, and to develop innovative curricular materials, but also to assert themselves, so that they take adequate account of their own needs, and do not accept ever more responsibility without appropriate support.

None of these issues is unique to work with training agencies, but experience shows that in this kind of work a teacher is more likely to be directly involved with them, and therefore needs to be fully aware of all aspects of the situation.

Acknowledgements My thanks to Sumitar Kaur, Roger Munns and Peter Sayers for help
with many of the ideas for this chapter.

References BROOKS, THEO AND ROBERTS, CELIA (1985) 'No Five Fingers are All Alike: Managing
Change and Difference in the Multi-Ethnic Workplace', In *English as a Second
Language in the United Kingdom*, ELT Document 121, Pergamon
CENTRAL POLICY REVIEW STAFF (1980) *Education, Training and Industrial Performance*
CHARNLEY AND JONES (1979) *The Concept of Success in Adult Literacy*, Huntingdon
Publications
FEY, SUSAN AND DAVEY, MARGARET (1985) *Preparing Proposals for Funding*,
Educational Centres Association
FURTHER EDUCATION UNIT (1978) *Developing Life and Social Skills*
NATESLA (1981) *Survey Report: Teaching English as a Second Language to Adults
from Ethnic Minorities*
ROBERTS, CELIA (1984) *ESL: The Vocational Skill*, NCILT

Section 3 Developing Effective Provision

Introduction

Learning English is not a hobby and it's not a qualification. It is only a very beginning of a long process in terms of job-seeking, confidence, knowing our rights and fighting for them, getting qualifications or doing the job we used to do in our own country.   (Radia)

One of the other difficulties for me while learning English was to decide what kind of English study I wanted. Was it for higher education, special skills or just for communication with the others?   (Arife)

Today, teachers are showing a new willingness to listen to the views of students such as those expressed above and to provide courses and methodology that reflect the students' view of language learning and education. This has not always been so.

As papers in Sections 1 and 2 describe, there has been a tendency until recently for the content and methodology of courses, and the range of provision available, to be based on teacher perception of student need. Now, however, teachers are re-examining their approaches and moving towards a position in which students are partners in the learning process. While this reflects a new understanding of equal opportunity and racism, and their operation in education, at the same time it is also a response to new developments in continuing education. There have been a number of influences on our profession including:

1. A realization in adult education, especially in adult basic education, of the need to 'empower' students by providing them with skills that will enable them to assume greater control of their lives.

2. A shift in curricular focus, particularly in FE and schools, away from the acquisition of a finite body of knowledge and towards transferable skills that can be applied in different ways at different stages of people's lives. This has been accompanied by radical changes in methods of assessment and a desire to assess the processes of learning rather than simply the product. Since language is seen as an underlying element of all learning, this has important implications for bilingual students.

3. Work in independent learning and student autonomy. This has occurred in a number of areas, including modern languages teaching, where it is recognized that most learning takes place outside the classroom, and in skills training where the need for learner training and study skills has been recognized. (Lancashire ILTU, 1986)

Two of the papers in this section adopt a historical approach to illustrate how these influences have been felt in ESL. Faine and Knight use case studies to show how provision for younger students has responded to a widening range of student background and expectation. McAllister and Robson look in more detail at issues related to the provision of language support for bilingual students following a variety of courses in further education. Their paper describes work in one FE college but the models they present could also be applied to work in skills centres and other training organizations as well as within the adult and community context. Ishmail-Bibby illustrates how the changing requirements of adult students have led to a diversification of provision in a large county with ethnic minority groups living in a number of small centres. Her account provides an interesting contrast with Faine and Knight's urban setting and with papers in other sections which also assume an inner-city setting.

References LANCASHIRE ILTU (1986) *Implementing Learner Autonomy*, NEC

A further education response — North-east London

Miriam Faine and Elizabeth Knight

Introduction The students in the following case studies live and study in an area of North London which is a typical inner-city area with high unemployment, declining industrial base and a large diverse ethnic minority population. Most 16- to 19-year-old late arrivals have come to join migrant worker parents; a few, especially refugees, come together with their families or by themselves. Those who benefit from English language support post-school are, broadly speaking, those who arrive at any age after 12–13, including those who arrive after the school-leaving age. Since 1983, it has been ILEA policy for all young people wanting to learn English in this last category to attend further education colleges (see Hoadley-Maidment, Section 2).

The three students we describe here have been chosen to reflect the relationship between individual progress and the range of provision available for young bilingual adults during the last ten years.

Chi, 1981–86

Chi's career illustrates provision in the early 1980s. He came to Britain from Hong Kong in 1977, aged 12, to join his father who had been in the country for some 10–15 years and who worked in a Soho restaurant. Chi's mother and younger brother and sister came a couple of years later and his grandmother came after the death of her husband in 1981.

School

Chi had not completed his primary education when he arrived in London from the New Territories. He went to a local secondary school. Initially he received intensive language tuition which meant that he did not have a full programme of subject study. After this period ended, he followed a very limited programme of study consisting largely of ESL with some mathematics and non-academic options. There were few bilingual students in Chi's year, so he must have been rather conspicuous. This no doubt contributed to the development of his clown persona. He put on a show of not caring about study and made jokes not really about, but rather to disguise his weaknesses, and to become more accepted by his peers. The latter became more important later in his secondary career when a bulge in the Bangladeshi population of the school made bilingual students more conspicuous. With the growth in racism at the school, Chi preferred to identify with, and be identified as one of, his white and black British peers rather than the newly arrived bilinguals segregated in their special ESL class.

Transition to college

Chi left school in 1980 at the earliest opportunity. He had a CSE Grade 5 in mathematics and a reputation for not being serious about study and for being slightly surly. Superficially, he was fairly fluent and his aural comprehension appeared good. His English was sufficient for surviving in London but he could hardly write; he had very poor reading comprehension and his oral presentation skills were only effective in a very limited range of registers and situations. His study skills were almost non-existent.

His ESL teacher knew of the pre-sessional ESL course for Easter leavers at North London College which had started the previous year and referred him to it. It was generally felt that he was not very bright and that work was his best option but that he was not yet ready for this. The one-term course led to an improvement in his literacy and other skills. More importantly, away from school peer group pressure, and in an environment which accepted his bilingualism as a positive rather than a negative attribute, the surliness gradually disappeared and, in a small group, his natural humour emerged as a quality in itself and not as a cover-up to weaknesses. The careers work showed him to be extremely keen to get into a skilled area of work. Unfortunately, the course had not then developed sufficiently to allow him access to maths, and other vocational subjects that would have made his goal more realizable.

Springboard At the end of this short course, Chi saw himself as wanting to work rather than study. He went straight on to a specially devised work experience course for bilingual students: Operation Springboard. Started in 1977 by Camden Committee for Community Relations, this endeavours to place bilingual students in areas of skilled and semi-skilled employment such as engineering, office work or new technology. After counselling, students choose their area of interest and, after a period of language instruction specifically related to work, they are matched to a placement in that area of work. They return to college once a week for language specific to their area of work, maths and world of work. They also go over, individually and as a group, their experiences at work. The placements are closely monitored by the project's Employment Liaison Officer and the language teachers to combat cross-cultural misunderstandings and instances of racism, and to ensure that placement and student are compatible and that worthwhile training is being provided. Springboard has been exceptional in the high rate of employment offered from placements — even in the 1980s.

Chi wanted to become an electrician so he was placed with a self-employed electrician. The placement had its ups and downs and the reactions of trainee and supervisor are typical of the Springboard experience. The electrician complained that Chi was slow to learn and not very sociable. Chi complained that he was not learning very much. Many of these difficulties were due to cultural differences. Some were due to Chi's age and inexperience. Like most 16-year-olds, Chi expected to go straight on to interesting work. He was unaware of the safety hazards of his chosen vocation and how these prevented the electrician from giving him more interesting, unsupervised, work. He was also not used to the peculiarly British concept of time-serving as an essential element of any 'apprenticeship'.

However, the whole experience confirmed Chi in his initial desire to be an electrician. It also induced a consciousness in him with regard to his own educational standard and made him want to improve on his formal qualifications.

Work At the end of the work experience period, the electrician felt he could not offer Chi a permanent job, so Chi joined in the course's intensive job-seeking options and was able to secure employment in semi-skilled electrical fitting work. At this stage Chi was interested in further education but had family pressure to earn an income. Getting the job boosted his confidence tremendously. He, and we, saw it as an interim stage though, if further training at the work place was not forthcoming, Chi could at this stage have chosen to follow a vocational course at college, such as CGLI 224. Experience has shown, however, that students like Chi who attempted this kind of course often did not succeed. What was required was special literacy/study skills support integrated in the course. This was not then available for his area of interest. As a result Chi attended a study skills course in the evening, aimed largely at ex-Operation Springboard students in employment who needed study skills and specific language for day-release courses on which they were studying alongside other English speakers. Attendance on the course kept Chi in touch with friends and teachers and improved his study habits, gave him strategies for coping with texts and introduced him to language specific to his area of study. After one year of work he had proved to himself, teachers and parents that he was a serious student. There were obviously not going to be any further training opportunities at his workplace so he began looking around at possible college courses. The year had greatly increased Chi's maturity and had given him time to decide if he was really prepared to give up a well-paid easy job in order to study for a number of years.

Linked skills

In 1983 North London College set up a specific integrated course in engineering for 16- to 19-year-old bilingual students. The course worked to CGLI 200/224. All the theory and some of the practical sessions were double-staffed with a language specialist and there was language follow-up as well as preparation for a language examination (CGLI Communication 772).

The course was well designed and the vocational teachers were impressed with the motivation and ability of bilingual students who, when offered a course with 'real' subjects and examinations, did extremely well. At first the skills teachers were a little reticent about the course arrangements, feeling that they were going to be asked to change drastically their ways of teaching. But as the year progressed and they saw how the linked-skills approach made the language of engineering accessible to the students, their attitude changed considerably and the increase in their own language awareness enabled them to anticipate possible areas of difficulty.

Chi passed all his subjects and gained credits in most. Moreover the course really fired his enthusiasm for learning. Chi saw the need and had the desire to continue his education. He could have continued on a craft course or transferred to the technician level. His choice was largely determined by the availability of language support. By the end of this substantial course he could write up notes and lab. reports and understand lectures and clearly written text books. With the aid of a personal set of some 100 key words, he could get round his poor spelling. Yet he would still need some language support for areas not covered in his course, such as the freer answering of short questions, or reading denser and more complex texts.

ESL support

Chi's path through further education was highlighting the need for 'a whole college' language policy and for language support on mainstream courses. Hackney College in 1984 offered such support on a BTEC course in electronics. So it was here that Chi went. He was accepted on to a native speaker course that also recruited bilingual students and offered a follow-up language class. In addition, there was careful monitoring of students' progress and counselling. The structured support offered enabled him to pass Level 1 in 1985 and to progress on to Level 2 without any specific support.

Ruhena

Background

Ruhena arrived in the UK from a large provincial town in Sylhet region, Bangladesh, aged just 16 in October 1983. After being admitted to the fifth form of a local comprehensive she was immediately sent to Hackney College's ESL reception course, the 'ESL General Education Course', as a 'school link' student.

Like most new arrivals in recent times, Ruhena had had schooling in her country of origin, in her case slightly more than most. She comes from a relatively prosperous and well-educated background. Her father, who had been in the UK some 20 years, is a post office employee. She had just started her tenth year of education in Bangladesh, in the science stream, and would have sat public examinations at the end of the year had she stayed. In the course of her school career she had been taught to read and write in the Roman alphabet and she had some passive knowledge of English vocabulary and structure. In terms of using language, she was a beginner. The reception courses had changed since Chi's arrival and they now contained the elements of any general education course — numeracy, general science, computing, vocational tasters, short work-experience tasters. The courses were still catering for recent arrivals, and therefore covered a wide ability range.

The courses were diagnostic and so could cater for 15-year-olds sent by their schools as well as 16- to 18-year-olds. While FE-based provision had, from the beginning, catered for some sixth formers on a part-time basis, in the part of London we are describing, schools began to refer all who arrived during their sixteenth year straight to an FE General Education Course. Here they were spared the alienating and frightening experience of coping with a large comprehensive, big classes, and the option system. At college they stayed with one group throughout the day, were with bilingual peers who could help them adjust to education in England, and received language support throughout their programme of study.

Ruhena's programme consisted of a core of English, including 'careers' and 'community studies', maths/numeracy, general science, computing, typing and electronics, and some recreation time. The value of the practical subjects was that they immediately put the students in a situation where they needed to communicate and, with more fluent students acting as facilitators, the students would in most cases acquire oral skills very quickly. In addition, some of the options were double-staffed by an ESL teacher. Their task was three-fold: to provide the students with the instant language they needed to cope with the class, to follow up the subject matter with the English language needed for that subject, and to help the subject teacher cope with a class of very recently arrived adolescents. As the course progressed, the whole of the course team could begin to assess the potential of each student. The 'careers' programme helped the students compare life and education in the UK with that in other countries as well as offering advice and information on job search and further education.

When the time came for a brief work experience in February, Ruhena went to a local unemployment advice centre, to do some translating as well as general office work. She had no great interest in clerical work but it was a chance to increase her confidence and her oral English skills in a slightly less protected environment. In the third term the students studied one chosen subject area in more depth. Ruhena joined the science group (the others were motor vehicle, electronics, office work). In the June examinations, six months after entering the country, she gained a CSE 2 in mathematics. Her English — and above all her study strategies in English — were now sufficiently developed to allow her to carry on learning her chosen subjects where she had left off. She had been able to transfer, and then build on and develop, skills that she already had in her first language.

Pastoral issues

The social and pastoral elements of college life for bilinguals were important in providing a 'safe' place for recent arrivals to adjust to life in the UK. To ensure equal opportunities it was especially important that the college recruited young women on to courses for bilingual students — and that they catered for their specific needs. For example, with a Bengali-speaking woman ESL teacher, all the students were closely supervised in order to reassure the girls and their families that their customs and traditions were respected and that the girls' reputations were safe in a mixed college. With a few exceptions — notably in the Turkish speaking community — this had an excellent response and young women were encouraged by their families to benefit from the course. This included the work experience, a variety of educational excursions, and theatre visits, both 'multi-ethnic' and 'English'. Two ESL discos a year, closely supervised and with transport home provided, helped former and current bilingual students establish their own networks and friendships. The General Education students also went on a residential course, where they developed their skills through shopping, orienteering on bicycles and organizing each other in groups to do the cooking. They also saw a part of Britain that wasn't like inner-city London. A fair number of girls participated and this showed that they and their parents trusted the college.

A programme of twilight community language 'O' level classes also provided an environment where, as well as mother-tongue maintenance and learning important translation skills, newer arrivals could mix socially with those who had been here longer and so slowly come to terms with living in two cultural systems. The Bengali students in particular, encouraged by their Bengali teacher, produced a series of cultural events and their own modern Bengali drama; in this environment Ruhena soon became an acknowledged leader.

GCE courses

In September 1984 Ruhena joined Hackney College's 'O' level science/ESL course. This is an offshoot from the original General Education course. Designed for students who have either studied science to this level before and/or show promise, it consists of substantial ESL support attached to a three-subject one-year science 'O' level/GCSE course already on offer in the college. Students study a core of ESL/study skills using an approach based on the work of McAllister and Robson (1985). As with other courses, sections of the science work were double-staffed with an ESL teacher. While this helped the ESL teacher gather material for 'follow-up' work based on students' observed difficulties in class, and to monitor the students' progress overall, it also led, over the years of partnership, to the development of teaching strategies by the science teachers that were more appropriate to students still learning the language.

The course also gives enormous attention to traditional study skills. Even able and well taught late arrivals such as Ruhena need to acquire very specific study skills implicit (and not explicit) in the British education system, and acquired by British students very early in their educational career. Ruhena was notable for her diligence on this course, always completing homework and studying several hours a night at home, and this is obviously a reason for her success. Ruhena talked of a career in medicine or teaching and, though this still seemed a bit unrealistic, we advised her to take physics and chemistry and see how she got on.

The 'English' language qualification

The bilingual students took the NWRAC (North Western Regional Test for ESL), (see Rosenberg, Section 5) because it specifically tested the language and skills areas our 'study skills' syllabus covered. Ruhena was most unhappy about this and asked to be allowed to do 'O' level English. The problem the ESL staff saw was that a student at her level of English proficiency — perhaps 'mid-intermediate' in ESL terms — could be taught to express herself clearly and correctly in a *limited* range of contexts and language functions, whereas 'O' level English was assessed on a range of features that are well beyond the minimum necessary to pass science 'O' levels. There was no reason why Ruhena should not take 'O' level English, with a much better prognosis, in the next two years while attempting 'A' levels. ESL staff explained this to her father and showed him examples of course material. Eventually Ruhena and her father both agreed reluctantly that she should take NWRAC. (The tutor heard later from our Bengali colleague that he had asked her privately whether he should take his children away from the college and place them in private education — which would have caused him considerable financial hardship. It was certainly to our benefit and, the ESL staff believe, to that of his children, that she convinced him to leave them at the college.)

Assessment of 'O' level /GCSE students

Like most of the students on the 'O' level course, Ruhena was recruited through the ESL network — in this case from the college's own General Education course which acted as a funnel on to a variety of other training or courses. How were students assessed for suitability for this kind of course? Firstly, on the basis of a very careful assessment of their previous schooling, based on the analysis of the college application form. Secondly, the ESL staff try and keep careful records of a student's progress through the system. A most helpful indication of the relative standing of x years' schooling is the use of a maths test. Though our college maths test is not perfect, it has been used so often for this purpose that responses can be standardized allowing for the language used in it (which is also a good test of applicants' reading ability). This gives an indication of what has been learnt and thus one can grade the standard of previous teaching from nil to pre-'O' level/GCSE standard.

In the end, the quality of students' education has proved a much better predictor of their future success than their language level at the beginning of the course. As with the General Education course, it is through the study of other subjects, and the resulting communication need, that even beginners have rapidly acquired fluency in English.

Like the General Education students the 'O' level/GCSE science students also have a careers programme. Its purpose is to help them and their families to come to a well-informed understanding over the course of the year of the options open to them and the advantages and disadvantages of each (e.g. BTEC, 'A' levels, YTS), and to recognize their own true capabilities; sometimes they scale down unrealistically high ambitions after having tasted academic study. In Ruhena's case it was clear that we had, if anything, underestimated her; her results in August 1984 were A in maths and Bengali, B in physics and C in chemistry, as well as a credit in her NWRAC English. She then progressed on to an 'A' level course in maths, physics and chemistry.

Zohra

Zohra is a refugee from an Iranian Jewish background. She conforms to the stereotypes many people have of refugee students; that is, she is from a middle class, prosperous background in Iran. Her originally elite background caused all sorts of tensions and traumas for her family in adjusting to the huge change in circumstances and opportunities when they had to leave everything behind and come to the UK, and these affected her career at college.

Exceptionally, Zohra had heard about our courses, not through the ESL referral network, but through general college publicity – her brother had seen the prospectus in the local library. She was just 18 and had arrived in the UK about three months before. She had briefly attended EFL classes in the outer London borough where she lived.

She had received an 'O' level equivalent education from one of Teheran's best schools. When she first came to the college, her level of English could be described as elementary, though she had better passive knowledge. She was given the usual college maths test, as well as the diagnostic English writing test. Her maths score was lower than one would have expected from the level of education she claimed; she said this was due to nerves. Once we got to know her better, it was clear this was true. She was therefore accepted for science 'O' levels, including computer studies. (In spite of her level of language, the General Education course would have been inappropriate for her educational level and maturity and her existing study skills. Almost all students with good educational background move up quickly in both English and the mainstream curriculum if they move straight on to a course with substantial language support, rather than taking a course at a level lower than that of their previous studies.) However, within a few weeks she said that her rather traditional family was expecting her, as the eldest daughter, to get a job and support her unemployed parents (both her older brothers were studying at postgraduate level), so she wanted to change to a more practical, office work course. She was transferred to the BTEC General Certificate, which was for the first time being offered to a group of bilingual students.

The way forward   The case studies we have described above illustrate that, with bilingual young people, unemployment has not led to 'a decline in the quality of student' as it is argued has happened in further education generally. Rather, we deal with a self-selected group. Of the 15-year-olds who have access to a further education college, a proportion (about 8 per cent) disappear every year — sometimes, sadly, because of economic pressures, sometimes advisedly in view of our assessment of their potential. For the rest of the group, our problem is to match their justly high expectations with the realities of inner-city Britain, remembering the sacrifices their families are prepared to sustain in order to help their children's future.

In order to match these expectations we need to understand how culturally based a conception of 'good' education is — both our conception and that of our students. Thus, we need to recognize a different view of education that may seem to us to value the academic at the cost of the experiential, the product rather than the processes, and to understand that qualifications may seem the only road out of the ghetto. And to teach effectively, we have to understand other cultural procedures of study and learning, of examinations, of classroom interaction and so on, as well as endeavour to reconcile our students to those procedures that, sooner or later, they must meet in mainstream English education.

It also becomes our responsibility not just to 'sell' our courses to a new market, but to accept a role as brokers within the system, a system which must change to accommodate the new types of student. In the short term, though, we are also responsible for the individuals, so all students must be advised on the most appropriate provision. Colleges must work together to develop a range of language-supported courses and not fill their own courses at the expense of individual needs. It is not the job of the ESL staff to fill 'unpopular' courses or use up the resources (e.g. engineering workshops) that have become redundant. And you cannot graft healthy ESL support on to ailing general provision. Nor, in the end, do 'special' ESL courses which do not have mainstream, recognized accreditation and equivalents, serve the purpose. If, for example, bilingual students want to do computing, they need access to the most current, recognized course of a significantly high level with *additional* support. 'Special' ESL provision, or low-level provision, or 'preliminary courses' will only perpetuate inequality. We need to look for the most popular, well-taught, over-subscribed and credible provision in our colleges and negotiate the ESL support there.

Acknowledgements   Both colleges were much indebted to the work of McEldowney and the application of that to ESL developed by J. McAllister and M. Robson at Shipley College in developing syllabuses.

References   CCCR (1979) *A Chance to Work*
McALLISTER, J. AND ROBSON, M. (1985) *Building a Framework*, NEC

A community education response — Northamptonshire

Zorina Ishmail-Bibby

Northamptonshire is a mixture of town and country. It incorporates rural areas such as those around Brackley and Towcester, small market towns like Wellingborough and Kettering, more recently established towns such as Corby and, of course, the major centre and county town — Northampton.

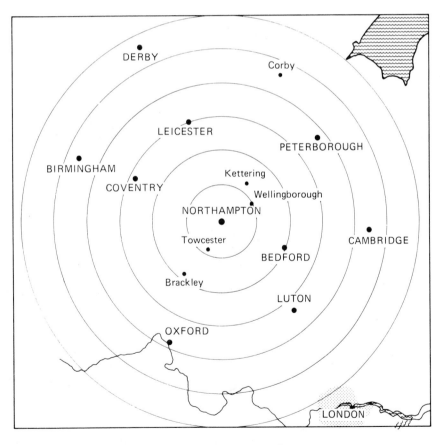

Large and small towns within a 60-mile radius of Northampton

ESL provision received its initial impetus from the TOPS courses established in 1976. The MSC-funded courses catered for more advanced bilingual students who were job-seeking. Less advanced students were not specifically catered for and were to be found in adult literacy classes or EFL provision.

However, with the appointment of an ESL tutor/organizer in 1980, ESL provision increased and became more directly concerned with the students' needs. By 1982 several daytime and evening classes were taking place in Northampton. Others were established in Kettering and Wellingborough. Provision was then extended to Corby and a home-tutor system set up to complement this network of community classes. Still, classes have tended to centre mainly on urban areas and a few rural areas. It has proved difficult to make ESL provision in more isolated rural areas.

The RSA Diploma TESL (FACE) was first run for part-time ESL staff in 1981 in Northampton. The RSA CIT TESL followed the next year. These courses, as well as further developments in volunteer and other in-service training, improved the quality of service and made it more relevant to student clientele. Links with NATESLA also helped to increase awareness of ESL training and other developments nationally, and made for good practice locally.

The background

Northamptonshire has grown in ethnic diversity since the 1950s. This is due to the accessibility of reasonably priced housing, the business opportunities available and what was, until recently, a strong industrial base.

Poles settled in Northampton immediately after the war and now have a flourishing community which centres on the Polish church and club. More recently another group of Poles has arrived: political refugees from the conflict surrounding the Solidarity movement.

The Italian community has also lived in Northamptonshire for a long time. Many originally worked in the Bedfordshire brick fields but then moved into the county to take up employment in factories or to work in restaurants or in the ice-cream business. More recently, some young Sicilians have settled in Northampton as a result of EEC legislation which has affected mobility of labour. Some may have family connections as well. These young people, some of whom were professionals at home, are keen students of English, seeing the mastery of the language as a key to good employment opportunities.

Asians of East African origin came to England in the 1960s. Some moved to Northampton because better housing was available. Many have bought corner shops and established successful businesses.

The Indians who came to Northampton were mainly young brides, semi-skilled workers or professionals, for example doctors who worked at Northampton General Hospital. Sikhs were attracted by British Steel in Corby and Weetabix in Burton Latimer near Kettering. They settled in and around Kettering and Wellingborough.

There has also been a small well-established community of Chinese from the New Territories, Hong Kong, connected with the restaurant business. A small number of Pakistanis also live in Northamptonshire.

The most recent ethnic minority group to settle in Northamptonshire are the Vietnamese. They come from both North and South Vietnam and, after spending some time at reception centres in Derby and Lincolnshire, were re-housed in various parts of the county.

Meeting student needs

In order to show how we have tried to meet students' needs over the years, I shall use a few Northampton case studies. These students arrived at different times over the last seven years and have both affected and been affected by the provision that was available at the time.

Tien came to Northampton in 1979. She is Vietnamese and has seven children. She and her husband came to classes at the centre, bringing their youngest child with them. They even rented a small house nearby so that they could attend as many classes as possible. Tien's husband was unwell and, as the classes became more difficult, he stopped coming. Tien, however, continued to attend classes until 1984 and progressed from speaking only a few words of English to taking and passing the RSA oral exam in communication skills.

During the time Tien was attending our ESL classes, we were following topic-based, functional syllabuses. Then in 1983 we began to experiment with some linked-skill classes. One of the first of these was a sewing class. Initially, it was only planned to run for a term, but the classes are still running at present.

The sewing class was taught in tandem by an experienced dressmaking teacher and an ESL tutor. It was a cheerful class where students were relaxed and enjoyed both the teaching and each others' company. One such student was Sumri who came from Gujerat in India. She had come to England as a bride the previous year but, because of problems with her in-laws, had come to Northampton to live with friends. When she first came to class she could not speak any English and was unable to read or write it at all. However, she persevered and, with tremendous patience, learned to read, write and speak enough English to get a job in a dressmaking factory. There is no doubt that the ESL/sewing class played an important part in increasing Sumri's confidence, as well as providing her with a marketable skill. The longer term effect was that her job enabled her to become more financially independent and to accept a place at a women's hostel. Eventually she and her husband were reconciled.

Other linked-skill classes followed on from the initial sewing class. A sewing class was set up in Wellingborough in 1985/86. Driving classes were started in Northampton and Wellingborough in 1984. They were similar to the sewing classes in that there was an ESL tutor and a driving instructor involved. Then in 1985 cookery classes began in the Sikh temple in Kettering. In this instance the ESL tutor, an experienced cook, taught the classes which specialized, at the students' request, in cake making and decoration. Knitting classes took place in Rushden. Flower arranging classes took place in Wellingborough in 1985.

In Northampton our links with MSC staff, with whom we have shared premises and expertise over the years, have always been good. A useful co-operative venture has been a recently run 10-week computer course, which taught students how to use software with reference to business. Amongst the students attending the May 1986 course were Ranjeet Kaur and Sohrab.

Ranjeet, a Sikh, came to Britain in 1973. At the time she spoke no English and she says she had little education in India. A few years after her arrival, she was widowed and left with two young daughters to bring up on her own. She started attending one of our community classes but because she needed to be available for her youngest child, who had a kidney complaint, and because there was no crèche where she could leave her, Ranjeet soon found it impossible to continue. She returned to the classes in 1985:

> I started English classes again because I had very great difficulty understanding English and finding work. This time it was easier since both my girls were at school.

Having attended classes for the best part of a year, Ranjeet commented:

> I understand how to help myself. I don't need to bother anybody. I can take my daughter to the hospital and I explain everything to the doctor myself. I can go to the shops. I can go everywhere myself. I don't want help.

Ranjeet was determined to learn English to cope with her child's illness and to get a job. One of the topics covered in her class was job seeking. This included form filling, letter writing, ways of finding work, and role-play interviews. Ranjeet was an avid participant and decided to apply for a job as a clerical assistant at the Barclaycard Centre in Northampton. As soon as the computer course was offered, she was eager to apply for a place since she felt it would further her ambition to obtain a job at the computerized Centre. The RSA Profile Certificate was introduced at our Northampton centre during this year. Ranjeet and other members of the class agreed to enter. This helped to give her more confidence and evaluate her language learning. She mentioned it in her letter of application to the Barclaycard Centre. She was interviewed and accepted for a clerical job. She has been working at Barclaycard for two years now and has recently been promoted.

Sohrab also attended the computer course. He and his wife, Iranian refugees, arrived in Northampton in 1985, having spent a year in Pakistan before coming to Britain. Sohrab had an extremely good formal education in Iran. He obtained a degree at university and was a chief accountant at a factory in Teheran. He was motivated to attend the computing class because he felt that a knowledge of computers would help him develop skills which would enhance his chances of finding a suitable job.

Sohrab is quite philosophical about his current position and sees this period without work as an opportunity to improve his language skills. He is certainly not a passive student and comments freely on the methods of teaching employed in ESL classes:

> In our class, we have many different nationalities. For example, Vietnamese, Mexican, Korean, Indian, Pakistani, Polish and Iranian. I think it is good to hear different accents. English has helped me to talk to people and to understand them. I hope it will help me to find a job in the future.

The teachers use different methods to teach us: tapes, cards, video and some printed worksheets. I think the printed worksheets are more useful than the rest.

Although we have always tried to make our teaching relevant to the needs of students, it is only recently that we have tried to involve students in the planning of course syllabuses. For example, in January 1986 we were approached by a group of doctors from Northampton General Hospital and asked if we would set up a class for them. They met with the ESL tutor who was planning to teach the class and discussed what sort of topics and language they needed. Their level of oral English was good. Three of them were studying for the English exams for the BMA. The tutor assumed that they needed English for medicine but they assured her that this was the least of their problems. They wanted the kind of English used when communicating informally with their patients, i.e. to talk about local and current affairs, to understand and use colloquial expressions.

It was initially agreed that the class would take place for six weeks and that, if the students were dissatisfied with the level and content, the tutor would be informed and the class discontinued. During this period, the tutor checked with the students carefully and they regularly evaluated what was being taught in class. At the end of the six-week period, the group asked for the class to be extended until the end of the summer term.

This was one of many attempts at collaborative learning and the success of the exercise strengthened the belief that we should continue to operate in a similar way in all the classes. It is obviously necessary to devise different approaches according to the level of English of the students concerned. For instance, at the more elementary levels it will be essential to have bilingual teachers, or to use other bilingual professionals such as community interpreters, to help in the process.

Special support and liaison staff have been used in Northamptonshire for several years. Bilingual interpreters and teachers have assisted, especially at the more elementary level. Some of the better students have been recruited and used as teachers and volunteers. This is an extremely necessary and important development.

Self Access Workshops were set up in Northampton and Wellingborough in September 1986. They take place twice weekly in Northampton and also in Wellingborough. They cater for students who work in the day, those who do not attend classes but have enough study skills to benefit from self-directed study, and students already attending classes who wish to supplement the work already covered. A teacher is available at each workshop to give advice to the students about suitable materials.

The course has been successful. In a letter to the teachers, one of the students, Oscar from Hong Kong, writes:

I have a very nice and beneficial time attending the workshop. . . I gained a lot from the workshop including some confidence in my English.

Conclusion   Over the years we have attempted to cater for student needs as best we can. In the past, this has been hampered by lack of trained staff and premises. For instance, we found it difficult to expand classes or facilities given our existing accommodation in Northampton and Wellingborough, and in the early days it was very difficult to find trained staff.

The situation has now improved, although many problems remain. New premises in Northampton have enabled us to diversify our provision as well as to set up a crèche. In Wellingborough, however, premises still remain a problem and we have had to cope with this by locating classes in schools, health centres, community centres and, in some areas, even in the homes of the students themselves.

We still continue to train home-tutor volunteers but we now have a scheme whereby, after they have gained some experience by assisting in community classes, we are able to offer them further training through the RSA initial certificate in TESL. For more experienced staff, we continue to run the RSA Diploma TESL (FACE). Both these courses have helped us build up an experienced ESL staff.

In evaluating the development of our scheme and deciding ways forward in the future, we have made considerable use of our contacts with professional organizations such as NATESLA and the RSA. In this way we have been able to participate in many of the national developments and to share in the many debates surrounding this area of work.

Acknowledgements   My thanks are due to Linda Murphy, ESL Tutor/Organizer, Northamptonshire, for help with background information about Northamptonshire, and Sukhraj Bajwa, ESL Tutor/Home Tutor Organizer, Wellingborough, for information about Sikhs and classes in Wellingborough.

Language support across the curriculum

Jean McAllister and Margaret Robson

In the last few years we have been working on the development of a theoretical framework for teaching communication skills, which has helped us in the practical task of developing classroom strategies for language support. The framework rests on a categorization of communication skills which integrates personal development and political literacy with language development and study skills, thus allowing us to develop communication skills for a range of purposes — academic, vocational or social. In our work we have drawn upon the idea of core functions developed by Dr Pat McEldowney. This approach to English for Academic Purposes underpinned much of our early language support work, and led us to develop a framework, described in detail in *Building a Framework* (1984), which has been of considerable help in syllabus and course design. We have learned though, in the course of our work, that good practice in the classroom is ineffective without the right organizational structures to back it up. So in this paper we have chosen to focus on:

— some of the issues which the institution has to address to make language support effective;
— the various organizational options we need to lobby for in our institutions;
— some of the necessary prerequisites for implementing non subject-specific language support.

Issues in language support

Policy Language support cannot be divorced from the policy context in which it operates, and therefore it will be of limited value in improving the access and performance of bilingual students unless it is accompanied by other aspects of institutional change. While many colleges now have not only policies for racial equality but also language policies, these will only be effective if backed up by plans for implementation and a clear institutional commitment to adequate resourcing.

Resourcing A number of demands on resourcing will be made, including the need for:
— double-staffing to ensure adequate language support for bilingual students in subject lessons.
— liaison time to enable language tutor and subject tutor to meet to discuss methodology, materials, etc. Arrangements which rely on the goodwill of tutors meeting in lunchbreaks are doomed to fail.
— enhanced student hours to ensure that bilingual students receive adequate support in terms of class contact hours or tutorial supervision. Time pared from subject classes or tutorials allocated during elective sessions simply serve to marginalize the provision and the students it is designed to serve.

Negotiation Students should be actively involved in the design and delivery of their language support programmes. This means:
— students should not simply be drafted into language support

programmes, especially on the basis of being bilingual, but rather their involvement should be negotiated with them on the basis of sensitive counselling and guidance by both subject tutor and language tutor.

— following this initial negotiation, the programme should be designed with students on the basis of an analysis of their individual level of competence in relation to the particular communication demands of the subject concerned. (An example of how an analysis of the communication demands of a subject can be achieved can be found in the FEU report on the Shipley College communication skills project (1988).)

Curriculum and assessment

There is a growing awareness of the need to eliminate ethnocentric bias and cultural assumptions from subject syllabuses (see Rosenberg, Section 5). However, new syllabuses should also take into account the need to incorporate more flexible learning styles and to accommodate adequate support into the learning programme so that bilingual students, and in fact all students, can benefit from a more student-centred approach where 'pressure of the syllabus' does not take precedence over other interests and issues. It is also important that all forms of assessment, especially the new exams, should reflect positively the interests of black and bilingual students and the requirements of a multiracial and multicultural society.

Staff development

Providing effective language support has implications for staff development. These include the need for:

— racism awareness training for all staff, based on a recognition that all involved in education for a multiracial society should have the chance to address personal, institutional and structural racism in order to achieve a better understanding of the history and function of racism in post-industrial Britain, to become more aware of their own attitudes and to appreciate the effects of racism on educational achievement.

— language awareness training for all staff, to ensure that both subject tutors and language tutors develop a shared understanding and a common framework within which the language demands of specific subjects and courses, and the needs of individual students, can be discussed. Imprecise statements such as 'Mohamed's problem is his poor English' should no longer be considered a sufficient analysis of a student's difficulties.

— curriculum and classroom strategies for all staff, to help them develop a non-racist curriculum and effective teaching methods and classroom practice.

Organizational options

At present there are a number of organizational models for supporting students on mainstream courses. We outline these models below and give examples of them in practice. The table on pp. 76 – 77 summarizes the implications of each option.

Option 1: General English language communications provision
Students pursuing mainstream courses, and also following communications/English/ESL courses, possibly leading to exams such as CGLI 772, English Language GCSE, etc. Language provision operates discretely and often has no links with other parts of the course provision. For this reason we are in fact reluctant to describe it as a language support option as such.

Option 2: Subject-specific support outside the subject lesson WITHOUT liaison with the subject tutor. No double-staffing arrangements
Language tutors attempting to provide 'English for . . .' support lessons — English for biology, English for sewing — but without contact with the tutor and without being in the subject lesson.

Option 3: Subject-specific support outside lesson PLUS liaison with subject tutor
Language tutors providing support lessons as in Option 2 but with the opportunity to liaise with the subject tutor.

Option 4: Double-staffing
Language tutors working alongside subject tutors in mainstream subject classes.

Option 5: Double-staffing PLUS liaison time
As Option 4 but with time made available to liaise with the subject tutor about the lesson.

Option 6: Double-staffing PLUS extra subject-specific language support
Language tutors working alongside subject tutors on mainstream courses, plus extra communications support tutorials. No liaison time with subject tutor.

Option 7: Double-staffing PLUS liaison time PLUS extra subject-specific language support
As Options 5 and 6 above but with liaison time.

Option 8: Non subject-specific language support with liaison as necessary
Language support based not on specific subjects but rather on developing a broad communicative competence for academic and vocational purposes. We envisage such language support as being both systematic and generic — systematic inasmuch as it is based on a clear analytical framework, and generic inasmuch as that framework is sufficiently shared with the students to enable them to see its application in specific subject areas.

When we first started to provide language support in our college we were delivering option 1. We then made what we felt at the time to be a heady leap forward to option 2! Since that time we have experimented with other options and have discussed with colleagues elsewhere the various systems they are operating. We now feel we have a much better idea of the relative merits of each and have itemized these in the table below. (You will notice that the table does not include option 8. This is because, to our knowledge, option 8, as we envisage it, is not being used anywhere at present. It is our preferred option and we will discuss it in more detail after the table.)

	General English	Double-staffing	Liaison	Subject-specific support outside subject lesson	Advantages	Disadvantages
1	✓				Students can gain a qualification in English	1 English provision tends to be marginalized from mainstream course provision 2 Provision tends to be dictated by examinations available, most of which are very monocultural, focus on 'social context' communication, and in the case of ESL exams, lack status 3 No possibility of identifying and remedying students' difficulties with subjects 4 No possibility of influencing subject teaching methodology or enabling subject teachers to be aware of language demands of subjects 5 Makes no political demands on institution
2				✓	Student motivation higher than for 'general' English	1 Time-consuming to find right materials 2 Danger of getting subject matter wrong 3 May be too wide a range of subjects to support 4 Very expensive if support is for each subject 5 Does not influence subject teaching 6 Makes few political demands on institution 7 Support can be quite random without a systematic language analysis 8 Lack of exams to validate such work
3			✓	✓	1 Recognition of liaison time important step forward 2 Suitable materials can be made available 3 Use of current materials may increase student motivation	1 Does not necessarily influence subject teaching. Danger liaison = simply handing over materials 2 Danger of re-teaching the lesson 3 Support could still be unsystematic 4 May be too wide a range of subjects to support 5 Lack of exams to validate work

#				Advantages	Disadvantages / Cautions
4	✓			1 Subject tutor may see another model 2 Individual help valuable to students 3 ESL tutor can identify difficulties 4 May signal the end of ESL provision as 'remedial', i.e. into the mainstream	1 ESL tutor may not have a role – especially true in teacher-led situations 2 Support essentially random – responding to individual student difficulties. Difficult to do systematic language development 3 Difficult to influence subject tutor methodology 4 'Integration' of language and subject may mean loss of language dimension
5	✓	✓		1 As above 4.1–4.4 2 If team teaching happens, and quality of liaison good, can be a successful option	1 4.1–4.4 may still be true. Depends entirely on quality of liaison. Needs to focus on teaching strategies not detail of subject matter or individual students 2 May be difficulties over relative status of ESL tutor and subject tutor. Difficult to comment on another tutor's teaching style
6	✓		✓	1 As 4.1–4.4 for subject lesson 2 ESL tutor can spot difficulties *and* follow up in support lesson 3 Motivation may be high for support lesson because of tutor's visible link with subject	1 As 4.1, 4.2, 4.3 for lesson 2 Range of subjects to support may pose organizational difficulties, and time difficulties for students 3 Re-teaching lesson a danger
7	✓	✓	✓	1 If real integration happens in subject lesson, will mark very positive option 2 Students may be more motivated for integrated language/subject programme 3 Represents positive commitment to support from institution 4 Individuals will get a lot of help 5 Difficulties can be identified in subject lesson and remedied in follow-up work 6 Support has not disappeared as a result of integration	1 Very expensive option 2 Quality of liaison is still crucial if real integration is to be achieved – still could be no role for ESL tutor and difficulties over relative status with subject tutor 3 If there are extra lessons for each subject, this will be very demanding for students and expensive for the institution. It could be a 'general' support session drawing out general areas of language from each subject area, but illustrating with subject-specific examples

Preferred options   At present we push option 7 since it seems to us to provide maximum support for students, given current circumstances. However, we would ultimately like to see a system of language support based on non subject-specific work as outlined in option 8. For us this does not mean a return to the 'drop-in' general type of communications workshop provision, which is of limited value to our students. Rather it means a language support programme which is based upon:

— developing competence in the communicative functions appropriate for academic and vocational purposes, i.e. description, description of process, instruction, narrative, explanation, classification, comparison and contrast, etc.

— developing a range of communication skills identified by subject tutors as important. This would be done in liaison with the language tutor and would include two kinds of skills analysis. Firstly, there would be the skills that were needed because of the subject teacher's own teaching style. For example, one subject teacher may expect students to take detailed notes from a talk while another would prepare a handout. These activities clearly require different skills — listening and note-taking, versus reading. Secondly, the skills analysis would also involve an identification of the skills inherent in the demands of the subject itself. Electronics, for example, involves a lot of information transfer, such as understanding circuit diagrams, whereas business studies involves a lot of oral work. The subject tutor and language tutor would work together to analyse these various skill demands. Through the FEU project at Shipley College, a skills check-list has been devised which aims to facilitate this.

The kind of support outlined in option 8 would be easier to organize and more cost-effective, since students from different subject classes could be brought together for the systematic, generic form of language support we describe. However, it would only operate effectively when the following essential conditions were met:

— Subject tutors would have the benefit of *language awareness training* so that they could:
  1. identify the conditions necessary for bilingual students to learn effectively.
  2. identify the language and communication demands of their own subject.
  3. identify the difficulties bilingual students have with their subject and modify their methodology and teaching materials accordingly, with the aid of language specialists as necessary.

— Language and communication skills teaching would be aiming to develop a *broad generic competence* in the language and communication skills appropriate *for academic and vocational purposes*. Subject tutors would be able to overlay subject-specific work on to this basic groundwork.

— Subject tutors and language tutors would, as a result of staff development, share *a common framework* in terms of developing communication skills. Clearly, although each would have different areas of expertise, a common framework for discussion could be established which was more precise than 'Mohamed's problem is his poor English.'

— *A new examination* which measured competence in the language and communication skills appropriate for academic and vocational purposes would be available at a number of levels, but particularly up to and including GCSE English Language.

Conclusion

We have itemized some key issues which need to be addressed if language support is to be effective. However, many of these issues are not exclusive to the field of ESL, but rather they are issues central to the development of the new FE. The emphasis on negotiation, integrated curricula, new forms of assessment, liaison time for course teams, etc. is fundamental to the development of the new forms of pre-vocational education. These shared issues could become the basis for cooperation between mainstream communication skills teachers, ESL staff and subject teachers.

An institution which is making a genuine attempt to re-evaluate its contract with black and bilingual students will be better able to provide a context within which good practice can flourish. In our experience the ingenuity and goodwill of individual subject teachers and language teachers often manages to overcome enormous obstacles in order to provide a supportive learning environment for all students.

References

ROBSON, M. (1988) *Language, Learning and Race*, Longman for FEU
McALLISTER, J. AND ROBSON, M. (1984) *Building a Framework*, NEC

Section 4 Current Classroom Issues

Introduction

Current ESL methodology draws on a number of curricular developments that have occurred since the 1960s. These include findings from linguistics and applied linguistics (see Roberts, Section 1), approaches in adult literacy drawing on the work of Freire and the deschooling movement, and frameworks applicable to the learning of 'foreign' languages produced by the Council of Europe Modern Languages Project.

In the seventies, most ESL teachers adopted a curriculum approach based on teacher-perceived needs of the many beginner and elementary students who attended classes at that time. This emphasized 'survival' English for everyday life in Britain. (Nicholls and Naish, 1980). More recently, however, there has been a growing awareness of the great diversity of students' aspirations, educational experience and language-learning requirements (see Naish, Section 2), and of the extent to which the traditional syllabus was Eurocentric and often implicitly racist (see Alibhai and Bhanot, Section 1). This has led teachers to question who has control of the curriculum — how far it is genuinely negotiated and how much simply an exercise in which teachers have collected auto-biographical detail about students and then used this to impose a syllabus based on a list of language and communication 'needs' in a model that owes much to the concepts of medical diagnosis.

The result has been to focus on shifting the balance of power in the classroom away from the teacher. The papers in this section examine this trend by considering a variety of new classroom approaches and techniques. Arguably the most influential development has been the recognition of linguistic diversity and the ways in which this can be acknowledged and built on in the classroom, and this is central to all the papers in this section. The papers are practical and based on classroom experience: the ideas presented are ones which teachers and students are currently exploring and which consequently change rapidly. It is hoped that they will stimulate readers to examine and evaluate their present teaching practice in relation to these developments. In such a dynamic area, however, it is not possible for the section to be comprehensive. Readers are therefore referred to the end of each paper, where already published material on issues such as linked-skills teaching is listed.

References   NICHOLLS AND NAISH (1980) *Teaching English as a Second Language*, (BBC)

Making use of students' linguistic resources

Monica Collingham

Britain is now more visibly a multilingual society than it was ten years ago. The linguistic minorities project (see Reid, Section 1) and biennial ILEA surveys have revealed the true extent of linguistic diversity in Britain; more languages are now spoken in London than in any other city of the world (172 different languages in ILEA schools, 1987). The ethnic minorities themselves have shown how it is possible to maintain a separate cultural identity within Britain: one can be a British Asian, in the same way as one can be Chinese American or Greek Australian.

Within educational circles, there has been some reassessment of bilingualism. It is now recognized that the languages that learners already know are, far from being a problem, a positive resource in the learning of other languages.

This growing awareness of the value of the prior linguistic knowledge that learners bring to the ESL classroom has led to a redefinition of the word 'bilingual', which is increasingly being used to describe *any* level of fluency in more than one language, rather than its more traditional sense of *complete* fluency in two languages. Jane Miller, for example, defines a bilingual as 'someone who operates during their everyday life in more than one language and does so with some degree of self confidence' (Miller, 1983). An ILEA document (1985) uses the term 'bilingual' to describe 'students who regularly use more than one language. Many of these students have some facility in languages other than their home language and English and could be described as multilingual. The use of the term "bilingual" does not assume any specified level of fluency in any of the students' languages . . . (and) is a deliberate shift in usage to reflect a positive attitude towards students' languages.'

This new awareness has resulted in a reappraisal of classroom methodology. Teachers are increasingly evolving ways of utilizing students' other languages and cultures in the learning of English. This has come to be known as a bilingual approach.

What is a bilingual approach?

In a sense there is nothing startlingly new about a bilingual approach in language teaching. British people have traditionally learned French and other languages through the medium of English. The main difference with the present approach is that it is just one aspect of a modern communicative methodology which aims to teach language *use* as well as language *usage* (Widdowson, 1978) and which assumes that learning a language is a complex activity which needs to utilize a variety of strategies.

Why adopt a bilingual approach?

There are many practical, educational and political reasons for adopting a bilingual approach in the teaching of ESL. These include:
1. Valuing and building on the knowledge that learners already have and bring to the classroom: the cornerstone of good practice in adult education.
2. Raising the status of the languages used by ethnic minorities in Britain, which in turn raises the self-esteem of the speakers of those languages, making them more confident and effective learners.
3. Raising language awareness. Learners already have some linguistic skills and knowledge; by thinking about their own and other languages (e.g. their history, structure, syntax, writing systems), a class will learn more about language and languages in general. This can speed up aspects of learning and increase learners' tolerance of one another's difficulties. In this way classroom cooperation is fostered and classroom dynamics are improved.
4. Using learners' first languages improves the pace of learning — an important feature for adult learners, for whom time is always at a premium.
5. There is less likelihood of the lesson content being trivial, patronizing or childish where the contributions students can make in their own languages are recognized as significant and valued.
6. Fostering cooperative and independent learning (see Hallgarten, Section 4).
7. Reducing learner anxiety and therefore increasing confidence and motivation.
8. Enabling every learner, no matter how limited their knowledge of English, to contribute to the lesson in a variety of ways, depending on their previous experience.
By adopting this 'bilingual approach', the ESL teacher is consciously moving away from the deficit model (see Cheetham, Section 2) to a more affirmative, anti-racist focus (see Bhanot and Alibhai, Section 1).

Using a bilingual approach

This approach has implications for classroom management and the interaction patterns that are used during a lesson. What follows is a list of practical teaching ideas which utilize learners' linguistic resources.

All of them can be used by any ESL teachers, whether bilingual or monolingual, although in the case of the latter, the bilingual knowledge will probably come from the learners in the class (or from other bilingual informants) rather than from the teacher.

Discussion/ negotiation of the syllabus

Learners' first languages can be used to do this in a variety of ways:
— using an interpreter to discuss learning needs.
— using a bilingual check-list or form, produced in both English and the first language of the learners.
— learners can write down what they want to do in the class in their main language. This can later be translated by a bilingual teacher.
— learners can be grouped according to their first languages, either to discuss what they want to do, or to work on a check-list. More advanced learners can report back in English or fill in a form/check-list. Learners can talk on to a tape in their first language. This can later be translated.

Role-play

Learners can role-play a situation, first in their mother tongue. If they tape it, they can play back the tape and gradually translate what they said into English. This can lead to comparison/contrast of the language and discourse patterning required, and the non-verbal communication and other socio-cultural rules operating in that situation in British English *vis-à-vis* the first language of the learners. This can also be a good way of removing 'blocks' on learners who first feel that they cannot do the role-play in English. If a tape-recorder is not available, learners can still do the role-play in their first language and then discuss the results with the rest of the group.

Worksheets 1 and 2, pages 86 and 87, were produced as part of a course for Bengali-speaking community workers. They illustrate how bilingual worksheets can be used both to plan the content of a role-play, and to elicit the language and discourse strategies to be used.

Teaching grammar

Comparative analysis of the structure of English and learners' first languages can be done using number coding, colour coding or visual symbols. This can highlight similarities and differences in word order, the omission or addition of words, and subject/verb agreement. (See worksheet 3, page 88.) Learners' own written or taped work can be used as a basis for error analysis, leading to an exploration of how different languages express certain concepts. (See Ferguson, 1983, for one description of this kind of process.)

Teaching language functions

Contrastive analysis of how certain language functions (e.g. making a request, expressing politeness) are realized in English and the learners' first language can highlight the relationship between form and function in different languages. Also, by revealing how direct translations do not always work, the question of appropriateness can be raised. (See worksheet 4, page 89.)

Teaching vocabulary   Again, by comparing words in English and the learners' first language, questions can be raised concerning the boundaries of translation (one word in one language may translate into two words in another, and vice versa).

Teaching phonology   Individual sounds as well as the patterns of stress, rhythm and intonation can be compared between languages. The relationship of the sound patterns to the writing systems in different languages can also be contrasted. Learners not familiar with Latin script, but who are literate in their own language, can use the known script to note the pronunciation of words or phrases in English. This is a useful memory aid, even if it is only an approximation. (See worksheet 5, page 90.)

Teaching literacy   The scripts of different languages can be compared when teaching writing (for example, Bengali 'hangs' from the top line, whilst English 'rests' on the bottom line). The formats and conventions governing text types, such as formal letters or reports, can be compared and contrasted. (See worksheet 6, page 91.)

Comprehension   Comprehension questions about a text or a tape can be asked in the learners' main language, (See worksheet 7, page 92.) Where they are available, parallel texts can be used, so that learners can first read a text in their mother tongue before tackling it in English. (See worksheet 8, page 93.)

Creative writing   Learners can tell stories in their first language. These can be taped, then played back and translated collaboratively (McLoughlin, 1986). This technique can also be used for producing factual writing such as reports or letters.

Record keeping   Learners can keep records of work in progress in languages other than English (see Lawson, Section 5). Bilingual worksheets can also provide a useful record of newly acquired words and phrases. (See worksheet 9, page 94.)

Providing information   Students can be given essential information in languages other than English where this is likely to minimize the chance of misinterpretation and misunderstandings, for example, information about the DHSS, NHS, child benefit, etc. Likewise instructions on worksheets can be translated. (See worksheets 10 and 11, pages 95 and 96.)

Sources of bilingual materials   Many bilingual materials already exist, which can be used in teaching English: bilingual dictionaries, phrase-books, brochures such as those produced by local authorities or product manufacturers, and books of stories with parallel texts in two languages. Other useful resources are books and newspapers in the learners' first language. These can be used as a basis for work in English (see Baynham, Section 4).

Implications

To adopt a bilingual approach will have many far-reaching implications, both at a personal and practical level, and also in the wider political context in which ESL operates. To value rather than ignore learners' bilingualism and to utilize it in the learning of English will lead inevitably to a relinquishing of the traditional power of the teacher in the classroom. Instead of being viewed as the sole repository of useful knowledge and the person who makes all the decisions and provides all the input for the language learning experience, the teacher will become more of a manager and facilitator, and the ESL class more of a collaborative venture, with more peer learning and teaching. Acknowledging learner contributions will modify the curriculum and make it less ethnocentric. Monolingual teachers will have to be prepared to allow the use of other languages in the ESL classroom, and not feel threatened by this as they often do at present. One effect of teachers not understanding everything that the learners are saying is to put them in a comparable position to that of their learners, and so raise their awareness of the enormous task faced by those learning a new language. Teachers will find that it is helpful if they try to learn something of their learners' languages.

By consciously employing them in the learning of English, ESL teachers can contribute to raising the status of the community languages spoken in Britain. This then leads to a consideration of the wider institutional implications of, for example, the possibility of teaching other subjects through languages other than English, or the provision of mother-tongue maintenance or literacy classes. Thus ESL teachers will find themselves involved in wider language debates within the institutions in which they work, and often the only people to confront monolingual attitudes and assumptions within educational management.

The other major question raised by valuing community languages is that of 'who is teaching ESL?' At present most ESL teachers are monolingual and white, and most learners are bilingual and black, and so the ESL classroom merely replicates the structural racism of most other social institutions in Britain. Clearly this is a situation which needs to change if ESL is to reflect the multiracial composition of British society more accurately than it does at present.

Teaching English is, as Harold Rosen pointed out in his keynote speech to the NATESLA conference 1983, never politically neutral, nor can it be carried out in a 'state of innocence',. but is 'always a cultural and political act'. In their work, therefore, ESL teachers have the choice, either to reinforce or to challenge the existing power relationships of British society. To treat adult learners as if they know nothing of language is to accept the imbalance of power, and so ultimately to collude with institutional racism; to adopt a bilingual approach and to value the knowledge that learners already have is to begin to challenge that unequal power relationship and, one hopes, thereby enable learners to acquire the skills and confidence they need to claim back more power for themselves in the world beyond the classroom.

Talking about your organisation

আপনি যে সংগঠনের সাথে জড়িত সে ব্যাপারে
আলাপ আলোচনা।

What do you need to say to visitors, when they
first arrive?

আপনার অফিসে কোন আগন্তুক (visitor)
এলে তাদের কিভাবে অভ্যর্থনা করবেন ?

What is the building like that your organisation
uses?

যে বাড়িতে (building) আপনার অফিস রয়েছে
তাকে কিভাবে বর্ণনা করবেন ?

What activities does your organisation run?

সংগঠন কল্যাণমূলক কি ধরনের কাজের সাথে
আপনার সংগঠন জড়িত ? সংক্ষেপে বর্ণনা করুন।

What other work does your organisation do?

এছাড়া অন্য কোন ধরনের কাজের সাথে আপনার
সংগঠন কি জড়িত ? বর্ণনা করুন।

What problems do clients bring to your organisation?

আপনাদের সদস্যরা (member) আপনাদের কাছে
কোন ধরনের অভ্যুত্থান নিয়ে আসেন ?

When politicians visit your organisation, what do
you want them to learn? What do you want to say
to them?

যদি কোন রাজনৈতিক নেতা (যেমন Minister, MP
অথবা Councillor) আপনাদের সংগঠন পরিদর্শনে আসেন
তবে কোন বিষয় সম্বন্ধে তাদের অবহিত করবেন ?
আপনাদের সংগঠন থেকে তাদের কোন শিক্ষনীয়
বিষয় আছে কি ?

Worksheet 1:
This worksheet was produced as part of a course for Bengali-speaking community workers. A list of questions for discussion, and the title, are put in both English and Bengali translation.

Phoning the DHSS to make an appointment for a client

What will you need to say during your call?

এই আসল আলোচনার নীচে কিছুকম হতে পারে
তার ব্যুলা ।

ঢুকিনা- ইংরেজিতে Greeting	Open (greet)
যার সাথে যোগাযোগ করতে চান তার খোঁজ করুন	Ask for the person you want
নিজের পরিচয় দিন	Introduce yourself and your organisation
সঠিক লোকের সাথে যোগাযোগ হয়েছে কিনা তা দেখে নিন ।	Check that you have the right person on the phone
যার বক্ষ থেকে কথা বলছেন তার নাম ও ঠিকানা দিন ।	Give your client's name and address
চিঠির Reference দিন	Give the reference number
কেন টেলিফোন করছেন তার বিবরণ দিন ।	Ask for an appointment (say why you are phoning)
Appointment এর দিন, তারিখ ও সময় ঠিক করে ফেলে নিন ।	Arrange and check the date and time
শেষকথা- ধন্যবাদ ।	Close (thank)

© Monica Collingham/Tassaduq Ahmed

Worksheet 2:
This worksheet was produced as part of a course for Bengali-speaking community workers. The list of language functions is put in both English and Bengali, as part of an exercise to plan the content of a phone call and to elicit the English to be used.

Some differences in past tense usage between English and Bengali

In English a completed action in the past is nearly always expressed by the simple past tense, e.g.

I came here yesterday

whereas in Bengali this can be expressed by the present perfect tense, e.g.

আমি কাল এখানে এসেছি ।

or by the past perfect tense, e.g.

আমি কাল এখানে এসেছিলাম ।

Is it possible in Bengali to use the simple past?

আমি কাল এখানে আসলাম/এলাম ।

Which one of the three examples above would be used most often?

Is the meaning any different in the three sentences?

In English it is nearly always WRONG to use the present perfect or the past perfect for completed actions in the past.

WRONG - I have come here yesterday.

WRONG - I had come here yesterday.

You could CORRECTLY say:

I came here yesterday, but I had come here often before that. Came is simple past. Had come is past perfect. In English the past perfect represents a step further back in the past from the simple past. How would you write the above English example in Bengali?

Worksheet 3:
From materials developed at City and East London College (unpublished)

কনে ঃ
মোছাম্মৎ হেলেন বেগম
পিতা ঃ মো: ছমরু মিয়া
ঠিকানা ঃ ১৩২ এ হাউজিং এস্টেট
সিলেট বাংলাদেশ

বর ঃ
মো: মাসুন আহমদ (রুহেল)
পিতা ঃ আলহাজ্ব ফরিদ উদ্দিন আহমদ
ঠিকানা ঃ মজুমদারবাড়ী, মজুমদারী
সিলেট, বাংলাদেশ

● অনুষ্ঠানসূচী ◌
তারিখ ৫ই জুলাই ১৯৮৭ইং
বর আগমন – বেলা ১২-৩০মি:
খানা – দুপুর ১-৩০মি:
স্থান – স্টেপনি মিটিং হাউস
১৪৫ স্টেপনি ওয়ে
লন্ডন ই১

আছ্ছালামু আলাইকুম

জনাব/জনাবা

পরম করুণাময়ের অশেষ মেহেরবানীতে আগামী ৫ই জুলাই ১৯৮৭ইং মোতাবেক ৮ই জেলকুন ১৪০৭
হিজরী, ২০শে আষাঢ় ১৩৯৪ বাংলা আমার দ্বিতীয়া কন্যা মোছাম্মৎ হেলেন বেগমের সাথে আলহাজ্ব ফরিদ উদ্দিন
আহমদ সাহেবের একমাত্র পুত্র মো: মাসুন আহমদের শুভ বিবাহের দিন ধার্য করা হয়েছে। উক্ত শুভ অনুষ্ঠানে আপনাদের
উপস্থিতি ও দোয়া কামনা করি।

পর্দানসীন নওয়াতুজ্জনিত ক্রটি মার্জনায়।

আরজ গোজার মি: এন্ড মিসেস ছমরু মিয়া

Bride : Mst. Helen Begum
D o : Md. Somru Miah
19 Linale House
Murray Grove
London N1

Groom : Md. Mashud Ahmed (Ruhel)
S o : Al-Haj Farid Uddin Ahmed
31 Silvester Road
London SE 22
Tel : 01-299 1339

-: PROGRAMME :-
Date : 5th July 1987
Reception : 12.30 pm
Lunch : 1.30 pm
Place : The Stepney Meeting House
145 Stepney Way
London E1

To... ....
The wedding ceremony of my second daughter, Mst. Helen Begum will be solemnised with Md. Mashud Ahmed (Ruhel), only son of Al-Haj Farid Uddin Ahmed on 5th July 1987.

You are most cordially invited to attend the ceremony and bless the newly wedded couple.

RSVP 01-250 0547

Yours Sincerely,
Mr & Mrs Somru Miah

Designed and Printed by *SURMA* 01-981 5571

Worksheet 4

Talking to the doctor about a cough

ডাক্তারের কাছে কাশি সম্বন্ধে বলা

Vocabulary   শব্দ

English		Bengali
cough	কফ	কাশি
chest pain	চেস্ট পেইন	বুকে ব্যাথা
wheezing	হুইজিং	নিঃশ্বাসে ফ্যাসফ্যাসানো আওয়াজ
breathlessness	ব্রিদলেসনেস	নিঃশ্বাস বন্ধ
sputum	স্পুটাম	থুথু
phlegm	ফ্লেম	
blood	ব্লাড	রক্ত

© Afroza Ali/Monica Collingham

Worksheet 5:
This vocabulary list (produced for a special medical class) has the English words to be learnt, the English word written in Bengali script, and a Bengali translation (where possible) of the English word. The titles are put in both languages.

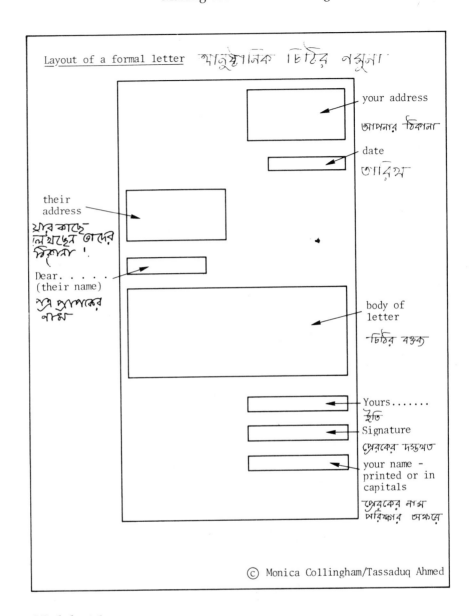

Worksheet 6:
This worksheet, showing the layout of a formal letter, has been annotated in both Bengali and English. The title is also bilingual.

Phoning for a job application form

ফেনেযোগে দরখাস্ত ফরমের জন্য আবেদন ।

Listen to someone phoning to ask for a form.

যিনি টেলিফোন করছেন তার বক্তব্য শুনুন ।

In the list below, put a tick (✓) by the things
the caller says:

নীচের তালিকায় কি অবর দিচ্ছেন তা টিক দিয়ে দেখান

his name - নাম

his age - বয়স

the job - কাজ

his work experience - অভিজ্ঞতা

his address - ঠিকানা

questions about hours and money - বেতন ও কাজের সময়

his present job - বর্তমান কাজের অবর

where he saw the job advertised - কোথায় বিজ্ঞাপন দেখেছেন

the name of a referee - রেফারীর নাম

Worksheet 7:

*In this exercise, the title, instructions and listening comprehension questions have
all been put in English and Bengali. The tape that the learners will listen to is in
English. (This is an adaptation of an exercise in 'Topics and Skills in English' by
Vivien Barr and Clare Fletcher, Hodder and Stoughton, 1983).*

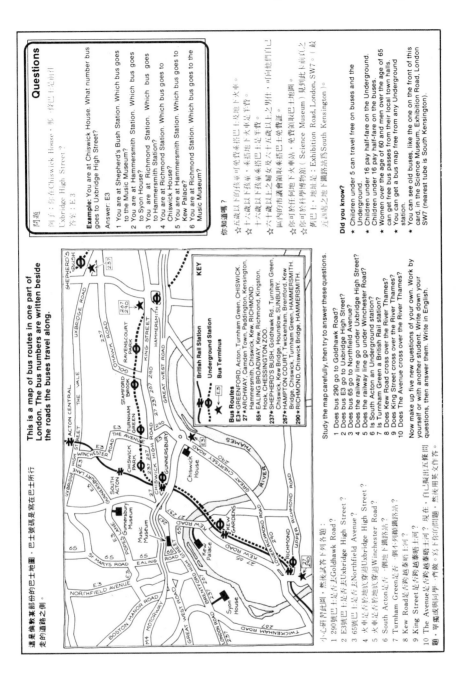

Worksheet 8:
This is from 'World in a City' teaching pack, ILEA Learning Materials Service.

Put the months in the correct order:-

মাসের নামগুলোকে কোনটার পর কোনটা হবে ঠিক করে বসাও।

February   June   August   January   April

March   May   September   July   October

December   November.

 1.

 2.

 3.

 4.

 5.

 6.

 7.

 8.

 9.

10.

11.

12.

© Suesanne Burgess

Worksheet 9:
Here the instructions to the learners have been written in English and Bengali.

JOB INTERVIEWS

Ordering interview questions

A job interview in the UK has a typical pattern.
Here are 8 interview questions, which are not in
the usual order. Put them in the order in which
they are usually asked (Number them 1-8):

চাকুরি সংক্রান্ত আক্ষাৎকারের একটি পদ্ধতি আছে ।
আক্ষাৎকার ৮ টি প্রশ্ন দেয়া হল । প্রশ্নগুলি ধারাবাহিক
ভাবে আজানোনস্য । ১ থেকে ৮ সংঞ্যা ব্যবহার করে
প্রশ্নগুলিকে ধারাবাহিকভাবে আজান ।

Are there any questions that you'd like to
ask us?

Tell us exactly what you do in your current job.

Good afternoon. Do sit down. I'm Mr Jones.

Thank you for coming. We'll be writing to you
over the next couple of days.

What are your interests?

Why do you want this job?

Could you tell us about the work experience that
you've had that you think would be relevant to
this post?

I'd just like to ask you to expand on some points
from your cv.

© Monica Collingham/Tassaduq Ahmed

Worksheet 10

Date: _____

Match the English and Bengali: Draw a line

একটা লাইন টেনে ইংরেজির সাথে বাংলা মাচাও ।

Monday   শনিবার

Saturday   মঙ্গলবার

Friday   সোমবার

Sunday   বুধবার

Tuesday   শুক্রবার

Thursday   রবিবার

Wednesday   বৃহস্পতিবার

© Suesanne Burgess

Worksheet 11:
This worksheet is a simple matching exercise where learners are asked to put together a list of English words with their Bengali translations.

References

BIRD, B. AND BRIERLY, C. (1985) *Switch on to English — A Handbook for Developing Reading and Writing*, BBC/ALBSU

FERGUSON, N. (1983) 'The use of mother tongue in teaching grammar at post-elementary level', in *ESL Issues* 1, ILEA Publishing Group

ILEA FHCE INSPECTORATE (1985) *English Language Provision for Bilingual Students in Colleges of Further Education*, Inspectorate Guidelines

ILEA News, 19 Nov. 1987

McLAUGHLIN, J. (1986) 'Developing Writing in English from Mother Tongue Story Telling', *Language Issues*, No 1 Spring 1986, NATESLA

MILLER, J. (1983) *Many Voices*, Routledge and Kegan Paul

WIDDOWSON, H. G. (1978) *Teaching Language as Communication*, OUP

The bilingual teacher in the ESL classroom

Krystyna Piasecka

Krystyna Piasecka

Introduction   Teaching bilingually does not mean a return to the Grammar Translation method (Piasecka, 1986), but rather a standpoint which accepts
that the thinking, feeling, and artistic life of a person is very much
rooted in their mother tongue. If the communicative approach is to live
up to its name, then there are many occasions in which the original
impulse to speak can only be found in the mother tongue. At the initial
stages of learning a new language, the students' repertoire is limited to
those few utterances already learnt and they must constantly think
before speaking. When having a conversation, we often become fully
aware of what we actually mean only after speaking. We need to speak
in order to sort out our ideas, and when learning a new language this is
often best done through the mother tongue.

Although more and more teachers are using the students' knowledge
of other languages as a language learning resource (see Collingham,
Section 4), only in a situation where the students and teacher share a
language other than the target language can the teacher teach
bilingually in a systematic way. A person who is able to speak both
languages can monitor the process of referring back to mother-tongue
equivalents which goes on in learners' minds. When this is monitored,
there is less likelihood of students making false analogies and students
are free to concentrate more fully on the target language instead of
seeking mother-tongue equivalents of newly encountered words.

If there is a common cultural heritage, there is bound to be a closer
understanding and sympathy between the students and the teacher.
The teacher is better able to understand not only their linguistic
problems, but also their predicament. Furthermore, a knowledge of the
routes students will be taking in their search for jobs, housing, etc., will
enable the teacher to focus on essential areas of access, and to discard
those which will not apply.

The class dynamics of a linguistically homogeneous group are completely different from those of a multilingual group. People get to know
each other very quickly, feel less restrained, less inclined to be polite,
and more inclined to be open about sensitive problems. The students
are able to give each other advice and support, and discuss different
ways of coping with all the tensions of resettlement. They may take
stronger likes or dislikes to each other than in multilingual classes.
Differences of opinion can often be exploited so that students stimulate

each other to voice their feelings, thus revealing their particular language needs and wants. However, where hostile feelings could emanate from deeper social or political differences, it is important that the teacher focus on areas of need, and utilize cultural aspects which unite all the students, thereby capitalizing on this unique opportunity to learn together in an atmosphere of mutual understanding. Prerequisite to this is a teacher who is not biased towards students from particular social, political or religious backgrounds.

My knowledge of Polish language and culture has provided me with valuable insights into social and political areas of some sensitivity. I do not inquire directly into students' personal lives, as many of them may wish to keep certain things to themselves. I have extended this practice of not collecting personal data into my teaching of multilingual classes.

Against this background of a common pride in a communal, cultural heritage, students will differ enormously in their levels of competence and confidence in English language, in their learning styles, personalities, ages, interests, and aspirations. This illuminates the absurdity of stereotyping a person's needs and wants according to country of origin.

When to use mother tongue

There are no hard and fast rules concerning the use of mother tongue. In effect, mother tongue will be used at moments of communicative exigency and one cannot predict where these moments will arise. The teacher can, however, predict points at which mother tongue is likely to be used, for example, when talking about a grammatical rule. When students are role-playing in English, on the other hand, one would discourage the use of mother tongue, but it is to be hoped that the English role-play would be an organic part of a lesson, in which mother tongue would be used either to comment on and discuss the English role-play, or used in a comparative role-play. The use of mother tongue will depend upon the format and the focus of the lesson. The most convenient way of approaching the question of when to use mother tongue might be to differentiate between two separate functions, the first involving the conveying of information and the second related to translation.

Informational use

The extent to which mother tongue is used will be a joint decision between the students and teacher and will largely depend upon the students' levels of proficiency in English. The students and teacher may prefer gradually to lessen the use of mother tongue, so that they move from a bilingual to a monolingual situation. Whatever mode is chosen, the fact that mother tongue can always be resorted to empowers the learners to a degree that cannot be reached in a multilingual class. The following list of possible occasions for using mother tongue might be helpful to bilingual teachers:

1. Educational counselling.
2. Publicity.
3. Negotiating the syllabus.
4. Negotiating the lesson.
5. Access skills.

6. Profiling and record keeping. (If the students and the teacher wish to keep profiles, the students can fill them in themselves.)

7. Integrating newcomers.

8. Personal contact.

9. Classroom management.

10. Setting the scene.

11. Language analysis.

12. Rules. Rules governing grammar, phonology, morphology, spelling, formal speech and writing can be arrived at collectively or explained by the teacher.

13. Cross-cultural issues. (A teacher of the same ethnic origin as the students is not only more aware of cross-cultural issues, but also has greater liberty to explain them.)

14. Materials. Worksheets and tapes with mother tongue instructions or prompts. Discourse chains can be drawn up with mother tongue prompts.

15. Correcting. Indicating the nature of the error.

16. Resolving individual areas of difficulty.

17. Assessment and evaluation of lesson.

18. Focusing on a particular skill. (Unless both the questions and answers of a listening or a reading exercise are either in diagram form or in mother tongue, one may not be able to make an accurate assessment of students' abilities in either of those particular skills.)

Translation/ comparative use

We talk of a communicative approach to language learning, but do we always know what a student wishes to communicate? Students are often limited to communicating that which they can express, or that which a teacher or textbook predicts they want to express. Language of the latter type tends to be cliché-ridden and conformist in nature, not allowing sufficiently, if at all, for individuality. The use of translation, however, can be a useful aid to a communicative approach. By this I am not referring to the method whereby translation passages are set in order to test whether particular linguistic items have been grasped, but a more creative use of translation. This approach can be demonstrated in relation to role play, a detailed description of which follows. (I have examined ways of using translation in the teaching of all four skills, but there is room here to look only at 'speaking'.)

Role play

Role-play is probably one of the best methods by which students may express themselves. Indeed, Denise Gubbay (1982) states that:

> Through role-play, the teacher can act as a bridge: . . . from the way people project their personalities in the medium of their first language to the way they would like to project themselves in English.

It seems to me that this can be achieved only by a teacher who understands the students' first language and culture.

If, in a linguistically homogeneous group, students role-play a situation first in mother tongue, then the rest of the class can observe their behaviour, and the students can discover for themselves what it is that they would like to say in the situation. Role-play is an exercise which demands imagination and, where students are free to use mother tongue, their imaginative powers can more easily be tapped. I have found that the memory of the emotional experience in the first language seems to be retained by the students, and carries them through the English version. Now, where the teacher speaks the students' first language, he or she is able to guide students towards choosing target language utterances which are appropriate to both the speakers' intentions and the situation.

Level of competence in English will, of course, also determine which utterances are learnt. Sometimes, it is useful to ask students to role-play in English initially. This will serve as a diagnostic test, revealing what they can say. The L1 version will then reveal what students want to say. The third stage will involve a synthesis of the two previous stages.

It is useful to tape the students role-playing in the first language. This can then be played back and translated into English as a class venture, encouraging other students to contribute their own language options. In a mixed-level class, it is possible to draw up a simple and a more complicated version of each option. This stage, where students volunteer options directly related to themselves, is essential. It is often revealed that students' vocabulary needs are very different from those usually predicted or those which are easily visually represented (for example, a role-play preparing students to talk to the doctor revealed that they needed words such as 'stomach ulcer').

This whole process of translating the L1 version into English alerts students to the fact that one cannot translate words separately, but only ideas or phrases. If the L1 version is transcribed alongside the English, this reality will be demonstrated visually. Thus, students will be able to develop an awareness of how the two languages differ.

Bilingual classes are often attended by people who have been in the country for a considerable period of time. They may have been reluctant to attend classes in which they could not use their first language, or publicity may not have reached them. These students often regard themselves as 'beginners' because they have not learnt the language in a systematic way. However, they may have a wide English vocabulary, and need help only in employing it. In my experience, such people respond particularly well to role-playing a situation first in mother tongue, and then translating it into English. In this way students can learn many much-needed idioms and colloquialisms. In this situation it is not necessary to teach simplified versions because it is mainly the arrangements of words, and not the words themselves, which have to be internalized. The high level of motivation accompanying the discovery of long sought-after phrases will greatly facilitate the learning process.

Needless to say, students will require plenty of practice in using the English equivalents. Where there is a point of difficulty, the teacher might devise a simple translation drill, and any structural or functional items which have caused difficulty can become the main teaching objectives of future lessons.

Differences in social conventions and cultural expectations will also emerge from acting out a situation in mother tongue. These too will need to be translated. Cross-cultural issues are present in almost every situation and students do need to develop an awareness of the differences.

The teacher will need to act

> *as a bridge from the student's culture to the culture of the host community by revealing the traditions and expectations underlying the language and by giving information relevant to the situation. (Gubbay, 1982.)*

This will enable students to understand better the motives of other people and to choose for themselves in each situation whether they will act according to their own tradition or to the traditions here. If the teacher is not aware of the differences in cultural conventions, then the students are at a disadvantage.

Gesture often accompanies speech. Role-play will illustrate para-linguistic features and the students and teacher can discuss those which might cause cross-cultural misunderstandings.

Conclusion

Although I have focused on role-play, translation can also be used in the development of other skills such as creative writing. The lesson plan at the end of this paper shows how the mother tongue can be used in a variety of ways in a mixed level class.

I believe that there is a pedagogical and a psychological need for bilingual classes. Some people will attend a class only if the teacher speaks their first language. For others, a bilingual class is a springboard or supplement to different sorts of class. Where the teacher cannot speak the first language(s) of his or her students, the 'bilingual approach' is of a completely different nature; inevitably it is more *ad hoc* but students should, nevertheless, be encouraged to use their mother tongue (see Collingham, Section 4).

The critical and vital link between language and culture is becoming increasingly apparent. It is recognized that encouraging students to use their first languages widens the choice of learning strategies available to them, as well as providing an atmosphere where the mother tongue is recognized as a positive contribution to language learning. This helps both the teacher and the students to develop a sensitivity to the values, attitudes, and customs of other ethnolinguistic groups.

References

GUBBAY, DENISE (1982) *Role-play: The theory and practice of a method for increasing language awareness*, Pathway Industrial Unit

PIASECKA, KRYSTYNA (1986) 'Using Mother-Tongue in Teaching Adult Immigrants', *Language Issues* No 1, Spring 1986, NATESLA

Lesson plan

Background information   All the students are from Poland. The class level is mixed, with most students at an elementary level. Some have been in England for a considerable time, are fairly well acquainted with the English system and have picked up a fair amount of English. Others have arrived more recently and have a very limited, or purely academic, knowledge of English. In order to accommodate students who are long-standing members of the class, the main focus over the past two years has been successively functional, access, grammatical and again functional. As all students have made it clear that one of their primary aims is to be able to mix socially with English people, we are now concentrating on telephone skills, involving the functions of inviting, refusing and accepting.

Aims   To help students make social contacts through the medium of English language and cope with making and receiving telephone calls of any nature. Also to improve receptive discourse skills and transactional skills.

Objectives   **System**   To increase students' awareness of differences between social conventions in Poland and England: different expectations regarding guest and host (for example, Poles might bring flowers if invited to dinner, not necessarily a bottle). Also rituals of children's parties (to the students to whom it applies).
Functional   Reinforcement of inviting and accepting. Also refusing and giving reasons, suggesting alternative times.
Transactional   Opening and closing telephone conversations (reinforcement of). Alternative ways of closing. Checking/asking for repetition.
Receptive discourse skills   Listening for essential information. Rejecting what's redundant.
Grammatical   Using future form for planned events (the difficulty is that there is no congruent construction in Polish. In Polish, the auxiliary is used for planned events. Thus students might incline towards the 'will' form).
Language patterns   Would you like to . . . ?

Yes   I'd love to.
That would be lovely, etc.   Thank you very much.

Easy: No, not . . .
Difficult: Sorry, I can't make it on . . .   I'm going to . . .

What about . . . ?
What did you say? etc.
Literacy   (If time) looking at language of formal invitations and replying.
Phonological   /θ//ð/ Thank you/That's . . . (integrated into lesson).
Register   Awareness of register and intonation — relating to different degrees of formality.

Stages of lesson   (Some students may be late, as they finish work late.)

1. Looking at homework (Polish diary and exercise practising inviting), while students arrive.
2. Setting scene (in Polish) and recapping on last week's lesson. Eliciting social conventions relating to invitations in both Poland and England — discussing in Polish.
3. Listening to contrastive tapes:
   (a) Informal — two builders arranging to go to the pub (some students work on building site).
   (b) Formal — woman invites couple to join her and husband for bridge (many Poles play bridge).
   Deciding how well speakers know each other. Listening to tapes separately. Answering worksheets in Polish (focus is on listening, *not* on reading or writing).
4. Focus on and practise:
   (a) Inviting and accepting.
   (b) Inviting, refusing and giving reasons.
   (More elementary students do easier version; more advanced students do difficult version. Focus on future form for planned events. Compare with Polish.) Practise as class and in pairs (using Polish diaries).
5. Focus on suggesting an alternative time.
6. Focus on asking for repetition (formally: *I'm sorry, could you say that again please?* and informally: *What was that?*).
7. Drawing up discourse chain (with options) using Polish metalanguage.

	A: odbiera telefon
(dzwoniący)	**B**: Przedstawi się i prosi o kogoś
	A: Przedstawi się
	B: Zaprosi A. na coś
A: Akceptuje i dziękuje	**A**: odmawia i podaje powód
i pyta o szczegóły	**B**: Proponuje inny dzień

. . . .
. . . .

A: żegna się	**A**: Akceptuje i dziękuje	**A**: odmawia
B: żegna się	pyta o szczegóły	**B**: Proponuje, żeby A zadzwonił w wolnym czasie
	A: żegna się	**A**: żegna się
	B: żegna się	**B**: żegna się

8. Role-play in pairs, according to ability. Teacher with less able students.
9. Less able students write out dialogue. More advanced students continue to role-play (with teacher). Most advanced students translate own role-play (taped last week in Polish) into English.
10. (If time) look at formal invitations — wedding/child's party — compare with Polish.

Homework   — Elementary: dialogue completion with prompts in Polish.
— Advanced: translation from Polish to English (based on expressions which came up last week in various role-plays in Polish).

Discussion (in Polish) of the kind of formal telephone conversations students have to deal with, so that next week's lesson is related to students' wants and needs.

Assessment in Polish.

Pierwsza   Rozmowa

1. Czy dobrze się znają? Skąd wiesz?

2. Dokąd John go zaprasza?

3. Czy John chce się spotkać z Jimmym dziś czy jutro?

4. Gdzie się spotkają?

5. O Której?

Druga   Rozmowa

1. Czy dobrze się znają? Skąd wiesz?

2. Na co Betty zaprasza Leszka?

3. Na Kiedy?

4. Czy Leszek i Jola mogą się wybrać wtedy?

5. Czemu (nie)?

6. Na Kiedy się zdecydują?

Worksheet 1:   *For stage 3 of the lesson plan*

Michelle Kirkman
i
Jerzy Domaradzki
mają zaszczyt zawiadomić Sz.P.
że ślub ich odbędzie się
dnia 28 kwietnia 1984 roku
o godzinie 16:00
w misji Św.Wojciecha
w Montrealu

— WEDDING —
INVITATION

request the pleasure of

Company at the Marriage of

to _____

on _____ at _____ o'clock

at _____ and afterwards at _____

R.S.V.P. _____

Acceptance

will have much pleasure
in accepting your kind invitation
to the Wedding of

on

With Regret

It is with regret that

cannot accept the invitation

to

on

Worksheet 2: *For stage 10 of the lesson plan*

Worksheet 3: *For stage 10 of the lesson plan*

PROSZĘ WYPEŁNIĆ

A : Hello.

B : Hello, can I speak to _____ (swoje imię) ?

A : _____ . (przedstaw się)

B : Ah, hello ! Henryk here. How are you ?

A : _____ (odpowiedź)

B : Would you like to come round for a drink tomorrow?

A : _____

B : What about Saturday ? (odmów i podaj powód)

A : _____

_____ (przyjmij i opytaj o której godzinie)

B : Oh, come round at about 8 o'clock.

A : _____

_____ (podziękuj i pożegnaj się)

B : Goodbye.

Worksheet 4: *Homework for elementary students*

PROSZĘ TŁUMACZYĆ NA ANGIELSKI

A: Halo!

B: Dobry wieczór, czy mógłbym prosić Annę?

A: Przy telefonie.

B: Cześć Anno! Tu Bohdan. Jak się masz?

A: Dziękuję, bardzo dobrze.

B: Chciałem Cię zaprosić na drinka, jutro u mnie.
Co ty na to?

A: Bardzo mi przykro, ale nie będę się mogła wybrać.
Jutro będę u Józka.

B: Trudno, to może byśmy spotkali się w innym
dniu, w sobotę, co?

A: Będę zajęta także w Sobotę. Ale ja
zadzwonię do Ciebie jak będę wolna. Do widzenia!

B: Do widzenia! Czekam na twój telefon

Worksheet 5:   *Homework for more advanced students*

Student autonomy — learner training and self-directed learning

Katherine Hallgarten

Introduction

The goal of education is the facilitation of change and learning. The only man who is educated is the man who has learned how to adapt and change; the man who has realised that no knowledge is secure, that only the process of seeking knowledge gives a basis for security. (Rogers, 1983)

This paper derives from experience gained and conclusions reached on the Independent Learning Project funded by ALBSU at Morley College, London 1984–86. The project was sited in the Basic Education and ESL Department with the brief of setting up independent learning facilities and independent learning programmes for students attending classes and for students unable to come to classes. The facilities consisted of a workshop with self-access materials for reading, writing, listening and computer work, for use by bilingual and monolingual students who were at post-beginner level in both speaking and writing. This workshop was open for individual work twelve hours a day, four days a week, and staffed by tutors for work with individual students six hours a week. In these individual tutorials, students worked with tutors at assessing their own work in order to set their own pathways or programmes of work, and learnt how to choose new targets arising out of work done.

The students

Students who came to use the workshop divided into three groups: students coming two or four hours a week to ESL or literacy classes at Morley, students on 'mainstream' or vocational courses in AE, FE and HE, and students who were not on courses but who wanted help with language for work or private study. The largest group was those seeking language support which was not being provided on other courses. Bilingual students were in a minority: more than half the students were Afro-Caribbean or students whose first language was English. In this paper we shall be concerned only with bilingual students whose first language was not English.

The wants and aspirations of bilingual students

Students who came to the workshop for individual study presented the same range of wants and aspirations as those coming for ESL tuition. There were students with immediate crises, such as M who was about to take a TOPS test, and Z whose essays on his 'A' level English

Literature course were being criticized as 'too long and flowery'. Or C, who had failed part I of a City and Guilds Leathermaking course but had been admitted to part II and released half a day a week for 'more English'. There were students who had identified their own wants, such as MT who wanted to write letters to her English mother-in-law, J who wanted study and discourse skills to do a degree in social studies, or L who needed writing skills for Grade 8 music which had not been necessary in Grades 1–7.

The language needs of bilingual students

Most of these students had significant disparities between their oral fluency and their writing skills. Individual study in a workshop seems a particularly good way to attack these disparities. Each student was at a different stage, and many of the areas of difficulty were directly connected to the student's first language structure and style of presentation. Bilingual work would obviously be an ideal way of tackling these areas, but the cost of developing such resources was outside our range. We also saw students who wished to develop oral skills to match their writing skills, but it was not possible to develop oral communication skills in a workshop.

The need for learner training

Within a very short time we identified a crucial area common to all students: the need for learner training in effective ways of learning, in ideas of taking responsibility for one's own learning, in strategies for learning language and evaluating progress. Until students had these skills, individual study was totally dependent on a tutor providing private tutorial sessions. It became increasingly clear to us, as we spent hours working with single students, that learner training for self-directed learning is central to the ESL curriculum and to student autonomy.

The place for this training is every ESL classroom, not a workshop. These skills must be explicitly taught, and it is the tutor's responsibility firstly to teach these skills and then to allow the student to practise them in the classroom by creating space for self-directed activities. We therefore worked with various groups of bilingual students, and students in literacy classes, to develop materials and a syllabus for 'Learning for Autonomy'.

Background to student autonomy

During the 1970s the perspective on adult education changed, influenced by Illich, Freire and Rogers. Using student-centred learning styles, adult education came to be seen as working towards goals of equality of opportunity, responsible autonomy, personal fulfilment and democratization of education.

From these ideas came the notion of autonomy as 'an ability to assume responsibility for one's own affairs' (B. Schwartz, L'Education Demain, quoted in Holec, 1979) within a wider context of responsibility for the affairs of the world.

Holec (1979) emphasizes that this ability is not inborn but must be acquired, most often by formal learning in a systematic deliberate way. So when we talk about the 'negotiated curriculum' or 'student-centred learning', what we often fail to appreciate is that these are skills which both tutors and learners have to acquire. This is what learner training is about.

The autonomous learner

All adults are autonomous to some degree. The autonomy of a newly arrived bride in Harrow may be less than she had in Baroda; choosing items from a supermarket in the Caledonian Road may seem a less autonomous activity than buying and selling vegetables in Sylhet district. The autonomy may be less than the individual would like and there may be no opportunity to increase it, but some control will be made by the individual over his or her affairs.

A curious thing, however, appears to happen to adults returning to learning! When adults (re)enter the classroom and sit again at a desk, they look initially to the tutor to control and process all aspects of learning. The purpose of learner training is to enable the student to make all decisions about learning, such as
— choosing the objectives;
— assessing progress and performance;
— selecting method and techniques.
The autonomous learner does not have to make these decisions all the time; he or she must have learnt how to make them and have the chance to practise them. At any time, however, an autonomous learner may choose to be directed by a tutor or by an outside evaluation such as an examination.

An explicit handing over of control by the tutor to the learner must be central to the ESL curriculum. The training necessary for this we see as the tutor's responsibility.

The learner training syllabus and materials

Learner training can be incorporated into any ESL syllabus and at any level of language work. As discussion is an important element, a language common to groups of students is essential, though this need not, of course, be English. We developed the materials with 'advanced' groups of bilingual students, as this was easier for us, but they have since been used in a mixture of Gujerati and English on a preparatory course. Learner training should be embedded in the current syllabus as one topic area among others: the resulting goal-setting, assessment, and learning strategies should then be used in conjunction with other topics, skills or functions.

A 'learning for autonomy' syllabus will go through three stages. It will depend on the group how much time is spent on each stage.

We have worked with some groups of students who had very developed learning skills, who understood immediately about goals and self-assessment and where we moved almost immediately into sharing strategies. The three interlocking stages are:
1. Looking at learning.
2. Goals and self-assessment.
3. Sharing the strategies for learning the subject with students.

Stage 1. Looking at learning

This stage is based on discussion and uses the student's previous learning experience to examine: what learner autonomy is, decision-making in learning, sharing responsibility between tutor and student, what makes for successful learning and motivation.

Research has shown (Wenden, 1983), and our own experience has confirmed, that it is essential to be completely explicit about why the learner training is taking place. We have to tell students why we see autonomy as a useful or valuable goal. Some of the reasons we see as useful are:

— Learning is more effective when the learner takes control — we all learn what we are ready to learn.
— As adults, learner and tutor are equal and power is shared.
— An autonomous learner can go on learning the subject outside the classroom at the end of the course and if there is a gap in attendance.
— An autonomous learner can transfer learning skills to other subjects.

The main techniques we use at this stage are stimulus materials such as charts and questionnaires, which enable students to concentrate on their own experience or are used as a basis for group discussion. The points raised in discussions are drawn together on a sheet to be used for future work or as a reminder that there is no fixed body of knowledge about learning, and that what students say is as valid as anything written in any study-skills book.

Examples of materials for looking at learning

Responsibility for learning: Worksheet 1, page 115, provides a stimulus for discussion on how tutors and students perceive the differences between learning as a child and as an adult. Worksheet 2, page 116, is designed to start students thinking about planning their own work relevant to their own needs.

Successful learning: Worksheet 3, page 117, helps students to identify their own particular style of learning and to see that different styles work for different people. There is no single best method.

Motivation

It is important to have some discussion about motivation before starting to identify goals and negotiate a syllabus. Lack of explicit motivation may mean that it is difficult for the learner to identify goals apart from 'wanting to improve my English' and, as a result, learning may not be as successful as it could be. This can be done in counselling sessions, but group discussions are also valuable in building towards a group autonomy and for students to compare their own reasons for wanting to learn.

Stage 2. Goals and self-asssessment

Setting goals and knowing when one has reached them is a skill just as learnable as those of speaking and writing. The first part of this is to understand that breaking a large goal into smaller objectives makes it more concrete and manageable. Doing a series of small tasks is easier than looking at one large and possibly overwhelming goal such as passing a TOPS test, or learning to drive. We did this item of training first in a familiar context (see worksheet 4, page 118) and then later on in the context of language learning (worksheet 5, page 119).

What one is doing at this stage is beginning to share the metalanguage of ESL so that students can identify their progress in terms of language skills as well as in topics and functions.

Worksheet 6, page 120, is the record keeping sheet which students chose on one course. There are many other types.

After looking at individual goals one can start on an exercise in gradually negotiating a group syllabus for a period of time. The group or the tutor can assemble the individual learning objectives on to a single chart. From this, criteria will have to be agreed for choosing what to do and in what order (perhaps refer back to sharing responsibility). One of the aims of this exercise is to reinforce the idea that the tutor is not the only person who can teach.

Correcting one's own work and proof-reading

Closely linked to self-assessment is the ability to correct one's own work and to decide which areas or skills one needs to work on first. Training, once again, is a group exercise, where the group either listens to a piece of taped speech or corrects a piece of written work from within the group or outside. We found, when doing this exercise, that there were enormous differences between members of the group about what was or wasn't a 'mistake' and this alone led into long discussions about the aims of communication.

Proof-reading skills are usually taught as part of a study skills syllabus. We have tried using them as part of the ESL-literacy syllabus and would encourage other tutors to try this at an earlier stage than is usually done.

Stage 3. Sharing the strategies of language learning

Remember that we defined an autonomous learner as someone who can continue learning using the tutor as one resource among many. It follows from this that, if we share responsibility for learning with the student, if we teach students how to identify their own goals and monitor their own progress, then we also need to share with them our skills as teachers.

There seems to be no reason why we know the difference between skimming and scanning, why we know the purpose of a gap-fill exercise as opposed to a multiple-choice exercise and students do not. Some course books such as *Reasons for Reading* and *Strategies for Reading* (Davies and Whitney, 1984) are incorporating these skills into the text. In discussions we have had with students about grammar, about spelling, about proof-reading, we found that students often have well established and well thought-out strategies for learning. By sharing these with the group, individuals are exposed to different strategies and the tutor can add any which seem to be part of ESL techniques. Worksheet 7, page 121, shows the strategies which students produced in discussion. The tutor then added a session on mother-tongue interference.

Sharing strategies with students is not a discrete part of the syllabus. It is more of a thread of explanation which precedes each exercise, or is built into each worksheet until it becomes a habit. For example, a teacher might say before a listening exercise, 'Today we are doing listening for specific information, that's only listening for the important bits which you know you want to hear. So if we are listening to a weather forecast, which bits are you likely to want to hear?' It's what we as teachers are actually doing all the time, but perhaps without overtly transferring our skills to students and explaining why we are doing so.

Description of a learner training programme

We carried out a learner training programme with an 'advanced' ESL group which was meeting four times a week in a large AE centre with graded classes. It was in the summer term, so the group knew each other quite well and was familiar with discussion and analysis of issues. It was a multilingual group with a variety of aspirations for further study and/or training. Most of the group had been a relatively short time (1–3 years) in Britain, and had finished school or college in their country of origin. We worked with the class tutor to identify the most relevant areas of learner training for the group, which already had quite sophisticated learning strategies. Some of the four sessions were taken by the visiting tutor and some by the class tutor. The topics we covered were:

1. *Who's responsible for learning?*
This provoked a discussion on previous learning experience and how it compared with adult education methods and ESL teaching methodology.

2. *Successful learning and motivation.*
Here the group identified the difficulties of learning as an adult; fear of failure, problems of making time to learn, the idea of taking risks and the idea of fluency versus accuracy.

3. *Self-assessment and choosing priorities for language learning.*
A piece of written work and a taped conversation were analysed for mistakes. The group set the following priorities for the oral work: grammar, confidence, listening, better presentation, clarity.

4. *Strategies for increasing confidence.*
This discussion produced a list which included items such as: go on an assertion-training course, learn to listen before speaking, role-play a situation before, for example, an interview, and take tranquillizers.

Overall the group felt that the sessions were useful in making them look more closely at what learning was about. The sessions would have been more useful at the beginning of the course than at the end, as they could then have influenced the rest of the syllabus.

Learner training as a central curriculum objective will affect both content and practice in ESL teaching. Parts of learner training, such as discussions about successful learning, or reading strategies, will be treated like any other topic, introduced at the right moment and used for extension activities. Other parts, such as record-keeping, will occur over a period of time so that evaluation can take place and will become part of continuing classroom activities.

Self-directed learning

An autonomous learner will require the opportunity to exercise the skills by directing his or her own learning in both content and method. The student will come increasingly to use the tutor as one resource amongst the many available — books, cassettes, a range of writing and listening exercises, video or computer, or individuals outside the classroom. Time should be set aside during class sessions for student-led activities which may be an extension of the 'taught' part of the lesson or a free activity. For example, after a group communication activity on talking to a child's school teacher, or reporting an incident of harassment to the police, students could be offered a choice of extension activity — or do something entirely different like reading or writing a story.

Conclusion

We must all be quite clear, however, that we are changing our role of tutor into that of facilitator. Together with staff teams and with students, we must develop resources which allow choices to be made. We must realize that we will no longer be spending two hours in eyeball-to-eyeball 'class contact' time with a group of students x times a week. Sometimes the group will work together without a tutor, sometimes tutors will have counselling sessions with individuals.

> *Tutors concerned with the facilitation of learning rather than with the function of teaching organise their time and efforts very differently from conventional teachers. Instead of spending great blocks of time organising lesson plans . . . facilitative teachers concentrate on providing all kinds of resources . . . (and) concentrate on making such resources clearly available by thinking through and simplifying the psychological and practical steps the student must go through to use the resources. (Rogers, 1983)*

Where does a workshop fit into all this? The Independent Learning Project started with a workshop and with the generous start-up funding essential for such a resource. At the end of two years, we see a workshop as an optional extra to the essential development of learning skills and the opportunities to practise self-directed learning in the classroom. All that has been written in this paper can take place perfectly well without a workshop; a workshop cannot be used effectively unless, as tutors, we train students to become autonomous learners and allow them to take control of their own language learning.

Finally, however, it is our archaic institutional frameworks which have to change to accommodate a curriculum which holds learner autonomy as central. Accountability in terms of student numbers in classifiable blocks of time is not possible when students drop in and out to use resources which may or may not involve tutors. We shall have to think again.

Student autonomy as part of the wider ESL curriculum has, however, not only the narrow language-learning goals which I have described in some detail above. Language learning is about acquiring skills in order to do something else. Access is about knowing what's on offer, about making choices, about evaluating the quality of a training offer made, for example, by MSC. Learner training will develop and practise these transferable skills to broaden the opportunities for autonomy in a wider area than the ESL classroom.

References

DAVIES, S. E. AND WHITNEY, N. (1984) *Reasons for Reading, Strategies for Reading*, Heinemann

HOLEC, H. (1979) *Autonomy and Foreign Language Learning*, Pergamon

ROGERS, CARL (1983) *Freedom to Learn*, Merrill

SCHWARTZ, B. *L'Education Demain*, quoted in Holec, 1979

WENDEN, A. (1983) *Learner Training for L2 Learners*, TESOL

Skill Responsibility

DATE

> Use worksheet 4a or b - "Me and my pottery."

1. Discuss this passage with another person.

2. Recall your own learning experiences—
both the good ones and the frustrating ones
-thinking about both the role of the
learner and of the tutor.

3. Role play the pottery tutor and the student
(or a situation experienced
by yourself or your partner.)

4. Report back how the role play went to the
rest of the class.
How did you feel - as the student?
as the tutor?

morley **Adult Literacy & Basic Skills Unit**
Independent Learning Project

BR

Worksheet 1

Skill Responsibility	Who is in charge of learning?
	DATE

TEACHER SICK
CLASS CANCELLED
SORRY !

Last night I went to my evening class.
There was a notice on the door to say
the teacher was sick.
We went and had a cup of tea, and then
we went home.

What else could we have done?

morley **Adult Literacy & Basic Skills Unit**
Independent Learning Project

K H

Worksheet 2

Skill	SUCCESSFUL LEARNING	
		DATE

Think about 2 things you have learnt + fill in the table

What have you learnt?	Why did you learn it?	How did you learn it?
1. Successfully		
2. Unsuccessfully		

morley **Adult Literacy & Basic Skills Unit**
Independent Learning Project

BR

Worksheet 3

Skill GOALS

DATE

What do you need to do?

Choose colour

Decorate a room

Put up shelves

What are you going to do first?

morley **Adult Literacy & Basic Skills Unit**
Independent Learning Project

K H

Worksheet 4

Skill SELF ASSESSMENT

DATE

What do you need to be able to do to write a letter?

Punctuation

Letter writing

What can you do?
What do you need
to learn?

morley **Adult Literacy & Basic Skills Unit**
Independent Learning Project

KH & BR

Worksheet 5

Skill ENGLISH AND ESL NUMERACY WORKSHOPS	WORK RECORD

DATE

NAME: _____

Date:

Work done:

How did it go?:

What do you want to do next?:

Date:

Work done:

How did it go?:

What do you want to do next?:

DATE:

Work done:

How did it go?:

What do you want to do next?:

morley **Adult Literacy & Basic Skills Unit**
Independent Learning Project

Worksheet 6

Skill Language learning strategies	Choosing your own strategy

Pronunciation

DATE

Strategies	Week 1	Week 2	Week 3	Week 4
Record yourself and pick out the mistakes.				
Listen to the radio and T.V. and concentrate just on the pronun-ciation.				
Practise with an English friend- listen and repeat.				
Record something and copy a few of the sentences. Stress it how you think it should be stressed. Listen to the tape again x check.				
Read aloud~with the teacher or a friend.				

morley **Adult Literacy & Basic Skills Unit**
Independent Learning Project

Worksheet 7

Talking from experience — writing and talk in the ESL classroom

Mike Baynham

One of the tensions inherent in ESL teaching, as in other forms of teaching, arises from the fact that the classroom is a place where power is not distributed equally. Who has the rights in the classroom — the right to speak, to organize others to speak, the right to start a topic and judge when it is finished, the right to have the last word? Common sense, as well as the findings of those who have analysed interaction in the classroom, tell us that power relations in the classroom are heavily weighted on the side of the teacher. Sinclair and Coulthard (1975), looking at interaction in the primary school classroom, found that the typical pattern of exchange was Teacher Initiation — Pupil Response — Teacher Follow Up (IRF). For example:

> *T: So what's the capital of Spain then?*   *(initiation)*
> *P: Umm . . . Madrid?*   *(response)*
> *T: Yes, that's right, Madrid.*   *(follow up)*

'Ah yes,' I can hear the reader say, 'but we're working with adults. We don't treat them like kids.' Yet David Dinsmore (1985), looking at classroom interaction in 'communicative' EFL teaching of adults, finds that this pattern of (IRF) exchange, typical of the primary classroom, is precisely the one that features most in teacher/student interactions in the classrooms he visited. Any ESL teacher who has listened to a tape of themselves teaching will perhaps remember a feeling of shock: 'Do I really talk that much?'

So why do teachers talk that much? Or, to put it another way, why is the right to speak so unequally distributed in the classroom? Why do students wait patiently, even as adults, for the teacher to interest them or bore them, instruct them or confuse them? David Dinsmore, thinking about the teacher's behaviour in the classroom, wonders whether 'this is an example of something learnt (or acquired) during our own school days which automatically takes over when we adopt the role of teacher'. We can perhaps say that both teachers and students approach the classroom with certain expectations about how business should be conducted, who should do what. In common with other roles and relationships where the right to speak is unequally distributed (typically professional/layperson relationships like doctor/patient, social worker/client, interviewer/interviewee), the teacher/student relationship of its nature tends to inhibit the development of dialogue in the classroom.[1] These roles, relationships and expectations will form the background to the ESL teacher's attempts to develop a communicative situation in which language learning can take place.

In addition to these background expectations about what ought to happen in the classroom, the ESL teacher's performance may well be conditioned by a desire to fill those awkward gaps and silences with talk, a natural wish to give value for money, not to waste students' time, a sense that those hours of class time should be packed full with useful language-learning activities. 'Maximize active practice.' Wasn't that what they said in our teacher training? Yet an over-active, interventionist style of teaching, emphasizing the teacher as performer and orchestrator of the activities that take place, may in fact inhibit the development of talk in the classroom, talk in which participants, students and teachers, can contribute on a more equal footing.

Too often as teachers we behave as if we were teaching people how to communicate (tell stories, request politely, insist), instead of recognizing that they already know how to communicate, they come to the task of learning another language with a lifetime's experience of communicating in one or more languages. We need to enter into a dialogue with our students which can include their experience as language users, their understanding of the process of learning a new language, their crises of adaption to the ways of another society, which may greet them with racism and the denial of opportunity. Teachers who have been through it themselves, who have been migrants or refugees, may be in a stronger position to initiate that dialogue, but it is up to all teachers to sensitize themselves, inform themselves, ground their practices in the classroom in the experience of their students.

ESL teachers, along with others in adult education, have tried to subvert the conventional expectations of the classroom where teachers talk and orchestrate talk, and where adults leave their experience and knowledge at the door. Instead they are working to develop a style of teaching in which talk, discussion, the sharing of experience, the evaluation of what has been learnt and what needs to be learnt, are the everyday grounding of dialogue out of which what is to be taught emerges. This leads to a looser, more exploratory style of teaching, emphasizing the teacher less as performer, as orchestrator of communicative practice, and more as initiator and knitter-together of discussion (how does it feel to be in such and such a situation, what happened, did you fail or succeed, are there other, better ways of doing it?), out of which the active language work (role-play or writing or whatever) can emerge.

Now this is obviously an important issue in adult education as a whole, as well as in ESL. Michael Norris (1985), in his report on language use in literacy and craft classes, examines the way that exploratory, sharing, dialogic forms of talk are handled in different groups. Indeed some of the approaches to learning we are considering have antecedents in work done on children's schooling (cf, for example, Barnes, 1976). It is perhaps a historical accident that when ESL emerged, the nearest available model was not this critical, questioning tradition, which held 'the language question' to be crucial to other kinds of educational development, but rather EFL, geared to the foreign market, with educated, youngish students in mind. ESL has had to struggle out of this particular mould, create its own boundaries and sense of what the work is. It may be that, as Norris suggests, in examining similarities and links with other areas of the adult education curriculum (literacy, numeracy, the teaching of crafts and skills), we can initiate a discussion on the functions of language in the classroom which will in itself benefit the users of ESL classes who want to move out into the educational mainstream. This paper will look at the ways that discussion and writing from experience can become part of ESL work. In a sense it is looking at the way that techniques and approaches used in adult literacy work can become part of the work done in the ESL classroom.

The development, in adult literacy, of ways of working with students which are grounded in their knowledge and experience, arose out of a recognition that the functional, skills-based approach to learning implied a rather mechanical concept of what the process of 'becoming literate' involved. Freire's emphasis (1973) on 'critical consciousness' stresses the ways in which we act to create the world (in this case the small world of the classroom): learning is something you do, you make happen, not something you wait to have done to you. Freire's emphasis on dialogue, the development of critical consciousness through talk and sharing, contrasts with the unequal 'anti-dialogue' in which one participant has power over the other. We can see the former approach in Herbert Kohl's *Reading How To* or Jane Mace's *Learning From Experience* with its assertion that

> *any room containing adults wanting to learn also contains a living resource: the accumulated life experience of the people there. The problem for the teacher lies in knowing how to build from that experience, and how to bring those people together in its analysis and expression.*

Out of this emphasis on work grounded in people's experience came publications of writing from literacy schemes, either in newspaper form like *Write First Time* or in small booklets of collected writings on a theme like *Every Birth It Comes Different* in which adult literacy students and tutors from Hackney Reading Centre give accounts of their different experiences of childbirth, or life history, like *Pure Running*, the autobiography of Louise Shore. These publications,[2] based on first-hand experience and arising from the day-to-day process of literacy work, in themselves provide material for reading, discussion, role-play and writing in other literacy groups, part of a wider process in which experience is recreated and exchanged, in a dialogue-on-paper, very much as Freire would have it.

So how do these developments in adult literacy relate to ESL? It is becoming increasingly obvious that the literacy needs of students taking up ESL provision are many and varied. The users of an ESL scheme may range from university graduates who come here as refugees, to people from village communities who never went to school, with many other permutations in between. There is a danger that, unless the different educational backgrounds of the users of ESL provision are taken into account, some group or other is likely to lose out. And the chances are that it will be the educational have-nots who will lose out, rather than those who may already have had more than one bite at the educational cherry. ESL provision which does not take into account these considerations runs the risk of replicating the structured exclusion from educational opportunity which it is designed to redress: the same students will repeat the same classes because their level of literacy hinders them from progressing on to classes suited to them on the basis of their level of spoken English. The 'advanced' classes of an ESL scheme will mysteriously consist of people with a high level of initial education, while those without will somehow never end up in these classes, however fluent they become.

In the last few years, it has been increasingly recognized that literacy work of one sort or another is part of the day-to-day activity in ESL classes and that you can no longer rely on the homogeneous group of similar educational background suggested to us by our graded EFL antecedents. Most schemes nowadays put on special literacy classes to supplement the core provision. The ALBSU/ILEA ESL/Literacy project began to set up a dialogue between ESL and literacy workers, producing such useful handbooks as *Literacy Work with Bilingual Students: a Resource for Tutors* (1985). Many ESL schemes now produce collections of students' writings as a matter of course. *Folk Stories*, a collection produced by students and tutors at Clapham and Battersea Adult Education Institute is an example of this approach: folk stories presented bilingually, arising out of work done during a summer scheme. *The NATESLA Catalogue of Resources for Teaching English as a Second Language* is a useful source of information about such reading material[3]. Outside the spectrum of ESL schemes, the experiences of migrants and refugees have been recognized in community-based publications like *A Place to Stay: Memories of Pensioners from Many Lands* (Age Exchange, 1984) in which the reminiscences of pensioners are presented bilingually. In her autobiographical *My Life as a Woman in Love*, Netta Campbell, from Italy, describes her marriage and settling in England. Young people's life stories are represented in *Our Lives* (ILEA English Centre, 1979). All of these provide materials for initiating the kind of dialogue referred to above, either in the process of learning to read through them, or else in using them with already literate students as a starting point for discussion and other kinds of related language work.

Approaches to literacy work in ESL contexts have been documented in articles like 'Creative Writing in English as a Second Language Work' (McLaughlin, 1985) and 'Mother Tongue Materials and Second Language Literacy' (Baynham, 1983) and there is now a much wider recognition of the literacy dimension in ESL work. But it is also fair to say that the 'literacy issue' in ESL has not been fully grasped, particularly in relation to potential users with little or no formal education, for whom joining an ESL class is not just a top-up of an already wide experience of education, but may be a first and crucial experience of schooling. So what are the factors that ESL teachers and organizers should have in mind in order that the literacy dimension is adequately recognized and planned for?

Organizers should be aware that lack of formal schooling may be one of the main reasons for people not taking up ESL provision in the first place. Publicity, fieldwork and contacts with community organizations should aim to reach those who have never considered school as part of their lives. At the interviewing stage, the interviewer should find out as much as possible about the new student's educational background. There should be literacy support within mainstream ESL classes, and effective and well thought-out specialist classes, in which literacy work is central. Too often the 'mixed level' label is used as a cover-all for impossible classes ranging from graduates wanting to brush up their essay writing skills to those just beginning the literacy process. Links with literacy schemes, knowledge about good practice in literacy work, are means by which organizers can inform themselves of what is needed to do good literacy work.

An effective teacher training programme is clearly a key factor in developing good literacy work in the ESL context. At present, the literacy dimension to ESL work is dealt with in short in-service training courses and as a component in professional training. It should be recognized that the literacy needs of those taking up ESL provision are just as wide-ranging as the needs of native speakers of English. Teachers setting out to do literacy work in ESL should be able to undertake a substantial professional training.

So much for the organizational context in which literacy has come to be seen as a crucial component of an ESL provision which is sensitized to the encoding of inequality into educational 'opportunity'. What about the classroom? How does work on reading, writing and discussion serve to create the atmosphere of dialogue in the classroom in which other types of language learning activity (learning effective ways of insisting, getting and giving information) can be grounded? Some examples of such work will follow, two drawn from work with adults, one in an ESL/literacy group, the other in a group of ESL tutors doing training. The third example illustrates this approach with a group of teenagers.

What sort of factors should a teacher bear in mind when choosing themes for literacy work? Firstly they should be close to the life experience of members of the group. This is why the student writing movement described above is such a valuable source of reading materials. You may choose to introduce a theme through reading a piece written by another student. You may choose to introduce a theme orally and develop it in discussion, with writing down as an outcome. With students not able to write for themselves, the teacher (or possibly another student) can act as scribe. Sometimes a group discussion can be synthesized into a text that can be typed up by the teacher for use as a reading text in the next lesson. For a useful and detailed account of what to look for in selecting materials, *Literacy Work with Bilingual Students: a Resource Book for Tutors*, mentioned above, is a useful guide. So in the three examples which follow, we will look at how a theme can be introduced and developed through literacy and oral work.

My bank account

It was pointed out above that professional/layperson relationships typically exhibit an unequal distribution of the right to speak, with power in the hands of the professional. Dealing with situations where you don't have institutional power, being able to assert yourself and get your point across, must be a strand in the ESL curriculum. Lack of confidence in speaking up can hinder someone's chances of communicating well just as much as not having the right choice of words or intonational nuance.

The object of this activity, based round a Stephen Leacock short story in a simplified version, *My Bank Account*, was to explore situations where members of a group (a literacy group, consisting of bilingual students with a post-elementary language level) had felt humiliated or embarrassed in a public, official setting, and to look at ways of increasing confidence in objecting, or answering back where the situation puts you at a disadvantage. Notice that this theme is not one limited to people who are learning English as a second language. Everyone (teachers included!) should be able to think of occasions when they were worsted by someone on the other side of the desk. The power invested in those who have 'gatekeeping' roles as interviewers in public, institutional contexts has been investigated by Erickson and Shultz (1982).

The Stephen Leacock story presents, in a humorous way, an encounter with some of these 'gatekeepers'. A prospective bank customer is humiliated and embarrassed by the snooty staff of a bank where he is trying to open an account, because he has an insignificant amount of money to do it with. It starts:

> When I go into a bank I am frightened. The clerks frighten me; the desks frighten me; the sight of the money frightens me; everything frightens me.

The discussion following the story can be used to evaluate the feelings of the hero in the bank. Has anyone ever been in a situation like that? If so, what happened? Each story told to illustrate the point enriches the discussion, gives it depth and meaning, creates a grounding in which the communicative 'point' that might emerge at some later stage (how to confront the rudeness and unhelpfulness of officials) can make sense. In addition to evaluating the subjective feelings of the hero/victim, the discussion can go on to judge the behaviour of the bank employees: what are the rules for treating people well in situations where you have knowledge and they don't, when you are an insider and they are outsiders? How should the bank manager have behaved? How should the hero of the story have challenged the bank staff? These issues can be dealt with in a number of ways, through discussion alone, through evaluative writing about the Stephen Leacock story, through writing about personal experiences, through working on the communicative problem via role-play. In fact, one student replied to the theme presented by the story by telling another story in which Mullah Nasreddin has the last laugh on someone who, quite literally a gatekeeper, refuses him entry to a smart party because he is looking scruffy! The process of this telling and writing down is described in 'The Moment of Telling: Bilingual Folk Stories in the ESL Classroom' (Baynham, 1986).

The themes introduced by this story were 'generative themes', in the same sense that Freire speaks of generative words: they encapsulate some deep-seated social process with which all participants can identify, in this case the abuse of power by insiders to embarrass and humiliate outsiders, the day-to-day enactment of inequality. Hitting on those themes, whether introduced speculatively by the teacher or contributed by the students, is the basis for developing a dialogue about what communication means, how it can be achieved, how we can learn to say what we mean.

My Friend

It was a cold winter morning.
I got up quite late.
It was 10.30 in the morning but it was still dark.

We had had some snow for a few days
and the footpaths were very slippery.
I was scared to go out and do my shopping.
I was alone in the house. It was freezing inside.
I looked for a box of matches to light my oil heater.
But I could not find one.
I could not even turn on my gas cooker
to make myself a cup of tea!
I felt miserable.
The whole world seemed to be very unfriendly
and cruel to me.
I started to think of my country,
those warm sunny days and the warmth of my people!

We were new in that area
and did not even know our next door neighbour.

I stood near my bedroom window and looked outside.
I watched peoples' faces, walking on the icy roads.
They all looked happy,
not miserable and cold like me.

I pulled myself together.
I put my coat on and went outside.
"Hello", I heard a voice calling me.
I looked back.
"I am your next door neighbour . . . . .
are you from India?" she went on –
"You must be missing your weather.!"
"Weather!" I said, "Oh no, it does not worry me at all.
Anyway, nice to meet you."
"My name is Bo-del. I am from Norway," she said.
"Would you like to come for a cup of tea?"

To me it was an invitation
and a welcome to warm friendliness.
I went to Bo-del's house.

Twelve years have gone past.
We have lost contact.
I still remember that bitter cold morning quite clearly.
But above all I remember the warm hospitality
of my friend Bo-del.

Santa Ghosht

My Friend   This is a piece of writing produced during a TESL teacher training course, in which the subject was producing reading materials based on personal experience. Those on the course were asked to try and write about something that had happened to them in a way that would be useful for literacy work in an ESL classroom. All the tutors on the course had had the experience of migration and settlement in this country. The story that Santa Ghosht brought back to the group raises many themes of isolation, loneliness, adaptation to a new country in the depths of winter, which might strike a spark in a group who have had similar experiences. In addition to this, embedded in the narrative is the basis for communicative work on inviting and accepting invitations which can be developed out of using the text for reading or listening. The narrative provides a context in which the interaction between Santa and her neighbour makes sense. Communicative work on initiating conversation and accepting the initiatives of others, can arise out of this narrative grounded in the experience of separation and isolation.

Notice the way that the passage has been laid out. It is typed in a jumbo typeface, which can make reading easier for beginner readers. The text has also been laid out on the page in a way that is generally thought to be helpful to beginner readers: great expanses of print can be a very daunting prospect if you are finding reading difficult. This approach aims to present the text in meaningful chunks, thus helping the beginner reader to get oriented. *Write First Time*, the adult literacy newspaper, written entirely by adult literacy students but now unfortunately no longer being printed, used this approach.[4]

So how might you use a passage like this with a group whose literacy level is quite mixed? For beginner readers you could tape the story, or read it to them, going straight into a discussion of the theme. You might get them to tell you and each other some of their own experiences of winter in England, the friendliness or unfriendliness of neighbours, and use this as a basis for a reading passage. This 'language experience' approach, first popularized for use with children in the Breakthrough to Literacy Project, is widely used in adult literacy work. It fulfils the criterion of choosing materials which are close to the life experience of students: the words on the page are literally their own words. This, it is argued, gives a new reader confidence to read for meaning, since the words, the concepts expressed and the context are already familiar ground. As mentioned above, the text can also easily lead into a role-play about introducing yourself, inviting and accepting or refusing invitations, all staple topics for oral work.

With developing readers, you might want to use the passage as a way of working on reading strategies like skimming for meaning. Questions about the text can send the reader back to it and also develop writing if they are asked to write their answers to the questions. Gap-filling (cloze-procedure to give it its official title) can help the reading for meaning process, and can also be an exercise for beginner writers. The example worksheet accompanying *My Friend* uses gap filling. You might want to use a discussion of the themes of the text to lead towards students writing their own accounts, or at least taping them so that they can be typed up for reading in a subsequent class. The knock-on effect of reading that really engages the attention of a group is considerable: other people will start to talk and write, producing new texts for other readers.

Fill in the gaps. Choose one of the words from the box.

I_____near my bedroom window and _____ outside.
I_____peoples' faces, walking on the icy roads.
They all_____ happy,
not miserable and cold like me.
I_____myself together.
I_____my coat on and_____outside.
"Hello", I_____a voice calling me.
I_____back.
"I am your next door neighbour . . . . .
are you from India?" she_____on –
"You must be missing your weather!"

pulled	looked
went	watched
stood	heard
put	looked
looked	went

Worksheet : *A gap-filling exercise*

With fluent readers, you might want to present the text rather differently: those who have internalized the conventions of writing often, understandably, think of texts using the line-breaking convention as poetry. You might ask this sort of reader/writer to do something like writing a letter to Bo-del, getting back in contact, writing about an incident in their own lives, or writing the story again, this time taking the perspective of Bo-del.

For further consideration of this way of approaching reading texts, I would again recommend *Literacy Work with Bilingual Students* as a way of learning more about the selection and use of reading texts with different kinds of readers and writers.

Fathers and sons

Sometimes reading can be used to generate discussion with no other end in mind than to explore the themes raised by what you have read: here the process is more important than the end product of more writing or answering comprehension questions. We will look at the way that *Dress Factory*, a story by Mahbubar Rahman, a young Bangladeshi boy, is used to start a discussion with a group of teenage Moroccan boys about their feelings on work and their fathers. In Mahbubar's story, Alal works in his father's dress factory. He has been invited to a party and wants to make a jacket to wear to it. He tries to make it without his father noticing, but his father catches him at it and forbids him to go to the party. His brother goes instead and wears the jacket. The story raises themes about work and play, a son's relationship to his father, and seemed like a good basis to start a discussion with.

Dress Factory

Alal and Abdul work with their father and mother. They lived at 88 Settles Street, and they make ladies dresses. They have a dress factory of their own. Alal's father works very hard and he wants his sons to work hard too. Alal is 17 years old and Abdul is 19 years old, they don't want to work hard. When they don't work hard, their father gets angry with them. But Alal doesn't want to work all day. Alal is a good tailor, he wants to make smart clothes for himself. Sometimes he makes shirts and trousers for himself.

One day Alal wants to make a jacket for himself. So he went to the market and bought jacket clothes, and went back to his home and he cuts it. Then he hid it behind some green dresses because he doesn't want his father to see it. Alal's father is angry when he doesn't work all day. Alal is making the jacket today because he is going to a party this evening. He wants to wear the jacket at the party. Alal's father is at the door, he is looking at Alal.
'Alal,' his father says.
'Yes Dad,' says Alal, and he puts the jacket under the table.
'What are you doing, Alal?'
'I am machining Dad,' says Alal.
'What are you machining?' asks Alal's father.
'I am machining the green dress,' says Alal.
'I can't see the green dresses,' says Alal's father.
'Brr, brr, brr, brr,' the telephone is ringing. Alal's father goes out.
'Whew!' says Alal, 'that was very close. I think the jacket will be ready for the party.' Then Alal is finished his machining and he is making the buttonholes and sewing on the buttons. His father comes in. He puts a green dress on top of the jacket.
'Alal,' says his father.
'Yes Dad,' says Alal.
'What are you doing?' asks his father.
'I'm making buttonholes Dad,' says Alal.
'these dresses don't have buttonholes, Alal.'
'I am not making buttonholes, I am sewing on buttons,' says Alal.
'Then why. .'
Abdul comes in and says, 'there is a man at the door Dad, he wants to see you.' Alal's father goes out.
'Whew!' says Alal. 'That was very, very close. The jacket will be ready for the party now.'
Now the jacket is ready and Alal is pressing it and he is talking to Abdul.

'Look at my jacket. It's ready for the party this evening. I made it today.'
'Alal,' says Alal's father. He is standing at the door.
'Oh! Yes Dad,' says Alal.
'What are you doing, Alal?'
'I am pressing, Dad.'
'What are you pressing, Alal?'
'I'm pressing a dress, Dad.'
'The dresses are green, not purple.'
'Well, I'm pressing my jacket, Dad. You see Dad, I'm going to a party this evening.'
'A party! You are not going to a party this evening Alal. When you don't work all day, you got to work all evening.'
Poor Alal!
Alal is not going to the party but his jacket goes to the party. Alal gives it to Abdul and Abdul wears it to the party.

Mahbubar Rahman, 13

The reading and discussion generated different kinds of talk, ranging from the youths talking and laughing together in English and Arabic, responding in a quite tangential way to the topic under discussion, through teacher/student interaction (the teacher asks a question which a student or a number of students respond to) to student/student interaction focused on the discussion topic (two or more students talking or arguing through a point). Here are some examples of the talk that came out of the discussion.

Teacher/student talk

Teacher:	*so I mean if you had a son in that situation you would do something you would say 'no don't go to the party'*
Student:	*no no I wouldn't because the father he didn he didn't know what the boy tried to do cos these old mens they I mean they don't know about putting new clothes or something-likethat they only want to work and make money but this boy he's young all right he wants to look smart and all that he want to make himself make a nice clothes for himself that I mean he could wear at a party people could say 'oh this is nice boy got nice clothes on' but his father he doesn't think that way he thinks only 'I want my son to work hard' and all that*

The following extract shows how a question initiated by the teacher is taken over by four of the students and becomes an argument between them in which each student bids to make himself heard.

Teacher:	*so if you were a father*
Student 1:	*yeah*
Teacher:	*with a son*
Student 1:	*yeah*
Teacher:	*how would you treat him*
Student 1:	*well all these fathers here all these boys here these young boys if when they going grow up they going to treat their children like not like these fathers now they hard innit I mean they not all of them but*
Student 2:	*yes I know what you mean*

Student 1:   *rigid I mean*
Student 2:   *very strict very strict very stiff*
Student 1:   *like we we know what it's like we we know like we say*
Student 3:   *listen listen don't say that because*
Student 1:   *we want to do*
Student 3:   *they had you dad had the same experience when he was young*
Student 4:   *no*
Student 1:   *that was look those days those days no cinema no nothing allright those days only*
Student 4:   *when you grow up right you'll be*
Student 2:   *does your father let you go to the cinema*
Student 1:   *yeah this is it*
Student 4:   *listen I'll tell you something*
Student 2:   *does your father let you go to the cinema*
Student 4:   *listen   listen*

The way this extract develops shows how the teacher's question is taken over by the four students and develops into an in-group discussion, which Student 4 is eventually bidding to get into with his 'listen   listen'.

There are perhaps two points about these interactions relevant to our discussion. The first is that the teacher's questions are genuine questions, asking for personal opinions, judgement and evaluation of the themes under discussion, not the unreal 'What is the capital of Spain?' type of question that David Dinsmore noticed in the classrooms he visited. The second is that this group of students demand and take space to develop the discussion, without reference to the teacher, who is certainly organizing what goes on, to the extent that he provided the topic and framed the question, yet who is also prepared to stand back and let responsibility for developing the discussion transfer to the group.

We suggested above that teachers have a problem in that they talk too much. Perhaps the corollary of this is that a basic teaching skill involves knowing when to be quiet!

Conclusion

This paper has examined ways in which teachers and students can develop a dialogue in the classroom, based on activities involving reading, writing and discussion. The power relations in the classroom, by which the teacher has the right to initiate talk, to organize others to talk and to decide when a topic has been completed, create a situation of 'anti-dialogue', in Freire's terms, and frustrate the active involvement of students in their own learning. Discussion, talking and writing from experience can be the key to developing, in both teachers and students, a better understanding of the dynamics of communication, both within the classroom and outside it. The 'literacy dimension' to ESL work is a vital strand in achieving equality of opportunity in education; it is up to ESL teachers and organizers to ensure that it is an integral part of the ESL curriculum.

Notes

1. Power relations in professional/layperson interaction have been extensively studied. See, for example, Erickson and Shultz *The Counselor as Gatekeeper: Social Interaction in Interviews* (1982), Mehan

Language and Role in Institutional Decision Making (1983), Sinclair and Brazil *Teacher Talk* (1982), Candlin, Coleman and Burton *Dentist–Patient Communication: Communicating Complaint* (1983).

2. A catalogue of writings published by community publishers is available from The Federation of Worker Writers and Community Publishers, Janet Burley, 16 Cliffend House, Cowley Estate, London SW9.

3. *The NATESLA Catalogue of Resources for Teaching English as a Second Language* can be ordered from National Extension College, 18 Brooklands Avenue, Cambridge CB2 2HN.

4. Back issues of *Write First Time* can be obtained from Avanti Books, 1 Wellington Road, Stevenage, Herts.

References

AGE EXCHANGE THEATRE COMPANY (1984) *Memories of Pensioners from Many Lands*

BARNES, D. (1976) *From Communication to Curriculum*, Penguin

BAYNHAM, M. J. (1983) 'Mother Tongue Materials and Second Language Literacy' in *ELTJ*, Vol 37 No 4

BAYNHAM, M. J. (1986) 'The Moment of Telling: Bilingual Folk Stories in the ESL Classroom' in *ELTJ*, Vol 40 No 2

CAMPBELL, N. (1986) *My Life as a Woman in Love*, Hanley Road Adult Reading Centre

CANDLIN, C., COLEMAN, H. AND BURTON, J. (1983) 'Dentist–Patient Communication: Communicating Complaint' in Wolfson, N. and Judd, E. (eds) *Sociolinguistics and Language Acquisition*, Newbury House

CLAPHAM BATTERSEA ADULT EDUCATION INSTITUTE (1983) *Folk Stories*

DINSMORE, D. (1985) 'Waiting for Godot in the EFL Classroom' *ELTJ* Vol 39 No 4

ENGLISH CENTRE (ILEA) (1979) *Our Lives*, ILEA English Centre

ERICKSON, F. AND SHULTZ, J. (1982) *The Counselor as Gatekeeper: Social Interaction in Interviews*, Academic Press

FREIRE, P. (1973) *Pedagogy of the Oppressed*, Penguin

GHOSHT, S. *My Friend*, unpublished

HACKNEY READING CENTRE *Every Birth It Comes Different*

KOHL, H. (1973) *Reading How To*, Penguin Education

LEACOCK, S. (1960) 'My Bank Account' in *British & American Short Stories*, Longman's Simplified English Series

MACE, J. (1980) *Learning from Experience*, Adult Literacy Support Services

McLAUGHLIN, J. (1985) *Creative Writing in English as a Second Language Work*, ALBSU Viewpoints No 3

MEHAN, H. (1983) 'The role of language and the language of role in institutional decision making', *Language in Society* Vol 12 No 2

NORRIS, M. (1985) *Hand to Mouth*, Lee Centre, Goldsmiths' College

RAHMAN, M. (1975) 'Dress Factory' in *Classrooms of Resistance* (ed) Searle, C., Writers and Readers Publishing Cooperative

SHORE, L. (1982) *Pure Running*, Hackney Reading Centre

SINCLAIR, J. McH. AND BRAZIL, D. (1982) *Teacher Talk*, OUP

SINCLAIR, J. McH. AND COULTHARD, R. M. (1975) *Towards an Analysis of Discourse*, OUP

TURNER, M. (ed) (1985) *Literacy Work With Bilingual Students: a Resource for Tutors*, ALBSU/ILEA

Section 5 Assessment and Accreditation

Introduction

ESL teachers are constantly and uneasily aware of the many formal and informal assessments of communication skills which students meet outside the classroom. These assessments are both inevitable and unpredictable, overt and covert; they may also be employed in the cause of both direct and indirect racism. They occur in all day-to-day interactions with the English-speaking world of shopping, the DHSS, the health service and the education service, but they are felt at their most acute when students try to enrol on or complete education or training courses, or to apply for jobs.

At the same time teachers themselves, inside the classroom, are constantly looking for assessment procedures which will enable students to measure their progress, and help them to move on to the next learning stage, while at the same time following the syllabus which most nearly meets their needs.

This, then, is the conflict which teachers face, conflict between what is wanted in the classroom and what is demanded by the world outside. The papers in this section examine various aspects of the dilemma, not to provide easy, simplistic resolutions, but to consider the issues involved against that shared assumption of what ESL teaching is really about: the provision of skills and strategies to enable bilingual learners who continue to need ESL support to achieve their full potential in work, training and everyday life.

First, it is important to confront the extent and range of assessment outside the ESL classroom. Teachers often despair, understandably, when they begin to consider the hundreds of local tests which exist across the UK in industry, commerce and MSC programmes, and how students may be inappropriately assessed. (In 1977, seven Bangladeshi workers won a case against the British Steel Corporation when it refused to reinstate them in posts they had already satisfactorily held down and for which it was now claimed their literacy in English was inadequate. BSC was found guilty of violating the 1976 Race Relations Act on indirect discrimination and had to reinstate the workers.)

The other main field in which bilingual students are assessed and have to demonstrate a not always relevant level is that of education itself. Only too often, entrance tests and examinations evaluate no useful skills and only erect discriminatory barriers. Enrolment on to courses as diverse as NNEB, catering, information technology, can entail taking an English test of questionable relevance but considerable difficulty. The problems involved in getting on to GCSE English language courses may only be matched by difficulties in achieving the standard demanded or finding qualifications which are equally marketable.

The papers in this section examine these issues in some detail: how assessment procedures inside the classroom measure student progress and motivate student learning; how assessment and recruitment procedures — formal and informal — can exclude bilingual students from courses and impede progress; the suitability, relevance and appropriateness to their needs of a range of national examination and profile assessment schemes.

Measuring student achievement — national examination and profile assessment schemes

Sheila Rosenberg

This paper studies national examination and profile assessment schemes and considers their suitability, relevance and appropriateness to bilingual students who continue to need ESL support. It is divided into three parts. The first is a general introduction. The second analyses a range of well-established, or at least tried and tested, tests, certificates and examinations under three headings: English as a mother tongue, ESL and EFL. The categories are self-explanatory and refer to the client group that the various national examination boards have in mind for the certification. The third part looks at two important new national forms of certification for which, at the time of writing, much less evidence is available: the Certificate of Pre-Vocational Education and the General Certificate of Secondary Education. An examination of these two certificates illustrates how criteria of both language and culture must be used when looking at assessment procedures from the point of view of bilingual students. However, it is useful first to define more precisely some of the general problems which they all in their different ways address and draw together the principles underlying possible responses. Six major issues arise, best expressed in terms of questions.

Introduction

1. How far does the assessment procedure/test in question usefully validate a good ESL course, whether in the adult or further education sector?

This is, of course, the question for which the ESL teacher has the overriding responsibility. Having established the learning needs of the students and drawn up the syllabus, the question of assessment inevitably arises. If the course is involved in some way with national examination or profiling certificates, CPVE, BTEC, GCSE, then the ESL teacher is involved in an exercise of tailoring, adjustment and accommodation, and his or her role is often one of broker or even advocate. This becomes increasingly true in courses validated by continuous assessment and profile certificates and where the ESL teacher is one of a team.

If the course is specifically for bilingual students, then the teacher must choose assessment procedures which measure the acquisition of appropriate skills, but which give qualifications which are then recognized and accredited when the student carries them on to the next stage or course. It is sadly true that tests and examinations which are widely recognized may be of little use in validating a good ESL course, while the few ESL specific assessments have yet to earn currency. What has been finally established, however, is the marginal currency of EFL qualifications when presented by bilingual students living in the UK.

2. How does the assessment procedure/test match the current skills of the aspirant and is it realistically within reach?
Answering this demands access to information about the test, and skill and sensitivity in interpreting and applying it. As important is the *equal* involvement of the teacher and the student in negotiating and making the final decision, against a realistic understanding of what the test is and what is involved. This can sometimes be extremely difficult, especially where, for example, the overwhelming currency of GCSE weighs heavily with a student and his or her family against all other indications that it is not, at least for the moment, appropriate.

3. How far does the assessment procedure/test recognize and validate the reality of multiracial, multicultural, multilingual Britain, so that it rewards bilingualism positively and does not penalize candidates by assuming cultural homogeneity?
All assessment procedures which seek to test skills via concrete, contextualized tasks (for example, CPVE) immediately penalize students by assuming cultural homogeneity. This does not apply only to assessing language and communication skills. The numerical presentation of the four rules is often easier to handle for the students under discussion here than the solving of problems presented in long and complicated language and culturally unfamiliar contexts, such as teenage budgets, shopping lists and recipes. This dilemma exists right through the education structure, but is ironically at its most acute at the basic levels. This is because the lower the level of educational ability that is assumed for the client group, the greater the amount of language used to present the material and test the skill, and the more likely the recourse to homely — and culturally specific — contextualization. So, bilingual students, already often assigned to a non-academic course by virtue of their language alone, are then further disadvantaged by having skills and concepts presented in language, and drawing on experience, which are in no way 'everyday' and familiar to them. One way of countering cultural hegemony is to make greater use of continuous assessment and profiling, devise appropriate tasks, and ensure well-briefed and sympathetic assessors. However, it still remains the duty of national examining boards to recognize and not penalize cultural diversity, and to reward bilingualism positively. If they do not address these issues then they will justifiably lay themselves open to the charge of indirect discrimination.

The last questions reflect the pragmatic considerations of the teacher and student, moving from the classroom to the educational and commercial marketplace.

4. How marketable is the qualification in terms of employment, education and training?

It has already been suggested that this is not easy to establish. Examining boards always hope their new enterprises will find currency; teachers and students have to contend with the obduracy or the idiosyncratic responses of employers and interview panels. However, nationally accepted certification is available across a range of courses and subject areas, and it may be a case of looking particularly carefully at the 'English' or communication tests of several group certificates, as well as at discrete language tests.

5. Are there any alternative strategies?

It may be possible to by-pass specific qualifications in English altogether, particularly with older students. The onus is then on the teacher and the student together to present a range of skills via a well-presented c.v. and a portfolio of work, plus oral interaction and interview skills, and in this way persuade interviewers of the student's suitability for the course, or job. (See Bagchi, Section 5.)

This strategy meets the demands of the final question.

6. How far does the assessment procedure/test establish the possession of real skills relevant to the particular course or employment to which it gives access?

It would be naïve not to acknowledge that this is the most difficult problem, not the least because its solution lies almost entirely outside the control of the individual teacher, and has to be tackled in a much wider arena.

Analysis of examinations

The tables that follow have been drawn up on the basis of the foregoing questions. (The sixth principle is not so relevant to this present account and some of the issues are dealt with in detail in 'The Enrolment of Bilingual Students in Further Education' later in this section.)

The tables indicate the varying marketability, accessibility and usefulness of the qualifications. Indeed it might almost be said that the marketability of certain qualifications varies in inverse proportion to their accessibility to bilingual students. More important, teachers frequently find themselves under pressure from students who do not understand all the issues, or from institutions geared to the teaching of certain courses. In this context the Burnham grading system, by which all EFL courses above a certain level are graded above all the other certificates listed in the tables, can be a disincentive to changing previous practice. The most important issues, however, are still the establishing and agreeing of criteria by which to judge the various certificates from the point of view of the bilingual learner.

Examination and profile certificates for native speakers

Name[1]	Characteristics	Marketability in the UK

Pre-Vocational and Basic Vocational Certificates: Tests in communication, e.g:
 	
C&G L1 361 I & II (course work and exam)
 	
Certificate of Pre-Vocational Education (CPVE) (profile and optional national assignment in communication)
 	
RSA Practical Skills Profile
 	
BTEC[2] First Award
	As a generalization, these courses assess overall communication skills in terms of behavioural objectives and are assessed by profiling and/or examination. They assume native-speaking oral/aural fluency and at least a basic familiarity with UK culture, organizations and systems. They need not be confined to the lower academic range (e.g. C&G 361 II and CPVE) but in reality FE and school students on these courses are not generally seen as academic
	    Bilingual students are at a disadvantage culturally and linguistically. If they have academic potential, but have been put on these courses because of language level, they can be further penalized since the courses do not emphasize academic skills. However, the clear identification of discrete communication skills can be to their advantage. On BTEC courses which have a group certificate, failing communication skills can mean being referred in the whole certificate
	    Finally, to date, communication assessments in business studies have tended to penalize technical inaccuracies as much as in GCSE English
		Nationally validated and accepted, with implications for progression still, in some cases, to be worked out

AEB Basic Test in English	Emphasis on demonstrating achievements, recognized by employers in reading, writing and listening. Although the test is norm-referenced, the certificate states what has been achieved in terms of behavioural objectives. It is seen as testing basic communication skills which should form part of any English course for students aged 14–16. Bilingual students benefit from the clear identification of basic objectives in three skills and by not having to deal with imaginative and figurative language Little continuous writing; accuracy up to functional level, e.g. letter-writing, indexing. Rather narrow	Becoming increasingly popular, which tends to show candidates, teachers and employers are finding it useful
'O' Level English Language Mode 3 Mode 1	Assumed and tested a wide range of usage, dialect and understanding of connotations, figurative language and cultural reference. Premium on accuracy. Mode 3 an advantage because folder could be put together throughout the course and because, in some consortia, teachers wrote the exam Mode 1 made the heaviest demands on bilingual speakers because the test was only by externally set exam	'O' Level English, Grade C, is a basic entrance requirement, whether appropriate or not, for many jobs, FE, HE courses and training. Ended 1987[2]

1 See Appendix 3 for names and addresses of examining boards
2 For GCSE see below

EFL, ESL examinations and profile certificates

Name[1]	Characteristics	Marketability in the UK
Cambridge First Certificate in English (EFL exam)	Assumes evenness of language skills, though listening and oral interaction count for only 30% of the marks. Emphasis on structural accuracy. Content material often simplistic. Writing tests demand surface accuracy rather than adult range and depth. Presents contemporary Britain from point of view of overseas student, assuming candidates are not resident in UK	Very limited in UK
Cambridge Certificate of Proficiency in English (EFL exam)	High level of structural accuracy and usage demanded, often beyond the experience of ESL students or even many native speakers! Content material more mature than First Certificate. No testing of language skills needed for study	Accepted by some HE institutions as entrance qualification, equivalent to 'O' Level/GCSE English Language, Grade C
RSA Examination in the Communicative Use of English as a Foreign Language (EFL exam)	4 Skills/3 Levels in each, to be selected as appropriate by the individual candidate. Exam tests communicative competence. Content still geared towards non-residents, though authentic UK material is used	Accepted by some HE institutions as entrance qualification, equivalent to 'O' level/GCSE English Language, Grade C
RSA Profile Certificate in English as a Second Language	4 Skills are assessed, the levels ranging from a point which a beginner may have reached after 100 hours tuition, to a level immediately below that at which the candidate can cope with mainstream tests. Syllabus geared to consensus of good practice in FE and AE ESL courses	Should be useful for referral on to other courses and, it is hoped, jobs. (See Dunman, Section 5)
NWRAC English as a Second Language (ESL exam)	4 Skills. Tests language for study, especially the sciences, and so provides a good framework, though *not* a total syllabus, for language support for students on science courses. No examination of figurative, affective language demanded	Was CSE equivalent. Still offered in FE
JMB Test in English Overseas (ESL/EFL exam)	More difficult than NWRAC (above). Still aimed at those studying science, but now at 'A' level. Cognitively quite difficult. Residence qualification: less than 10 years in the UK	Accepted as equivalent to 'O' Level/GCSE English Grade C by many HE institutions
AEB Test in English for Educational Purposes (EAP exam)	Aimed at a broader spectrum of students than JMB: sciences, arts, social sciences. 4 Skills and study skills. Long and complicated	Accepted by some HE as equivalent to GCSE/'O' Level English Language, Grade C
University of London 'O' Level English Syllabus B	Eschews dialect/regional variations and material with specific cultural bias. Concentrates on English as a lingua franca, *not* as bilingual students might experience it in the UK. Demands of continuous prose writing less than in other English 'O' Level exams	'O' Level/GCSE English Language, Grade C. *NB* Cannot be taken in the UK

3 See British Council: English Language Requirements (1988)

Abbreviations: C/A – Continuous assessment   EMT – English as a Mother Tongue   EAP – English for Academic Purposes

CPVE and GCSE

As has already been indicated, it is essential that, in examining any national scheme of education and training, attention is paid to all assumptions about cultural norms, as well as to issues of language. Only from this perspective is it possible to examine the Certificate of Pre-Vocational Education and the General Certificate of Secondary Education from the point of view of young people with a mother tongue other than English, who are impeded by their communication skills in English from achieving the education and training they are otherwise capable of.

In examining the CPVE and GCSE from the point of view of this client group, it immediately becomes clear that the most important characteristics that give rise to concern are, in fact, common to both:
— both are based on a system of national criteria;
— both assume a uniformity of previous educational experience in candidates;
— both make passing reference to a multicultural student body, which they fail to follow through in the detailed working out of the scheme;
— neither, so far, shows any real understanding of issues related to bilingualism, or credits bilingual competence adequately.

The two studies below, in their detailed examination of these characteristics, should be seen as case studies, suggesting through their examination of issues of both language and culture, approaches that would be equally applicable in looking at other forms of national certification.

The Certificate of Pre-Vocational Education

The CPVE framework provides for learning through experience and assesses student achievement on a programme of pre-vocational education which integrates core skills and vocational studies (see chart). Thus, for example, communication and numeracy skills should be developed and assessed within the context of such vocational areas as caring for the elderly, travel and tourism or building construction.

The target population for this certificate is clearly identified as young people who have just completed the compulsory period of secondary education. This assumption of homogeneity among 16-year-olds clearly places recent arrivals in the UK at a disadvantage and not only in the immediately obvious areas of culture, language and curriculum. The basic philosophy of CPVE may in itself present considerable barriers to such students. The principle of students being actively involved in the learning programme and taking a responsible part in the assessment of their progress and achievement, by way of continuous assessment and profiling, is almost always a greater change for them than it is for even those who have been used to 'traditional' schooling in the UK. For recent arrivals, such student intervention is unthinkable and normal modesty is reinforced by powerful earlier social and educational expectations to make it difficult to adjust quickly to a student-centred approach, with active student participation. This could crucially affect their performance on a year's course.

The particular problems facing bilingual students who continue to need language support on CPVE schemes can be identified as follows. Assumptions about homogeneity of previous experience penalize all of them, but especially late arrivals to the UK. Some bilingual students will

Certificate of Pre-Vocational Education

The Core Competences

Personal and career development
Industrial, social and environmental studies
Communication
Social skills
Numeracy

Science and technology
Information technology
Creative development
Practical skills
Problem solving

Vocational Areas

Category		Cluster
Business and administrative services	Control of organizations	Audio typewriting
		Typewriting
	Services to business	Word processing
		Book-keeping
		Accounting procedures
		Clerical services
		Enterprise skills
		Reception duties
Technical services	Information technology and micro-electronic systems	Product design
		Engineering drawing
		Electronics
	Service engineering	Electrical and electronic systems
		Micro-electronic systems
		Information processing
		Data handling
		Computing
		Motor vehicle engineering
		Engineering processes
		Installation and maintenance
Production	Manufacturing	Physical science
		Materials technology
	Craft-based activities	Fittings and furnishings
		Design and graphics
		Fabrication and welding
		Building construction
		Construction service installations
		Finishes and decoration
Distribution	Retail and wholesale	Customer service
		Merchandising
		Wholesaling and warehousing
		Stock control
		Buying
		Display
Services to people	Health and community care	Childcare
		Nutrition
		Human development
		Health care services
		Health studies
		Care of the handicapped
		Care of elderly
		First aid
	Recreation services	Geography of tourism
		Travel and tourism
		Leisure services
		Beauty therapy
	Hospitality including food and accommodation	Food preparation and production
		Home economics
		Food service
		Accommodation services
		Home management and institutional management

continue to have considerable difficulties in every area which involves communication skills in English. This may well mean that, whatever competence they may have shown in a complex range of skills needed to complete appropriately chosen and relevant assignments — problem solving, practical skills, information technology — the level of their final certification seems likely to be determined by their achievement of communication skills, examined against nationally set criteria. This is counterbalanced by a token only recognition of competence in other languages. Finally, the framework does not validate and recognize racial and linguistic and cultural diversity. So, though experience has shown that effective CPVE schemes for students from minority ethnic backgrounds — including those who continue to need language support — can be developed, they depend rather on the awareness and skill of the teachers than on explicit guidelines from the Joint Board.

The General Certificate of Secondary Education

The GCSE shows some similar difficulties, though at the time of writing there is insufficient practical experience on which to draw. The national criteria and syllabuses do, however, provide an opportunity to look at issues of language and language variety.

The GCSE amalgamates the General Certificate of Education Ordinary Level with the Certificate of Secondary Education and this may seem the most significant change. More important, however, has been the drawing up of national criteria both for the overall certification (the General Criteria) and for individual subjects (Subject Criteria). Candidates will achieve against these rather than compete against each other — criterion-referencing rather than norm-referencing. Again, as with CPVE, there tend to be assumptions about the homogeneity of experience, at least of 16-year-olds.

These are probably most important in the areas of language and culture. In any important recognition of this the General Criteria warn against 'bias':

> ... every possible effort must be made to ensure that syllabuses and examinations are free of political, ethnic, gender and other forms of bias, and provide the opportunity for some recognition of cultural and linguistic diversity.

The implementation of these criteria, however, is left to the individual subject criteria and the syllabuses produced by the local Regional Examining Groups. For example, in the National Criteria for English there is the following statement under Aims:

> The implications for English in a multicultural society are considered in what follows in this document and in the General Criteria.

However, the only recognition in the next seven pages of any linguistic and cultural diversity occurs in the section on English (sic) literature which declares that:

> Examining Groups may extend the scope of what is traditionally regarded as the canon of English Literature in recognition that aware-

ness of the richness of cultural diversity is one of the rewards of the study of literature.

There is no recognition here that such works may have a major value in their own right, separate from their role in increasing cross-cultural awareness.

The complex issue of language varieties in this cultural diversity is not covered at all. The assumptions are that this is an 'English' certificate and no hints are given a perplexed teacher, aware that assessing whether a candidate is 'speaking clearly and coherently with appropriate tone, intonation and pace' might be anything other than straightforward. This of course will affect the assessment of all students, but particularly students under consideration here.

The GCSE criteria in fact usefully highlight the problem inherent in all assessment schemes measuring the achievement of young people in the area of communication: the confusion between monitoring the acquisition of complex and maturing language skills on the one hand and the learning of a specific language and its literature on the other.

ESL examinations

One way of meeting the needs of second language students might be thought to be through a specific ESL syllabus. However, there are dangers in such courses and certification: the disadvantages of artificially constructed hierarchies of functions and skills which do not in fact recognize that 'learning English as a second language, goes on, necessarily, within a bilingual context'; the importance of placing learning 'within the context of multiculturalism, so that literature, film, television, sport and school activities of all kinds contribute to and motivate language learning'. Then the question of the 'usefulness' of the language taught presents difficulties because too often

> *the acquisition of such a 'useful' language is divorced from the processes in first language learning which allow us to become the best judges finally of what is 'useful' to us for particular purposes. (London Association of Teachers of English, 1980)*

Most significant in practical terms, however, is the fear that any examination in English as a second language, even with the GCSE label, will be seen as second class and not have anything like the currency of the English Certificate.

Conclusion

Both CPVE and GCSE schemes are important initiatives, welcomed by many teachers, including ESL teachers, for their emphasis on a more practical student-centred approach, with the focus on process rather more than product and content. However there is still far too little in the schemes to validate the achievement and experience of bilingual candidates. Those who continue to need language support also continue to be penalized in the levels of their overall final certification because their achievements in the crucial communication skills in the CPVE and English in the GCSE are measured against national criteria drawn up to assess the native speaker.

Teachers cannot ignore these realities and their efforts to encourage the Examining Boards to develop and introduce syllabuses that positively assess bilingual skills must for the time being be matched by strategies to help students, who will not achieve a Level 3 in communication in CPVE or a Grade C in GCSE, to persuade the gatekeepers of their ability to progress through to the next stage.

Postscript

At the time of going to press the National Council for Vocational Qualifications (NCVQ) is publishing clear instructions on the need for all validating bodies to ensure equal opportunities and some guidelines on how to achieve this (*Criteria and Related Guidance*, and Information Note 3 — *Access and Equal Opportunities*).

Further information

Addresses for the following can be found in Appendix 2 and Appendix 3:

AEB Basic English and Test in English for Educational Purposes, Southern Examining Group

Joint Matriculation Board Test in English Overseas, Northern Examining Association

GCSE English (ESL) and Cambridge First Certificate and Proficiency, Midland Examining Group

NWRAC ESL Examination, North Western Regional Advisory Council for Further Education

The Certificate of Pre-Vocational Education, City and Guilds of London Institute

References

BRITISH COUNCIL (1988) *English Language Entrance Requirements in British Educational Institutions*
DAVIES AND WEST (1988) *Longman Guide to ELT Examinations*, Longman
DES *GCSE. The National General Criteria, The National Criteria for English, The National Criteria for Welsh, The National Criteria for French*, HMSO
FEU (1985) *CPVE in Action: A Project Report*. Evaluation of the 1984–85 Pilot Schemes, FEU
LONDON ASSOCIATION FOR THE TEACHING OF ENGLISH (1980) *English Exams at 16*
NATIONAL INSTITUTE OF ADULT CONTINUING EDUCATION *GCSE and the Mature Student*: Information Bulletin

The enrolment of bilingual students in further education

Apu Bagchi

Introduction

It is possible to believe that today we have a situation in the post-16 education sector where all students, regardless of race, class, gender, linguistic and cultural background, have equal opportunity to study as advocated by the Crowther Report of 1958. The FE sector claims to be truly comprehensive in nature and, as Raffe (1979) pointed out, FE has been identified as offering the 'alternative route' of social mobility to those who had less opportunity in traditional schooling. In fact, an early claim was made by the DES (1970) that FE should enhance the opportunities of 'immigrants' because of the flexible, open-access and comprehensive nature of the system. However, when looking carefully at the structure of FE, it becomes clear that equal access to courses in FE for bilingual students is far from reality.

Reeves (1983) argues '. . . the comprehensive pretensions of further education are likely to be severely challenged by close examination of the racial factor operating in industrial and college departmental selection procedures, in channels of allocation, in the distribution of students between courses and levels, in the resourcing of courses, in success, failure and drop-out rates'. This impressionistic evidence has been backed by other researchers in this field. Gleeson (1983) pointed out that there existed two distinct strands within FE, one to do with training, and the other with education, but both routes remained highly selective. It therefore poses the question whether the issue is about colleges keeping prospective bilingual students out or encouraging them in. The process by which bilingual students enter FE is complicated and often highly hazardous. It has to be said that colleges readily committed to the idea of accepting bilingual students may not realize what hurdles the students have to overcome.

Gaining entry to college courses

The background

Let us first of all look at the structure of any FE college offering courses to all the 16 plus age group.

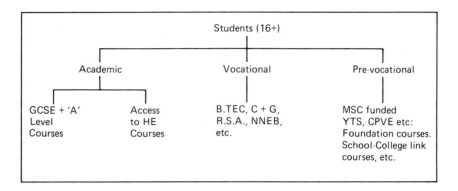

Fig. 1: *Structure of course system at FE colleges*

From the diagram in Fig. 1, one has to appreciate that any FE establishment is very complex because its clients do not conform to any particular type. The point here is that, unlike schools, where pupils are clearly defined in terms of age-range and course of study, no such strict procedures are followed in the FE sector. Each FE college is usually composed of a number of distinct departments (e.g. business studies, engineering, general studies, etc.) and each department in turn recruits students (part-time and full-time) to the various courses it runs. It is possible for one department to run courses in academic, vocational and pre-vocational areas, whereas another department may cater for students on academic courses only.

In addition, the diversity of the student body in relation to age, educational background, employment status and so on is also enormous. One must bear in mind that, by and large, further education institutions recruit a large number of students (often several thousands) undertaking a wide range of courses on a full-time, part-time or block-release basis.

Entry hurdles   As mentioned above, there are many possible hurdles awaiting prospective college students trying to gain entry on to a college course of study or training. These can be illustrated by examining the various stages students probably pass through from the moment they decide to apply to college to the point when they actually start on their chosen course of study.

It must be pointed out that the process outlined in Fig. 2 should not be regarded as necessarily the norm but rather a combination of steps that usually occur. What is important, however, is to recognize that at each stage of the above route, students will have to pass through a barrier, and that barrier may be synonymous with a member of the college staff — a secretary, clerical officer, admissions tutor, head of department, etc.

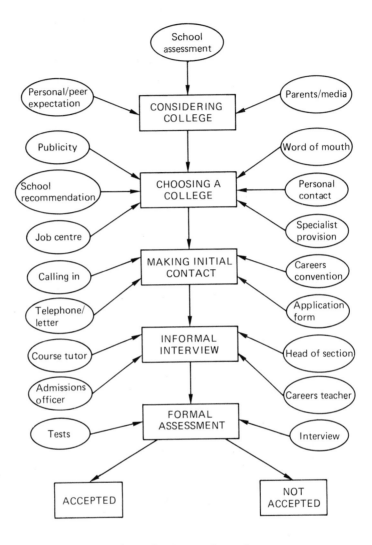

Fig. 2:   *Possible scenario of a student's entry into college*

Gatekeepers   It is how these gatekeepers perceive their roles that will have an important effect on whether or not prospective students gain entry into the college and admission on to their preferred courses. For example, gatekeepers can supply or withhold information, devise tests that assume similar or contrasting educational experiences, establish assessment procedures which take account of, or deny, differences in students' backgrounds, and use criteria to credit or ignore cultural or linguistic diversity.

The function of the gatekeeper becomes particularly difficult when dealing with bilingual students, the reason being that at each stage of the above process neither procedures nor standards may be shared between gatekeeper and client.

This problem stems from the fact that gatekeepers have to rely heavily on common ground and shared expectation. Unfortunately, many bilingual students do not have the same sort of experiences or background as that of the gatekeepers. Above all, they often lack confidence, knowledge and understanding of the very system they try to use successfully. (See Roberts, Section 1.)

It is questionable, therefore, whether a commitment to fairness to everyone, together with formally laid down procedures, could bring about a desired change in the recruitment of bilingual students, either into the general range of college courses or on to any special access courses. The issues are much more complex and need our careful consideration.

Institutional racism

We have to bear in mind that any process of publicity, interview, selection, and so on, is essentially a process of interaction. For instance, producing a leaflet in a community language about any particular course may not produce the desired objective because probably neither the purpose nor the significance of the course has been understood by those for whose benefit the course was intended in the first place. Moreover, educational structures limit disproportionately, and sometimes destroy, the opportunities of bilingual students. It is in this context that the damaging effect of institutional racism to existing education provision and practice needs to be recognized. The Swann Report has admitted the prevalence of institutional racism in our society which 'operates through the normal workings of the system and has the effect, if not the intention, of depriving ethnic minority groups of equality of opportunity and access to society's resources'. (Swann, 1985.)

Although the Swann Report does not make any specific reference to the further education sector, we may, nevertheless, take account of the fact that institutional racism has an important bearing on such procedures and practices as those involved in selection, assessment, admission and subject choice for bilingual students in FE. As Baker and Thomas (1985) argue, 'further education suffers from the same problems endemic in the school system — the racial prejudices of staff and students, a preoccupation with language problems to the exclusion of the wider issues, and the racialist content of materials and methods'.

It seems obvious that interviewing, testing and assessment procedures cannot be left to chance or simply to goodwill. Moreover, the assumption that the model which has catered for so many English-speaking white students for so many years must also work for the bilingual ethnic minority students can no longer be accepted. We need to appreciate that the process of interaction and evaluation takes place in a relatively short space of time, which in turn influences the life chances of the individuals concerned.

Gender

We must also address ourselves to the other factors which may affect the recruitment process. Are we, for instance, asking too much from some of our bilingual students and, on the other hand, pitching courses at too low a level for others? Is there a mismatch between what is on offer and what is needed? Do we take account of the varying social, economic, educational and cultural backgrounds from which most of our bilingual students come? In this context the gender issue has a special significance. Present studies have highlighted the tremendous problems that exist for Asian women when trying to take advantage of the opportunities that are present in the further and higher education sector. We have evidence from a number of studies about the very small take-up of courses by Asian women. The percentage of Asian women in the Access to Higher Education courses within ILEA during 1982/3 was only 0.6% compared to 42.8% of Afro-Caribbean women. The present situation is no better, as pointed out by Hinman (1985). There are many reasons for this situation, but it appears that the main reasons include family pressures, the position of Asian women as derived from religious, cultural and social factors, lack of knowledge or understanding of the British education system and inadequate crèche/child care provision.

In this context the Bradford College report on Asian women and FE has highlighted the disadvantaged and critical position of Asian women within wider British society. The report rightly claims that 'the structure of FE in Britain is, for historical reasons, closely linked to the occupational structure with its built-in class and sex bias. These biases are manifested in the set of formal rules and regulations relating to access, transfer and eligibility to qualify'. (Bradford College, 1982.)

Progression through college

Having gained entry to a college course, what chance do bilingual students have of progressing through the system? What happens to them at the end of their initial course? Unfortunately there are no reliable figures available because no systematic work has been done in this area, but personal experience and the experience of colleagues working in this field tell us that the situation here is rather disturbing. What we can say is that not only do bilingual students encounter difficulties at the point of recruitment, but they also suffer from lack of progression through their courses. This is borne out by the Bedford study which confirms that many students are concentrated on low-level basic courses, social and life skill courses and courses which are not directly linked to jobs (Bagchi, 1983). Lack of coordinated and systematic language support has aggravated this situation. (See Hoadley-Maidment, Section 2.)

Recommendations

Recruitment and selection procedures

Existing practices should be examined. Close monitoring should occur from the point of initial application to ensure that aspirations as well as abilities can be matched and that bilingual students are realistically assessed. This should lead to bilingual students being admitted to all courses and not only to foundation courses. We have to bear in mind that the structural inequality which is apparent in our society has limited opportunities in education for many people and for ethnic minorities in particular.

Access to employent   The fundamental issue to which we must address ourselves is that all ethnic minorities, including bilingual students, must have access to all levels of employment. Further education must therefore enable them to acquire appropriate 'marketable' industrial and commercial skills. This requires us to review not only our admission procedures but also the range of courses we offer. At present ethnic minorities are under-represented in higher level occupations. (PSI, 1984.)

Publicity   The college must produce publicity materials with a view to attracting more bilingual students on to *all* courses. This means using community languages to publicize new and existing courses. The importance of a systematic use of networks in order to disseminate information through school-liaison officers, outreach workers and other relevant bodies should be fostered. Moreover, 'a programme of bilingual outreach to create a better working relationship between the college and the local community should be embarked upon' (CELC, 1983).

Entrance tests and procedures   We must make a concerted effort to see that tests are designed to bring out the best in each of our applicants. At present many tests are full of culturally-specific elements and therefore discriminate against ethnic-minority students. The idea of bilingual assessment should be looked at seriously and adopted whenever possible. There are a few colleges which have done this and which are piloting bilingual assessment. There is therefore no reason to rule out the possibility of bilingual applicants writing out an application form in their first language. The same can be said for the interview. Bilingual applicants often find difficulty in expressing their ideas in English, particularly in a formal interviewing situation. It has been found that they frequently sell themselves short, both at interviews and when filling in the application forms. For instance, at City and East London College many of the bilingual students for the Special Access course failed to answer successfully such questions as 'Why have you chosen this (B.Ed. Access) course?' Many students replied to this in a single sentence, such as 'This course was the only one which would give me a grant', or 'I wish to be a teacher'. These replies may well be simple and truthful but are not adequate or full enough answers for the interviewers. However, when the same question was asked in their first language these applicants made several good points and responded well.

Language policy   A clear language policy is essential for furthering the ideals of equality of access for bilingual students. In this vein we need to give due recognition to all community languages, not just French, German or Latin, as has been the case in the past. It must be borne in mind that a successful bilingual assessment can only be possible *after* a college has already established a practice which allows both English language support across the curriculum and the maintenance of mother tongue. It has been rightly pointed out in the FEU's recent document on *Language for All* (1986) that 'any curriculum which takes student needs seriously would have to make available fully validated components in the major community languages'.

Staff development   This is needed above all by the gatekeepers (teaching and non-teaching staff) at both initial training and in-service level. As we have already seen, this group has power and gatekeepers are often forced to make value judgements on imperfect information, misinformation and false assumption. The other factor to be reckoned with is that, because of the present economic climate and lack of resources, gatekeepers are obliged to restrict access to certain courses and this invariably works against bilingual students. It is, therefore, important that we provide in-house training for all those involved in recruitment.

Obviously colleges should devise their own training programme, starting with their key staff, who should return to their own departments to work with the course tutors and others responsible for interviewing, testing and recruiting students. It is not possible to prescribe a particular form of training strategy that can be readily adopted, but the following criteria may form the basis of such an in-service training session. A checklist of the kind presented below may be given to the staff in a workshop situation (CELC, 1985).

Recruitment Policy for Bi/Multilingual Students

Checklist	Please Comment
Phone call	
1. How are inquirers dealt with who sound 'foreign'? Do you feel anxious when you don't understand people?	
2. How often are inquirers referred to other colleagues?	
3. How often does the inquiry result in written information being sent?	
Letter	
1. How are letters which do not identify a specific course dealt with?	
2. Do you get any feedback re whether or not the course of action you take, based on the letter, is appropriate for the inquirier?	
Application form	
1. Do you take these at face value, i.e. refer all applications to the person dealing with the course identified?	
2. Do you make any judgements in order to re-route, based on (a) previous qualifications (b) standard of written English on the form?	

Checklist	Please Comment
Test	
1. What does your test seek to do?	
2. Do you tend to judge the intellectual level of the applicant on the basis of his/her present standard of written English?	
3. How useful would a test be that included the applicant's facility in his/her written first language, if this was not English?	
Interview	
1. What kinds of records are kept of interviews?	
2. Is any other agency/institution involved in the interviewing process?	
3. How far are you influenced by the applicant's facility in spoken English?	
4. Would you consider including evidence from an interview in the applicant's first language as part of the interviewing process?	
5. How do you advise/counsel applicants if they appear to be inappropriate for the provision for which they have been interviewed?	
6. Do you get any feedback re how useful this referral has been?	

© Apu Bagchi, City and East London College

External factors However, we must acknowledge that there are other wider issues which prevent bilingual students from participating in FE. Discriminating practices such as demands for passport checks, withholding grants, and not recognizing qualifications from the country of origin contribute towards a negative perception of the education system as a whole for bilingual people (see Faine and Knight, Section 3). As for cultural issues, this paper cannot discuss all these in detail but we need to take account of the cultural implications when recruiting bilingual students, particularly women.

Conclusion Finally, we must remind ourselves of the fact that up until now assessment, testing and recruitment have been primarily concerned with students from the majority community (indigenous whites), without taking any account of the different experiences and requirements of ethnic minorities. It is now high time to review seriously our recruitment procedures and to make any necessary adjustments to ensure equality of access for all students wishing to enrol in further education.

References

BAGCHI, A. (November 1983) *Further Education and Ethnic Minorities: A Critical Appraisal of 'Second Chance'*, Research Thesis, Cranfield Institute

BAKER, C. AND THOMAS, K. (Spring 1985) *The Participation of Ethnic Minority Students in a College of Further Education*, JHFE, Volume 9, No. 1

BRADFORD COLLEGE/EOC (February 1982) *Asian Women in FE*, Project Report, Bradford College/EOC

BROWN, C. (1984) *Black and White Britain*, Third Policy Studies Institute Survey

CITY AND EAST LONDON COLLEGE (1983). *Multi-ethnic Policy Statements*. Section 8.2

CLARK, J., HARDING, K. AND BAGCHI, A. (March 1985). Exercise designed for an In-Service Training Course at City and East London College (abridged version)

DEPARTMENT OF EDUCATION AND SCIENCE (1970) *The Education of Immigrants*, Survey 13, HMSO, London

Education for All (March 1985). Swann Report on Education of Children from Ethnic Minority Groups, HMI

FEU (1986) *Language for All*

GLEESON, D. (1983) 'Further Education, Tripartism and the Labour Market', in *Youth Training and the Search for Work*, Routledge and Kegan Paul

HINMAN, J. (September 1985) *Opportunities for Adult Students of Asian Origin*, FHE Curriculum Development Project, ILEA

RAFFE, D. (1979) *The 'Alternative Route' Reconsidered*, Sociology, Volume 13

REEVES, F. (1983) *Race Relations: Ideology and Practice in Further Education*, JFHE, Volume 7, No 2

Record-keeping in adult education

Liz Lawson

Introduction

As developments such as self-assessment and independent learning have become part of the curriculum, so record-keeping has become essential. In order to progress, we need to look back with our students and evaluate both the appropriateness and the effectiveness of the learning already attempted. This is impossible without accurate records, kept by both student and teacher. For the purpose of this paper, record-keeping is defined as the process of collecting, storing and sharing information, related to the requirements of students, teachers and interviewers in adult education. The paper aims to:

1. explore the reasons for developing systematic methods of record-keeping;

2. describe some of the methods currently being used in adult education.

Background

The record-keeping systems outlined below have evolved in response to the requirements of students, teachers and interviewers in a large, mixed-sex, daytime centre, offering intensive provision four days a week. The examples would require modification if used in other contexts.

Four crucial areas were identified to provide the framework round which the record-keeping system was built. Expressed simply, these are:

1. *Appropriate provision*. Records and statistics are needed, both to demonstrate a demand and to match the educational offer to what students really want.

2. *Development of curriculum*. Independent learning, collaborative learning and negotiated assessment require systematic record-keeping on the part of the student and/or the teacher. All students need to be able to measure progress.

3. *Ongoing educational advice*. The provision of educational advice requires comprehensive systems both for the retrieval of information on training/employment opportunities and for the overview of student goals and progress.

4. *Evaluation and change*. As providers, teachers and interviewers require systematic methods of evaluating their own work, in order to judge how far aims and objectives are being achieved, and to incorporate feedback into planning for the future.

Design A record-keeping system needs to start with *people* and address itself to their information needs. The design of such a system requires consultation with those people affected by it, e.g. students, teachers and interviewers. It will be much less effective if imposed without this consultation process.

Records kept by the student

Purpose A record of *what* is done and *when* encourages individual students to look over work at home and ask questions about things that are not clear. It also enables students to revise for informal tests and exercises, which can help them establish for themselves how much they have learnt. Students can make better-informed decisions over what to do next if they have a record of previous achievement. If students play an active part in looking back and planning for the future, discussions about comparative methods of teaching and learning are more likely to arise.

Requirements It is useful to start by looking at record-keeping requirements voiced by students themselves. These may range from the need for a record of the time and place of their new class after the initial interview to the desire to keep a permanent record of oral work. Individuals have very different requirements.

Examples of records kept by students

'Your class' card At the end of the initial interview, the essential information about the new class can be given to each student, printed on thin card, so that when they start class the following week, there need be no confusion. (see Fig. 1)

Student information sheet When students join a class, there should be a discussion, with either the class teacher or the interviewer, about what to expect. An information sheet (see Fig. 2), preferably translated, could be one way into this discussion. Students should know in advance whether or not their class uses a textbook and something about what teaching methods to expect. Some centres may want to ask students to attend regularly or phone in if they are absent for several days. Students' attention should also be drawn to the equal opportunities policy (if one exists) so they know what action to take if they encounter racist or sexist behaviour while on the premises.

```
┌─────────────────────────────────────────────────────────┐
│                                                         │
│    Student name:                                        │
│                                                         │
│  Class: _____│
│                                                         │
│  Teacher: _____│
│                                                         │
│  Room: _____│
│                                                         │
│  Days: _____│
│                                                         │
│  Time:  morning  _____│
│         afternoon _____│
│         evening  _____│
│                                                         │
│  Start Class on: _____│
│                                                         │
│  If you have any problems,                              │
│  ask for  _____ Date    │
│                                                         │
└─────────────────────────────────────────────────────────┘
```

Fig. 1:   *Student class card*

Crèche information sheet   If a parent is bringing a child to the crèche, it is important that there is information about crèche procedure, i.e. whether or not it is acceptable to go in to see the child at break, whether spare nappies should be brought, what to do if the child feels poorly, etc. This information should be translated and discussed at the initial interview, so that no misunderstandings arise. Crèche workers should be consulted about the information they would like passed on to parents.

Ring-binder   If the class is using worksheets rather than a book, every student needs a ring-binder (or equivalent) and access to a hole-puncher. Without a filing system, worksheets which have taken energy to prepare and complete may well be left lying on the table.

Good study skills facilitate learning. Students may already have acquired study techniques . . . some come to their first class equipped with a ring-binder, notebook, dictionary, etc. If possible, students should have the opportunity of buying a ring-binder at the initial interview. Inside the file, students can have a copy of the plan of work negotiated by the group, worksheets in date order, evaluation sheets and 'memory joggers' (records of what was tackled and how it went). Copies of worksheets missed through absence should be available in the classroom in cardboard folders, so that students can collect them when they return.

A–Z notebook   A small A–Z notebook can be very useful for vocabulary, spellings and grammar points. Information can easily be retrieved. It is essential that, once bought, they be used regularly and referred back to. It is also a good idea if the teacher uses one herself, so that vocabulary items, etc. are systematically recycled in the syllabus.

INFORMATION FOR STUDENTS

1. ILEA Adult Education classes are for people settled in this country and for people waiting for refugee status. Further Education Colleges have classes for au pairs and short-stay visitors.

2. You cannot take First Certificate or Cambridge Proficiency exams at this Institute. Ask the interviewer for information if you wish to take an exam. [e.g. RSA Profile Certificate].

3. These classes cost £   a year for ILEA residents. They will cost a lot more if you live outside the ILEA. [The interviewer can check your address.]

4. Our classes are small and friendly. Our teaching methods may be different from the way you were taught in school; most of our classes do not use one text book. In your English class, you will listen to tapes, work in groups, talk and discuss, and do some reading and writing. Our classes aim to give you practice in dealing with real life situations.

5. If you would like extra help with writing and reading, maths or English please ask the interviewer.

6. There are lots of other interesting classes in the Institute, e.g. clothes making, pottery or computing. All classes are open to speakers of all languages. Please enrol for any class and ask for language support or help. Ask your interviewer.

7. If you need a creche place for your child [daytime only] don't forget to tell the interviewer.

8. Islington Institute has an Equal Oppotunities policy. If you have any complaint about racist or sexist behaviour in this Institute, please tell your tutor, Head of Centre or interviewer.

STUDENT RESPONSIBILITIES

1. If you:
    * are absent for longer than 2 weeks
    * stop coming to the class

    please inform one of the following:

    * The office at your branch [tel:]
    * The student interviewer at your branch [tel:]
    * Your tutor

    If you are absent for longer than 2 weeks and don't inform anyone, you may lose your place in the class, or your creche place. *If a class gets too small it may have to be closed.*

2. After you have joined the class, you can see the interviewer again if you have a problem or if you need any advice about further training, study or work.

3. Please attend regularly and on time, and bring a ring binder and pen with you to class. The teacher will give you worksheets which you keep as a record on your progress.

    ENJOY YOUR CLASSES!

Fig. 2: *Information sheet for students*

Negotiated plan of work   Once a syllabus or plan of work has been negotiated between teacher and students, every member of the group should receive a copy. The plan should be consulted regularly to establish:
1. how much of it has been covered;
2. whether it is still relevant to the group;
3. what to do next.
A plan of work negotiated and subsequently never referred to is absolutely useless. It is also frustrating for students to feel that they were 'consulted' as a token gesture.

Student's personal tape   A C90 tape brought in at the beginning of the session can provide an invaluable record of individual progress. Most students have cassettes at home, so the financial outlay need not be too great. Students can use their own tape in role-plays and other oral work. They are a useful way of record-keeping if, like anything else, they become part of the regular routine. If one item is taped each week or fortnight, habitual errors can more easily be noticed and self-corrected. The tape can be a permanent record of progress in oral work.

Memory joggers   As adults, we need to look back at a piece of learning several times before it has a chance of being remembered. As a guide, most of us need to be reminded of an item an hour after presentation, then the following day, then the following week and finally, several weeks or months later. It is useful to ask students after tea what they can remember from before tea, at the beginning of each class what they remember from the last class, and at the beginning of each week what they remember from the previous week. If the teacher gets into the habit of asking, everyone gets into the habit of remembering.

Memory joggers help the student and the teacher give a shape to these 'remembering' sessions. They can take many different forms. It can, for example, be useful for the students to record where they spoke or listened to English outside class in the previous week (see Fig. 3). Beginners and elementary students can use the 'What did we do?' sheet (Fig. 4) to remind them of the previous class. If not literate, they can tick the box beside the picture; if students are literate in mother tongue or English, they use the space to fill out the details. Intermediate and advanced classes can use the 'work tackled' sheet (Fig. 5), which is kept at the front of the ring-binder. It is interesting to compare the scheme of work planned near the beginning of the session, with the retrospective syllabus which emerges from these memory joggers.

Checklist/ evaluation sheets   Evaluation is one of the most crucial parts of teaching. It creates a dialogue, airs problems, empowers the student and gives the teacher a sense of direction. It is important to make a regular space for evaluation and to keep a record which the student shares. There should be feedback on the opinions voiced and the decisions reached.

It is often difficult for learners in any situation to feel confident about offering feedback and criticism without offending the teacher, much

Where did you speak or listen to English this week?						
	Monday	Tuesday	Wednesday	Thursday	Friday	Weekend
SHOP						
WORK						
DOCTOR						
?						

Fig. 3: *Memory jogger*

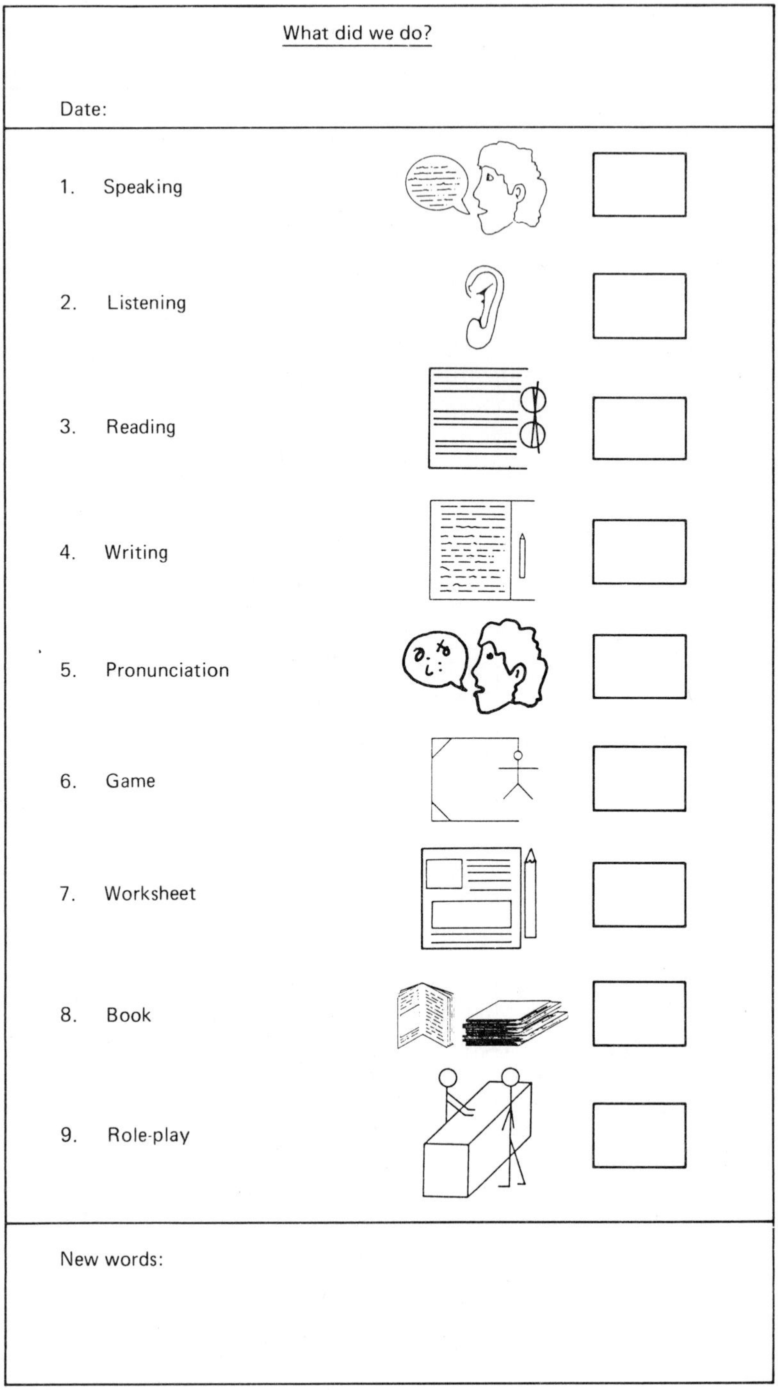

What did we do?

Date:

1. Speaking
2. Listening
3. Reading
4. Writing
5. Pronunciation
6. Game
7. Worksheet
8. Book
9. Role-play

New words:

Fig. 4: *Memory jogger*

Advanced Class					Record of Work	
Use this form to fill in the details of what we do each week						
	Listening	Discussion	Functions	Grammar	Reading	Writing
Week 1						
Week 2						
Week 3						
Week 4						
Week 5						
Week 6						

Fig. 5: *Memory jogger*

more so when students are concerned that language could cause communication problems. For this reason, evaluation should be raised as an issue in the classroom from the beginning. Discussion can be used to compare learning and teaching methodology and the roles of teachers in different cultures; the feelings around giving criticism can be shared and explored; the benefits of feedback and course modification can be explained. The group should choose the method of evaluation it feels most comfortable with. Such methods might include:

1. a checklist to open up general discussion (see Fig. 6);
2. a series of statements with 'like/don't like' boxes to tick;
3. small structured group discussions with a note-taker;
4. open questions to answer;
5. a blank sheet of paper to use in pairs or groups;
6. multiple-choice questions;
7. a questionnaire designed by students themselves.

One of the most useful ways of incorporating student-based criteria into the evaluation is to ask one group to design an evaluation sheet for another. This enables learners to focus on the most important issues for them and creates a group discussion of the different elements of

```
┌─────────────────────────────────────────────────────────┐
│                   CHECKLIST FOR STUDENTS                 │
│                                                          │
│   1. What are the aims of the course?                    │
│                                                          │
│   2. What are your language objectives?                  │
│                                                          │
│   3. Which topics and situations are relevant to you?    │
│                                                          │
│   4. How did you and your teacher decide the syllabus?   │
│                                                          │
│   5. In a lesson, how do you feel about ......           │
│          a) working by yourself                          │
│          b) working in pairs or small groups             │
│          c) working as a whole class                     │
│                                                          │
│   6. Do you use your first language in the class?        │
│                                                          │
│   7. Do you make choices about what to do during         │
│      the lesson?                                         │
│                                                          │
│   8. How do you keep records of ......                   │
│          a) your work                                    │
│          b) your attendance                              │
│          c) your progress                                │
│                                                          │
│   9. Do you study on your own?                           │
│                                                          │
│  10. How do you and your teacher evaluate the            │
│      lessons?                                            │
│                                                          │
│  11. How do you choose what to do next?                  │
│                                                          │
│  12. Do you feel you are making progress?                │
│                                                          │
│  13. Will you get a certificate or take any exams        │
│      at the end of this course?                          │
│                                                          │
│  14. Can you talk to the teacher or interviewer in       │
│      private, outside the class?                         │
│                                                          │
│  15. What would you like to do at the end of this        │
│      course? Have you got the information you need?      │
└─────────────────────────────────────────────────────────┘
```

Fig. 6:   *Checklist for class discussion*

learning prior to the completion of a subjective evaluation sheet. A lively class discussion can give feedback on many different aspects of the class. The following checklist provides a useful basis for anyone designing an evaluation sheet for their own class.

Do I want feedback on:
  (i) methods?
 (ii) materials?
(iii) content?
 (iv) classroom environment?
  (v) students' sense of own progress?
 (vi) students' feelings about the group?
(vii) students' feelings about the teacher?

Self-assessment   Self-assessment helps students evaluate for themselves how far their goals are being achieved. It should also help to introduce a vocabulary for discussing different ways of teaching and learning and encourage the student to participate in the planning of the course.

One of the simplest ways of encouraging students to assess themselves is to develop the use of simple record sheets which ask the learner to note down the date, type of work done, how it went and what they remember. With the addition of a column asking the student to suggest the next piece of work, this record sheet could also be used in self-access workshops and independent learning situations.

A more ambitious way of keeping self-assessment records is to use a modified profiling system, with specific objectives agreed by the teacher and students. At the end of each class students record their performance in relation to the tasks undertaken. This method of self-assessment provides a clear record of student achievement and improvement; it also enables students to feel more confident about judging their own performance. Most students start the year by vastly underrating themselves. By the end of the session, they come up with fair assessments of how each task went. Such record-keeping reflects what students *accomplish* rather than what is taught and what they *do* rather than what they know.

Group record-
keeping   If a class has agreed a number of objectives, such as those mentioned above, it is useful to display them in chart form (Fig. 7).

Reading objectives	Topics			
	Money	Social	Health	Travel
R1	✓			
R2			✓✓	
R3				✓
R4			✓	
R5	✓			
R6				
R7				
R8				
R9	✓✓		✓	
R10				
R11	✓			
R12				

Fig. 7: *Chart of objectives for group record-keeping*

At the end of each class, the group decides how the activities they have practised fit in with the objectives and these are marked on the chart. This method does not attempt to assess the achievement of the individual student, but aims to provide a record of tasks attempted by the group.

Records kept by the teacher

Purpose A record of the initial interview and a checklist of the skills needed by the group help the teacher keep track of what individuals need and how they are progressing. This helps in forward planning. Records of work done help the teacher to recycle language items and test informally. Worksheets can be more consistent in their style and 'instruction' language when past copies are kept for reference. The register can be used creatively to record student addresses and telephone numbers, reasons for absence, etc. This can help reduce drop-out or explain why a student has left.

Requirements Every teacher has a 'system' of record-keeping for his or her own classes. Sometimes, especially at the end of one academic year and the beginning of the next, it is useful to sit down and start afresh.

Examples of records kept by teachers

Advance copy of interview form If there is no interviewer at the site of the class, new students may well arrive at any time without warning. If an initial interview has taken place, it is important that the teacher receives advance warning of the new student's arrival and a copy of the interview form. This practice benefits both student and teacher − the teacher can plan activities to make the student feel at ease within the group and start to assess skills levels and needs.

Skills analysis Although in some cases an initial assessment has already been made, it is important to allow the time to draw up a more detailed analysis of language needs. The results of the assessment help in drawing up a relevant syllabus and in recording progress through the class. (See Fig. 8).

Profile records If profiling is relevant to a class, either under the auspices of the RSA scheme or more informally as a method of measuring achievement and encouraging student self-assessment, the teacher needs a way of recording achievement for each individual in the group. The teacher's profile record sheet has the profile objective written at the top and the names of the students down the side. Grades are inserted under relevant topic after negotiation with the student.

NAME			© Sharon Maconie
SKILLS NEEDS	Student A	Student B	Student C	Student D
---	---	---	---	---
Speaking	fairly incomprehensible simple functions O.K.	fluent good functions sometimes difficult to understand	clear functions O.K.	clear limited functions
Pronunciation	s/sh r/l stress final consonants	vowels pause stress	final consonants intonation ?	final consonants s/sh not a great problem
Structure	negatives questions tense reminders	word order tenses negatives (remedial)	good needs more complex eg: reported	questions tenses
Lexis	everyday quite wide	good	good everyday	very limited
Confidence	gets what she wants	confident in class	not very confident	very lacking in confidence
Listening	poor listener doesn't recognise questions	good except questions	needs to understand faster speech	understands more than she says
Reading	large sight vocabulary needs phonics	fairly fluent reader	needs to develop lexis	basic needs sight phonics
Writing	neat needs spelling word order plurals	spelling word order verbs	good needs fluency	neat can copy

Fig. 8: *Grid to show individual student needs*

Register record sheet   It is a good idea to keep a single ruled A4 sheet with the register on which to note what was done each time the class met. That way, if a different teacher takes the group, there is a record of the work the students have been doing. A single line of description and the date is all that is necessary.

Staff meeting/ progress sheet   Ideally teachers should have the opportunity of meeting regularly in paid time to discuss issues relevant to their work. This might include sharing feedback on student attendance and progress, discussion of the curriculum and methods and materials, planning trips out or suggesting improvements to the centre. This forms an alternative means of support to that provided by a 'line manager' and enables people to share good ideas and materials and learn from others' experience.

Progress sheets can provide a way of recording student attendance, progress and movement between classes. Each sheet has a list of students in a particular class, is kept in a central place and regularly updated. The sheets chart each student's progress through the class term by term. The staff meeting gives teachers the opportunity to add information about absence or progression on to other courses and to discuss the movement of students between classes.

Student record sheet   When a student progresses from one class to another, there should be an accompanying record of what s/he has already covered, together with a copy of the previous teacher's needs analysis. With this information, the new teacher can make a more thorough assessment and build a more relevant plan of work. The student record sheet should be based on the model of the RSA Profile Certificate (see Fig. 9) which concentrates on what the individual student *can* do.

Records kept by the interviewer

Purpose   There is an increasing awareness of the need to provide bilingual students with regular educational advice and support on an individual basis. Although not all adult education institutes have the resources to provide regular interview and advice sessions, some centres now provide interviewers/counsellors for this purpose. These people have several roles:

1.   to interview and admit students to adult education provision and pass on the information gained through this initial interview to the relevant class teacher;

2.   to advise and refer-on students who would benefit more from other courses, e.g. in colleges of further education, skills centres, etc., and to follow up where possible;

MANUEL GONZALES has demonstrated the ability to:

READING
Understand a variety of signs and short public
notices
Recognize where to write items of personal information on simple printed forms or questionnaires
Identify text and topic from such clues as layout
headings, typeface, etc.

WRITING
Fill in a form for self and immediate family given
some assistance
Copy short written details accurately
Write a simple notice, note or message
Complete mail order payments, cheques, giros and
other every day financial transactions

LISTENING
Recognize the essential facts of a sequence of
events given orally
Recognize relationship, context and topic in
dialogue
Follow simple instructions given orally

ORAL INTERACTION
Exchange greetings and personal details with
sympathetic interlocutor
Offer and ask for help, respond to offers and
requests for help
Pass on to a third person information given
orally
Make appropriate apology and response
Make arrangements involving time and location

Fig. 9:   *Student record sheet, based on the model of the RSA Profile Certificate*

3.   to support students and teachers working at a particular site. This support may vary from explaining to a student how to find and use the local law centre to discussing materials with a teacher or providing extra tape-recorders;
4.   to keep track of student progress and drop-out and provide some statistics at the end of the academic year.

   If the counsellor is to perform these very varied functions well, then s/he must be given the hours and training necessary. At a big site, the counsellor is an important link between students, teachers and middle management. Student details should be immediately accessible to the class teacher and the interviewer. Current class attendance figures need to be accessible so that the interviewer can admit sufficient new students to keep the class numbers healthy, but prevent the teacher being burdened by a massive influx or an impossible mix of levels and student needs.

Examples of records kept by the interviewer

Initial interview form

It is difficult, in a thirty- or forty-minute interview, to make a detailed assessment of a student's language level. However, some things should become apparent:

1. whether the student can respond to personal information questions;
2. whether the student can offer additional relevant information;
3. whether the student can initiate questions of his/her own;
4. whether the student can recognize where to write personal details on a printed form;
5. whether the student can give personal information in writing.

A form of some kind can act as a record of the first interview with a student. Some interviewers prefer to remember the details and fill in the form after the student has enrolled, while others have the form translated and discuss with each student the reasons for gathering the information. Some students may well prefer not to give personal information.

An interview form should be thoughtfully designed and regularly evaluated. Students, community outreach workers and teachers can give vital feedback on its effects and implications. Questions about date of arrival in Britain and number of children, routinely included on interview forms, should be avoided wherever possible on the grounds that they are intrusive and often perceived as racist. Space is needed for update, if the form is to act as a central record of student progress.

Central file

A central file contains all the student initial interview forms, filed class by class and copied if a student attends more than one class. Copies of the original form are also passed on to the class teachers, providing them with information about the new student, including the enrolment number. Detailed information can be added to the central record as the student progresses through the course.

The central file should also keep a record of students referred on to colleges and skills centres for interview. Sometimes these students come back to the AEI to take a part-time class alongside their new course or until the course begins.

Advice sessions and update of interview form

Naish (1986) points to the central role of ongoing educational advice. 'Student counselling . . . is necessary in order that students see the range of the offers open to them, a clear way through, and a number of possible exit points. This means that counselling has to take place on an individual and regular basis.' These sessions can cover any aspect of a student's progress and wellbeing, so the interviewer needs contact lists of professional advice agencies to hand. Details of the discussion can be recorded on the reverse side of the initial interview form, if the student agrees, so that information about a student's situation, progress and goals is constantly being updated.

Course information   As the interviewer provides a wide range of educational advice, there may be a wealth of information to organize for student advice sessions. Often this has to be in files so that it is transportable from one site to another. Lever arch files with an index and tabbed plastic pockets for each college, training centre etc. are probably the most practical answer.

Evaluation sheet for interview procedure   Interviewers need to collect feedback from students about how the first interview felt; this evaluation can help to modify interview procedures.

Interviewing register   The creative use of an interviewing register can make statistics much easier at the end of the year. In the register itself a record is kept of each time a student meets the interviewer and letters represent the kind of consultation that took place, e.g.

   I — initial interview.

   T — a telephone call on a student's behalf.

   If necessary, a separate register could be kept to record interviews with students who are referrred on by the counsellor to other types of provision. It is vital that AEIs produce statistics which do not neglect their very important role in educational counselling.

   The counselling register enables a relatively straightforward report of the year's work to be produced each summer. The figures give an interesting profile of take-up, turnover and progression. It is useful to record:

1.   the number of students enrolled;
2.   the number of students referred elsewhere;
3.   the number of male and female students respectively;
4.   the number of students who were in class for three terms, for two terms, for one term or less;
5.   the average age of students attending class;
6.   the number of students referred-on to other courses;
7.   the average number of advice sessions for each student throughout the year.

Conclusion

There are five issues which emerge as crucial to the consideration of record-keeping in adult education. These are:

1.   the necessity for consultation with community groups and students regarding interview procedure, enrolment and provision;
2.   the continuing need for empowerment of the student within the classroom;
3.   the importance of regular advice sessions and a good system of record-keeping to enable students to progress and achieve their stated goals;
4.   paid time for staff meetings and work support sessions for all teachers;
5.   the need for regular monitoring and evaluation of all record-keeping.

All this may seem a rather daunting task. However, once a record-keeping system has been established, both students and teachers will benefit from its use and value the support it provides.

Acknowledgements   I would like to thank Lynette Oliphant (Islington AEI) for many hours spent on the information sheet; Flick Thorpe and her colleagues at Neighbourhood English Teaching, Edinburgh, for lots of ideas on the student checklist and Sharon Maconie (Islington AEI) for allowing me to include her 'skills needs' sheet.

References   NAISH (1986) *From Need to Choice* (English Language Provision for Bilingual Students in ILEA's Adult Education Service), ILEA Language and Literacy Unit: Occasional Paper No 3

The RSA Profile Certificate
Sheila Dunman

Introduction   The school hall was packed with parents who were concerned about the proposed closure of this comprehensive school. Closure would involve pupils travelling further, into the centre of the city. The chairman of the education committee and other councillors were there to answer questions and listen to viewpoints. One of the many speakers that evening was a middle-aged Asian woman, Shantaben, whose daughter went to the school and whose son was due to go the following year. She put forward her opinion against the school closure and was listened to by the councillors. It was a situation that would daunt many fluent speakers of English. Shantaben's English was quite limited, although she had attended an ESL class for a few years, and she was normally shy and diffident, but she felt strongly enough about the subject to speak out. She was a member of an ESL class that had worked for the RSA Profile Certificate during the pilot year. She was awarded the certificate after that year. If her tutor had been at the meeting, she might have recorded that Shantaben had achieved the oral interaction profile objective 12: 'give a point of view in group discussion.' The school was spared from closure, though maybe not as a direct result of the RSA Profile Certificate.

This incident illustrates the achievement of the RSA Profile Certificate in giving confidence to students, particularly those in community classes, and enabling them to use their English outside the class situation. Shantaben's level of English would have meant that she could not have worked for any other existing examination. The involvement throughout of the students in the profile assessment meant that they knew what they had achieved and saw it recorded. Tutors also had a constant focus for their work with the students. Shantaben's tutor commented: 'The whole framework would, I hoped, provide me with better quality feedback on my teaching, give welcome direction both to myself and my students and help in bringing about a more "open" approach in the classroom.'

Background

The RSA Profile Certificate for ESL Adult Students is a comparatively recent development in the field of assessment. The assessment process was developed by a working party set up by the RSA to look at the needs of adult students for whom existing assessment procedures did not seem appropriate or easily accessible. Members of the working party were very much aware of the problem of the certificate being regarded as a second-class qualification: they regarded it not as a substitute for existing examinations for native speakers of English, but more as a stepping-off point for students who wished to go on to other forms of assessment. They also recognized that for some students it would be their only certificate, as they would not wish to continue with other forms of assessment.

Target population

The main group of students in mind throughout the development of the profile certificate was the large number attending community classes in all areas of Britain. Many of these students might have been attending classes for several years with no clear final aim in mind. If they were able to acquire a certificate that demonstrated their competence in English, many might gain the confidence to join other classes, either award-bearing or recreational. Several existing forms of assessment for ESL and EFL students were looked at, but it was felt that none of them was appropriate for community class students who met on average for four hours a week throughout a college or school year. These forms of assessment were also considered to be inappropriate to many other ESL students, from those on full-time work-seeking courses operating in FE colleges or industrial language training units to those on a range of part-time courses in a variety of institutions. It was felt that adult ESL teaching needed a form of assessment that took into account the particular concerns of the students, and that tutors would welcome a target for their students to work towards and which would give a sense of purpose to their learning.

It was important that the certificate should reflect different levels of achievement in English, as well as the variety of needs of students, and that each of the four language skills should be assessed separately.

Profile certificate It was decided that the most appropriate form of assessment was a continuously-assessed certificate: students would work towards a set of profile objectives for each of the four language skills. The final certificate would not include a level achieved by the student, but would list the profile objectives achieved. The level of each objective would be implicit from the wording and content. A student could decide to be assessed in only one language skill or in all four. (See RSA Profile Certificate objectives, pages 178–180.)

Examination Initially it was decided to retain an examination element in the assessment, but to offer it as an option. The examination was to be divided into four separate tests of listening, oral interaction, reading and writing. Although three levels were built into each test, students would not have to opt to take the tests at a particular level. They would all take the same tests, which would become progressively more difficult. Students could also opt to take any number of the tests. No student could take the examination if she or he had not been entered for and assessed in the profile certificate. The tests would not require additional objectives to those included in the profile objectives: students would not need to acquire 'examination techniques'. After consultation, the examination was discontinued after 1986.

Guidance to centres The RSA Board sends out detailed information about the scheme to all centres considering entering students.[1] This includes entry requirements, administration, suggested areas of course content and items on the profile objectives, record-keeping and examples of student performance.

Assessment of achievement An important element in the assessment was clearly to be the record-keeping undertaken by the tutor and, in some cases, the student. Careful record-keeping would keep the inevitable element of subjectivity in profile assessment to the minimum. A record-keeping sheet was devised for use in the pilot year of the scheme even though it was recognized that no one method of record-keeping would suit all tutors and students (see Lawson, Section 5). Tutors' previous experience of keeping records varied considerably: some MSC-funded courses required that detailed records of each student's progress should be kept, whilst some community class tutors were not required to keep specific records of progress. It was an area that had not been generally developed in ESL teaching and problems were foreseen for the pilot year. Self-assessment by students was also seen as an important element in record-keeping.

The pilot year: 1983–84 profile certificate

During the pilot year, seven centres entered students for the profile certificate. Courses ranged from skills centre intensive courses, courses for work-seekers and several community classes based in FE colleges or in local centres. The levels of ability in English also varied considerably. The tutors of the courses generally found that the certificate enabled them to plan the work for the students in a more coherent way, whilst still taking into account the students' needs and interests.

The Coventry experience

In Coventry, students from two very different types of class took part in the pilot year of the certificate. One class was attached to the industrial language training unit and was designed for job-seekers. The class met for two hours each weekday morning for 40 weeks. The students included several young Indian and Pakistani women and men and also several Vietnamese refugees, recently arrived in Coventry from reception centres in different parts of the country. The other class was a community class for women that met in a parents' room that had once been a pottery room in a local primary school. The majority of the class were Gujerati–Hindu women in their forties and fifties (one of them was Shantaben), together with a few Punjabi–Sikh and Hindu women and an Urdu-speaking Muslim woman. Some of the women had attended the class for several years. Both class tutors were experienced in ESL teaching. They were also very enthusiastic about taking part in the pilot year of the certificate.

The tutor on the work-seekers' course became aware early on in the year that her teaching had become more purposeful, with the specific goals of the profile objectives in mind. Her students became very much involved in their own assessment. Their assessment sheets were pinned around the classroom walls as a constant reminder of their goals and the tutor found that they were interested in each other's progress without it becoming a competitive process. She also involved others in the assessment of her students. All the students did a three-week placement during the course: 'They took a sheet with them, which outlined a few relevant profile sentences. Their supervisor was asked to sign and date the sheet each time the student had achieved one of the objectives successfully.'

Attendance on the work-seekers' course had always been quite high, but it improved as the students became aware of the importance of regular attendance. The whole atmosphere became more dynamic. The tutor summed it up herself by saying:

> *This is the first time, after six years of different students, that my students can actually receive something tangible following six months to a year in my class. This is very satisfying for the students and also allows the teacher to share in their pleasure and sense of achievement.*

The tutor of the community class noted an even more dramatic change in her class, since she knew many of her students well:

> *. . . early in the course, the first sign of change was in group dynamics. It had been the custom for some students to rely heavily on fellow students and, in fact, anyone available to act as scribe, messenger, interpreter.*

There was a sharp move away from this dependency in order to acquire a skill and/or achieve a profile objective.

The increase in the confidence of the students was noticeable, as highlighted by the incident described in the Introduction, and they became keen to develop their independence outside the classroom and to be in control of the situations they encountered. Also, the tutor noted:

Back in the classroom, there was a slow, not so quiet revolution taking place regarding notes and handouts. They began to disappear from the bottoms of bags and the back of notebooks into neatly organized ring-binders. Students said that now they were on a proper course it was felt appropriate to arrive carrying a binder. They became very organized.

Their attendance at classes was noticeably more regular.

Record-keeping

As was anticipated, problems arose over compiling effective records of achievement by individual students. The two Coventry tutors tackled this in different ways. As already mentioned, the tutor of the work-seekers' course pinned up in the classroom a copy of the profile objectives for every student. Each time a profile objective was success-fully carried out, it would be ticked off by the student or the tutor. When several ticks had been entered against a profile objective, it was agreed that the student had achieved that objective and that it would be included on the final record sheet.

The community class tutor compiled record sheets according to the tasks presented to the students. Each task was on a separate sheet and one lesson might contain several tasks. These task sheets indicated whether individual students had successfully completed the tasks or needed additional help with them. The tutor would then record at the top of the task sheets which profile objectives they contributed towards and in this way gradually built up a record of students' achievements.

Other centres devised other methods of record-keeping, such as gradually colouring in a grid to denote the extent of a student's achievement towards a profile objective.

The pilot year: examination

At the end of the pilot year, the majority of the students who had entered for the profile certificate also opted to take one or more of the four tests that made up the examination. The test that proved to be the most difficult was the listening test. It became apparent that ESL tutors had not given as much attention to this area of language and some students could not perform quite simple listening tasks with accuracy. Good authentic and relevant listening material is not so readily avail-able to ESL tutors: this is an area that needs development in teaching as well as testing.

Both the Coventry tutors commented that students showed less anxiety about the examination than they had anticipated. In fact, one of the students in the community class decided to enter for all four examination tests, against the advice of her tutor who felt that she would not achieve a level 1 pass in reading or writing. She passed only the oral interaction test, achieving a level 1 pass, but clearly felt that it was a worthwhile experience. That student was Shantaben.

The effect of the certificate and examination in the pilot year may be summed up by this tutor's words:

> *Having taught the course, watched the students' increasing confidence and voluntary participation in the exams, the attraction is still there and growing.*

Expansion of the scheme

The success of the scheme has been demonstrated by the fact that the number of centres entering students for it has snowballed. Students have gained personal satisfaction from working towards the profile certificate: some registered again in the following year and added to the objectives they had already achieved. In some cases these students entered for examination tests they had not attempted in the previous year, or took tests again to try and achieve a higher level.

From 1987, students could also be awarded Dual Certification with the RSA Practical Skills Profile Scheme if they achieved profile sentences that equated to a specific Practical Skills Profile sentence.

Student involvement in assessment

It is considered essential to involve as many students as possible in their own assessment. As a Coventry tutor commented:

> *Throughout the course there was one difficulty which I always pushed to one side — how to help the students relate to the profile sentences — which are written for teachers. Somehow we managed to have meaningful discussions about progress and choice of tasks, whilst charting progress on their final record sheet opposite finely expressed but complicated sentences.*

This problem has been tackled in two ways:
1.   One institution in London translated all the profile objectives into several community languages, so that students could understand them more easily. The obvious difficulties of this method of involving the students in assessment are that the translators need to have a very clear understanding of the language concepts of each objective and the students need to be able to read their mother-tongue to a high level of competence. This would exclude students without that competence.
2.   A working party of assessors of the certificate looked at ways of simplifying the language of the profile objectives. They encountered the problem of simplifying the language without altering the meaning of the objectives and reducing their content. The revised set of profile objectives was introduced in the 1986/87 session.

Guidance for tutors

Record-keeping
As already mentioned, many tutors developed their own ways of keeping effective records during the course of the year. Examples of good practice were gathered together and are available from the RSA in

booklet form. Tutors have been encouraged to involve their students in self-assessment and discussion about their progress throughout the year. Some students keep their own record sheets and compare them with the tutor's records of achievement.

Standards

Tutors were also concerned about standards of performance: what were acceptable and how their students compared with those in other classes. It is important that in a nationally recognized certificate there should be parity of standards across different parts of Britain. With this in mind, a booklet has been produced that gives detailed criteria for the assessment of each profile objective and guidelines about how the evidence of achievement can be demonstrated.

The future

The target group of students defined at the beginning of this paper must be kept in mind continually as the certificate develops. Community classes have problems with a constantly changing population of students, numbers, time allocated to classes and the other commitments of their students. The certificate would have failed in its purpose if the needs of this large group of students, once recognized, were not met because of these problems. The feedback from centres, especially with regard to increased motivation of students and, therefore, improved attendance at classes, has been very positive and demonstrates the need for such a certificate.

An upward drift in the level of the profile certificate should be avoided. There has been a tendency to select higher level classes to enter for the certificate; this could have been partly due to the uncertainty of tutors as to what is expected of students in a profile assessment certificate. It has prompted assessors to ask 'Where are the "Basic Level" students?' Students at a higher level should be encouraged to enter for certificates with native speakers of English. If students are selected for the profile certificate because they are at a high level of language ability, the more basic level students' needs will again not be met as the certificate becomes more difficult.

The final word is from a student who completed the profile certificate and took the four examination tests in 1985, at another centre in Coventry:

> *I enjoyed very much taking part in this year's certificate because daily conversation and discussion are most interesting. These topics helped me to speak good English. In future I would like to join Social Services or teaching . . . I hope that the Certificate will help me in future life.*

Notes

1.   Further information about the certificate is available from the Royal Society of Arts Examination Board, see Appendix 2.

RSA Certificate Profile Objectives

The Profile Objectives for each skill allow the student to demonstrate achievement on a continuous basis in relation to the Profile Objectives.

Centres may wish to submit suggestions for profile objectives in addition to those determined by the RSA, to allow for their particular circumstances. The assessor will discuss any suggestions with the centre before submission to the RSA for consideration and approval. It should be noted that the lists below are not in any order of priority.

Reading

R1   Understand a variety of signs and short public notices.
R2   Recognize where to write personal details on printed forms.
R3   Get information from simple diagrams, timetables, timesheets and street plans.
R4   Recognize the purpose of a text from layout, headings, typeface and other visual clues.
R5   Read a text for general meaning.
R6   Use an alphabetical index.
R7   Use dictionaries to find words and check meaning.
R8   Use dictionaries to check or find pronunciation or spelling.
R9   Use reference books such as atlas, encyclopaedia, etc.
R10   Get information from simple handwritten texts.
R11   Get information from simple printed texts, e.g. posters, leaflets, letters, timetables, advertisements.
R12   Get information from simple printed information, e.g. newspapers, booklets, magazines.
R13   Get information from a wider range of articles and other printed information including detailed notices, complex forms.
R14   Follow simple written instructions from text or diagram, e.g. recipes, electrical wiring diagram.
R15   Follow more difficult written instructions from text or diagram, e.g. for a washing machine, answer-phone.
R16   Read and evaluate a range of information from a variety of graphic displays, e.g. computer, graphics, typefaces.

Writing

W1   Fill in a form for self and family with some help.
W2   Fill in simple forms, questionnaires, time sheets, etc.
W3   Copy short written or printed details.
W4   Write a simple notice, note or message.
W5   Draw and label a simple map or diagram.
W6   Write down a simple message or piece of information.
W7   Write a simple informal letter.
W8   Write a short formal letter.
W9   Give the most important facts about an event in the right order.
W10   Fill in cheque, girocheques and mail order payments.
W11   Write a letter of application giving relevant personal details.
W12   Change writing style when writing to different people or for different purposes.
W13   Write a set of clear instructions.
W14   Put into writing information from simple diagrams and time-tables.
W15   Put into writing information from graphs, tables and notes.
W16   Make notes on a topic or event.

Listening

L1   Get information from a broadcast or announcement, delivered in a familiar accent.
L2   Get information from a conversation or announcement delivered in an unfamiliar accent.
L3   Get the gist of a conversation or discussion between 2 or 3 people.
L4   Recognize the relationship between speakers in a conversation.
L5   Get the gist of a conversation, discussion or meeting, involving several people.
L6   Recognize simple markers in conversation, such as then, so, after that.
L7   Recognize some difficult markers, such as pauses, stress and intonation.
L8   Recognize clearly expressed feelings from the way people speak.
L9   Recognize feelings from the way people speak.
L10 Follow simple instructions.
L11 Follow more difficult instructions.
L12 Get details from a telephone call or recorded message.

Oral Interaction

O1   Greet someone.
O2   Offer and ask for help.
O3   Respond to offers or requests for help.
O4   Pass on a spoken message.
O5   Respond to and make complaints and apologies.
O6   Ask and respond to a number of related questions to get information.
O7   Ask and respond to a number of related questions to get advice.
O8   Respond appropriately to clearly expressed feelings and attitudes in a conversation.
O9   Express a range of feelings and attitudes.
O10 Give a description of an object, person or event.
O11 Give a point of view in conversation with 1 or 2 people.
O12 Give a point of view in a group discussion.
O13 Make, receive and close a brief telephone call.
O14 Leave a message on an answer machine.
O15 Make an arrangement involving time and place.
O16 Ask someone to repeat or explain what was said.
O17 Agree or disagree or put a point of view in discussion as appropriate.
O18 Talk about personal interests.
O19 Give a set of instructions.

Section 6 Teacher Training and Staff Development

Introduction

From the early seventies, when ESL first began to develop as an independent field of education, it has adopted a dynamic approach to the training of teachers. As Nicholls says in Section 1, in the late sixties 'there was little, if any, specialist training'. However, by the early seventies there was a recognition that developments in curriculum and provision had to be paralleled by the development of schemes of training which would ensure that staff were able to respond to the changing requirements of students, and which would provide them with the skills required to work in an area where there were few, if any, curriculum guidelines and teaching materials. At this point teachers of ESL generally came from one of two backgrounds: those who had experience and training in EFL (the RSA had established its Cert. TEFL course in the late sixties), and those who had begun as volunteers and received some introductory training in their local scheme. The strengths that these two groups brought to the profession differed but it can be said that, together, they provided the base line from which teacher training programmes have developed during the seventies and eighties.

In the mid-seventies, as the number of classes increased rapidly, there was an urgent need to recruit staff who already had the confidence to handle a group of students, and whose existing skills could be applied in the new context while they received training in new skills, such as handling mixed-level groups and teaching basic literacy. The result was a number of training programmes which emphasized the transference of skills, for example, the ILEA 'conversion' course for people holding the RSA Cert. TEFL and the New Staff Training programme of Industrial Language Training. At the same time, the development of the RSA Certificate in Teaching English to Adult Immigrants provided a certificated course for teachers with some experience.

An important feature of teacher training at this time was its close integration with curriculum development. The need to develop materials meant that working parties were established on which trainers and less experienced staff worked together, and short workshops were offered in many schemes so that teachers could be informed about the latest developments in curriculum, teaching approaches and classroom methodology. This was aided by the small size of the field: networks built up quickly and people who had developed expertise or materials on a topic found that they were frequently asked to travel to other parts of the country to share their knowledge with teachers and volunteers. In this way the principle of 'practitioner as trainer' became established and has remained one of the strengths of ESL approaches to teacher training.

However, as Evans describes in this section, only the largest organizations could afford to mount coherent programmes of staff development. The radio programmes for teachers which accompanied the BBC series *Speak For Yourself,* and the publication of *Teaching English as a Second Language* by Nicholls and Naish (1980) which accompanied them, helped to fill some of the gaps that were felt by teachers who had no access to an RSA course.

The next development came when the Home Office funded a national project to train teachers for the Vietnamese in 1980. The project team consisted of regional teacher trainers who acted as facilitators and built up patterns of training that responded to local need. Around the same time there was a growing realization that there was now a body of knowledge in ESL which all new entrants needed to acquire and that this called for the development of a framework of stepped provision. A distinction was required between *training* and *staff development,* the latter being designed for staff with some experience, and maintaining its close links with curriculum development.

Teacher training in the eighties has mirrored the increasing diversity of provision for bilingual students and reflected fundamental changes in philosophy and approaches. The papers in this section focus on current concerns and new developments. Evans describes the range of training currently available to those who define themselves as ESL teachers and raises a number of important questions as to the continued relevance of these programmes. Spiegel outlines one approach to the training of bilingual teachers who enter the profession with a very different range of expertise and experience to that of monolingual British teachers. Frame and Hoadley-Maidment describe staff development programmes for subject specialists who teach bilingual students in further education. Underlying all these papers is a common philosophy on teacher training which includes the following principles:

1.   Recognition that in a dynamic field, teacher training must be flexible and able to incorporate new developments as quickly as possible.
2.   Recognition that there is now a body of knowledge relating to teaching English to bilingual students and that new teachers need to acquire this.
3.   Recognition of curriculum-led staff development which enables teachers to update themselves through working on materials development, curriculum projects etc., as well as through formal training.
4.   Recognition that there is a place for a number of training formats, including small group projects, classroom observation and research, and distance learning.

5.   Recognition that one of the strengths of teacher training in this field has been the 'practitioner as trainer' approach.

6.   Recognition that, if ESL is to be removed from its low-status position, teachers must have the opportunity to take certificated training, both within the subject speciality and in order to gain recognized teacher status in either adult or further education.

Current approaches and future directions in training teachers of ESL

Elizabeth Evans

The background

The in-service training currently available to teachers of ESL falls into three categories: courses leading to nationally recognized certificates or diplomas, staff development programmes for specific ESL provision and informal training sessions. This sounds like a very healthy training position; however, the reality is not so rosy. Specialist training courses are generally only offered in areas where there are considerable numbers of bilingual students in ESL provision and consequently a sizeable group of teachers, usually a minimum of ten per course, seeking to gain specialist certification. In practice such courses are run in large urban areas or on a county basis. Some higher education establishments do offer a TESL component in their degree or PGCE courses, but these mainly focus on schools rather than adult education provision. In-service staff development programmes are only offered within the Industrial Language Training (ILT) Service and the Inner London Education Authority (ILEA), where the scale of ESL provision is large enough to warrant a central servicing unit with an advisory and training brief.

The majority of ESL training is conducted on an informal, one-off basis by such organizations as NATESLA, the Adult Literacy and Basic Skills Unit (ALBSU), Community Relations Councils (CRC), LEAs or the RSA examinations board. In 1984, the DES ran its first one week training programme for teachers of ESL to adults. This does provide a welcome 'official' precedent of the recognition that ESL teachers require training. But the situation that gave rise to the national emergency training project for teachers of the Vietnamese in 1981 remains largely unchanged and in a number of areas little training has been provided since this initiative, despite the growth of a range of new ESL provision since this time. It is important to view the descriptions of currently available training against this background.

Current training provision

There are two specialist training courses offered at present to ESL teachers of adults. These are the RSA Diploma in the Teaching of English as a Second Language in Further, Adult and Community Education (RSA Dip. TESL (FACE)) and the RSA Certificate of Initial Training in the Teaching of English as a Second Language (RSA CIT). The RSA Dip. TESL (FACE) scheme is designed for practising teachers of ESL who have a range of ESL teaching experience and who wish to acquire a professional qualification. RSA Dip. TESL (FACE) courses are run on a part-time, 100 hour minimum contact basis over one or two academic years and demand high levels of performance from trainees in both practical and theoretical terms. Trainees following an RSA Dip. TESL (FACE) are generally employed on a full or part-time basis in a variety of institutions. Attainment of the RSA Dip. TESL (FACE) indicates an ability to work in all types of ESL provision. As such, the RSA Dip. TESL (FACE) has high credibility for employers. It does not count towards an increment in salary. The RSA CIT is designed for relatively inexperienced ESL teachers who wish to acquire basic skills for teaching a particular type of ESL class. RSA CIT courses consist of a minimum of 36 hours class contact and are run on a variety of patterns — weekly, fortnightly or residential/weekend blocks. Their focus is principally on practical classroom skills. The majority of RSA CIT trainees work in adult education centres and a sizeable number are volunteer classroom assistants. Attainment of the RSA CIT indicates an ability to work within a specific type of ESL provision.

Staff development programmes which provide in-service training to meet emerging needs and post-professional updating needs are somewhat thin on the ground. Most LEAs provide some training opportunities but these are not generally structured to take account of different levels of training need or training for new forms of ESL provision. A notable exception to this is the ILEA staff development programme which provides a framework for both new and experienced teachers working within the field. The ILEA runs in the region of 40 per cent of UK ESL provision and its size allows funding for a central advisory and training unit, the Language and Literacy Unit. Training is organized at local, area and central levels in a variety of patterns, such as sponsorship to accredited specialist courses, short training courses, weekend residential or working groups. Attendance at training sessions is normally free.

The ILT service also provides a staff development framework organized on a similar basis with national, regional and local training. There is an annual budget allocation per full-time employee for training purposes. The National Centre for Industrial Language Training co-ordinates the staff development programme. It also encourages the publication and dissemination of research/materials to all units within the service. The strength of both these staff development programmes lies in their providing flexible, continuous, professional updating in a relatively new field where provision is constantly being developed and modified.

The majority of ESL training takes place on an informal basis. A range of examples can be cited. NATESLA regions normally run training days three times a year. These days generally mean Saturdays! Participants pay a small fee and receive no travel allowance. NATESLA also runs a national annual weekend conference with training workshops. ALBSU generally runs an ESL-focused training day/weekend once a year on a regional basis. The unit also encourages indirect training where Special Development Projects are running. Attendance at training is free and travel allowances can be claimed. Local CRCs organize training courses for volunteer home tutors in some areas. Many LEAs provide Saturday, evening or end of term training sessions, usually via the adult education network. Finally, the RSA examinations board mounts training sessions for teacher trainers with its Open Meetings for the two specialist training schemes and with occasional training days on particular topics such as Racism Awareness. Such training is free but travel expenses must be recouped from the employer. All these forms of informal training can serve a useful purpose; however, such training often lacks coherence and structure and does not meet the needs of many teachers working with bilingual students.

Current problems in training provision

The 1986 NATESLA Project on the Training of ESL Teachers in the Post 16 Sector highlights three fundamental problems in current ESL training provision. First, many teachers are unable to attend training sessions because of practical considerations of distance, time and finance. Attendance at formal training courses, or indeed at informal training sessions that tend to take place at the weekend, is often not feasible for the largely female ESL workforce, particularly as crèche facilities are rarely available. Funding arrangements also deter teachers from attending training. For example, full-time staff following the RSA Dip. TESL (FACE) usually have their course and examination fees paid by their LEA and obtain some remission in their teaching contact hours. Although the LEA Training Grant Scheme has improved matters, part-time or volunteer staff often fund themselves and obtain training in their own time. Again, full-time teachers can often claim fees for attendance at the NATESLA annual conference whilst part-time or volunteer tutors are unable to do so. This situation is clearly unsatisfactory in a field where the ratio of part-time staff to full-time is in the region of 7:1, and 17:1 if volunteers are included. (NATESLA, 1986.)

Second, present training tends to be either too specialist or too unstructured or simply not available for many of those now working in the field. Four examples provide an illustration of this problem. The growth of education and employment-related provision in the 1980s has brought many teachers who are new to working with bilingual students into the field. These teachers come into ESL work from a wide range of entry points; they may have specialist qualifications in a related field or in non language-based areas such as mathematics or computing. This group rarely wants or needs initial or specialist training; they require orientation or 'topping-up' training which is not generally provided. Skills teachers such as those working with bilingual students on MSC-funded courses often need language awareness training; their needs are not currently being met. The 1980s have also seen a growing awareness of the need to encourage bilingual teachers into work with ESL students; however, training in the use of bilingual teaching techniques and the development of bilingual support materials is largely undeveloped. There is also only minimal provision for pre-service training to encourage suitable bilingual teachers into the field (see Spiegel, Section 6). Lastly, many full-time ESL teachers who have attained specialist qualifications are given few opportunities for relevant professional updating in this young and rapidly diversifying field.

Third, the channels of communication are generally poor in ESL. There are few LEA advisers with a specific responsibility for ESL for adults. Although NATESLA tries to fulfil a function as an information resource agent, it is severely handicapped in this role because all its work is voluntary and the Association has no premises. Efficient training requires sound materials and curriculum guidelines; however, there is currently no central base for ESL resources and little in the way of curriculum guidelines, even in well established areas of ESL provision. This has two detrimental effects. First, a good deal of time is wasted on reinventing the wheel up and down the country. Second, the theoretical base of the field is slow to advance because many innovative local research and materials development projects remain unknown. The present lack of regional/national channels of communication works against the development of appropriate training and staff development programmes, as well as the development of more appropriate ESL provision.

In conclusion, ESL training has not kept pace with changes in ESL provision. Previous papers in this publication show clearly that present ESL provision is diversifying rapidly. But outside of the ILT and ILEA models, the training pattern tends to reflect the picture of training needs as perceived in the 1970s, i.e. specialist courses for ESL language teachers and *ad hoc* training for a largely volunteer or part-time workforce. This pattern is inadequate in that it makes no clear distinction between those who wish to enter ESL work, those who are already working in the field and those who wish for training only in specific elements of ESL that are relevant to their work.

Future directions in ESL training

In a time of stringent financial constraints, it is clearly unrealistic to envisage the development of large-scale, innovative training schemes; however, more efficient and effective training for teachers of adult bilinguals could be achieved by the rationalization and modification of resources that already exist. A prime need is to develop 'middle-ground' training. Current training tends to be at two ends of the spectrum: the RSA training schemes for ESL specialists, or informal training sessions, which lack coherent progression and are not formally accredited. Accreditation is an important issue. Many involved in work with bilingual students are at the lower end of the employment scale. In the past, goodwill has been a motivating factor for those seeking training. However, morale has been lowered in the current economic climate and it is unrealistic to suppose that teachers will undergo training which does not in some way enhance their careers.

A modular approach

A new approach is needed to tackle the present problem. Given the current market, a modular approach to training would enable teachers to follow courses that were relevant to particular aspects of their work only, or, if they wished for ESL specialist accreditation, to build up a series of modules to this end. There are two accrediting bodies that could develop a modular approach: the RSA and the RAC network. The adaptation of the current RSA Dip. TESL (FACE) scheme to a modular basis could cater for both ESL specialists and teachers who are now working with bilingual students on specific mainstream courses. For example, teachers working with bilingual students on CPVE courses could attend a module on Supporting Bilingual Students in Further Education alongside ESL specialist teachers who are ultimately aiming at the specialist RSA Dip. TESL (FACE). This approach would have the added advantages of bringing together subject/skill and language teachers to share their different perspectives.

Flexibility is the keynote for future ESL training. A modular approach encourages this. The development of modules which subject/skills teachers could follow within the RSA Dip. TESL (FACE) course and which ESL specialists could follow within the framework for general training of teachers of adults (i.e. ACSET/Haycocks) would give training opportunities to a large number of teachers currently unprovided for.

Regional/national coordination

The RACs also have an important part to play in terms of national/regional coordination of ESL training. Without such coordination, the consolidation and development of training seems unlikely to occur. Regional involvement is crucial in order to avoid gaps and overlaps in provision.

There are currently a number of organizations which have involvement and expertise in ESL. However, these organizations have different priorities and perspectives and different ways of implementing training programmes. The formation of a national body with representatives of these organizations is urgently needed to coordinate TESLA staff training and the development of appropriate curricula.

References

NATESLA SURVEY REPORT (1981) *English as a Second Language Teaching for Adults from Ethnic Minorities*, NATESLA

NATESLA (1986) *Training of Teachers of English as a Second Language in the Post-16 Sector*, NATESLA

RSA (1983) *Certificates and Diplomas in Language Teaching*, London

The recruitment and training of bilingual ESL teachers

Marina Spiegel

An ESL organizer:

> But why do we need bilingual ESL teachers? . . . After all there are lots of bright, trained, experienced teachers who yes are white and mono-lingual but are broadminded and have very sympathetic attitudes to the students. Lots of them have worked abroad or come from Australia and are anxious to use their experience in a community context. And they just walk through the door looking for a job. Why bother to recruit bilingual teachers?

An ESL student:

> I don't want a foreign teacher. I want an English English teacher, you know. He will speak the best English, perfect. I want to speak perfect English with a perfect accent.

These views are not uncommon and while the assumptions and attitudes which inform the reasoning behind both statements are widely held, there is also a growing movement to challenge this thinking by recruiting and training black and bilingual ESL teachers who are drawn from local black and linguistic minority groups. This is a genuine reflection of the dislocation in attitudes within ESL teaching in Britain at the present time.

For years many of us were trained into believing that modern languages could and should only be taught by 'native' speakers. The influence of the direct method and behavioural theories of learning told us that students needed to copy and repeat 'correct usage' at all times. Teachers were warned off using the students' first languages in the classroom, for this, we were told, would hinder and confuse. The implication was that students might be tempted to think and translate from one language to another in an attempt to make sense of the new jumble of words. Instead, they were to be made to listen and repeat. At their most extreme, these theories encouraged teachers to think of their students as blank boxes, programmed into learning language through repetition and audio-visual contextualization.

What was meant by correct usage was rarely challenged. Teachers and students alike believed that Received English Pronunciation (RP) and the standard grammatical forms of the English middle classes — BBC English — were the only correct forms of English.

Modern linguistic thinking challenged this prescriptive view of language and contemporary methodology stresses communicative use of language rather than linguistic accuracy. It is, however, our growing awareness of the need to counter racism and to put equal opportunities policies into practice which has done most to make us review what we are teaching, how we are doing it and, most importantly, who is being employed to carry it out.

The impact has been felt in various ways. In recent years we have begun to accept that for both children and adults the use of the first language in the ESL classroom can be a positive help rather than a hindrance (see Piasecka, Section 4). A growing body of bilingual methodology is beginning to inform our practice as teachers and students have begun to reap the benefits of this (see Collingham, Section 4). Progress, however, is slow, due in part to the lack of bilingual teachers in ESL.

It is still the case that since the majority of ESL teachers are white they can have little in common with their students' experience of life in Britain — an experience determined by racism and culture shock. At best they can revive their experiences of working abroad and attempt an imaginative leap into feelings and situations vaguely envisaged.

It is felt by some that black and bilingual teachers who share a common experience with their students and who are drawn from the ranks of the local black and linguistic minority groups are less likely to see the end product of ESL as neat language packages: health today, travel and shopping tomorrow. But rather that their own experience will help inform their attitude to the students, to their communicative needs, as well as to their own role as teachers in the classroom.

It is clear that both bilingual and monolingual teachers can each bring a range of benefits and strengths to the ESL classroom. However, until quite recently, the experience, skills and expertise of black and bilingual teachers were either belittled or not recognized as qualitatively different. The following is a summary of some of those skills:

1. **Student–teacher relationship**
— Empathy with students.
— Knowledge of problems, situations, anxieties (e.g. frustration, depression, homesickness).
— Experience of how it feels to be an adult learner, an ESL student in an ESL classroom, learner of a foreign language.
— Knowledge of expectations of learning from other countries and expectations of the role of the teacher, etc.

2. **Methodology**
— Knowledge of learning a foreign language in terms of speed, pace, amount of practice needed, etc.
— Shared language with some students, even all students in a monolingual group, leading to the use of bilingual techniques (access information, discussions, grammatical explanations, language for study and study instructions, clarifications, etc.).
— Understanding of students' experience of methods of teaching and learning — thus acceptance of different learning styles.

3. **Curriculum**

— Firsthand experience of communicative strategies.
— Firsthand experience of using, bending, managing the system.
— Experience of institutional and/or individual racism, harassment, prejudice.
— Experience of alienation and marginalization.
— Understanding of cultural expectations, preconceptions and cross-cultural communication.
— Awareness of preconceptions regarding 'correct' English among some students.

In ILEA, courses specifically designed to increase the number of black and bilingual ESL staff in the field have been running in various boroughs since 1985. The main aim of these courses has been to provide an entry point and a properly devised and supported access route into paid ESL work. (See Fig. 1.)

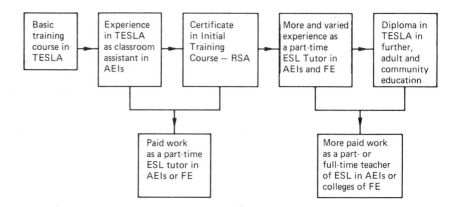

Fig. 1

Recruitment for the courses is begun a term in advance. All local linguistic minority organizations and groups are contacted and the rationale behind the course explained and discussed. A leaflet advertising the course with an accompanying information sheet is also distributed throughout the borough's institutes and colleges. Criteria for selection include:
— A strong interest/background/training or experience of teaching in this or any other country.
— An interest in and empathy with the educational aspirations and needs of adults who speak English as a second language.
— A strong command of spoken and written English.
— A sense of enthusiasm and a fair level of confidence.
Most of the recruitment is by referral, and all prospective candidates for the course are interviewed prior to the start. Many are counselled on to other types of training courses; some experienced English teachers from other countries are referred directly to Heads of ESL in the local institutes and colleges.

On completion of the course some experienced participants may be employed immediately. Others with less experience or confidence are offered the chance to gain practical experience of teaching ESL as a classroom assistant in a local AEI. This involves working with an experienced part-time tutor who will teach with the classroom assistant, offering him or her support and the chance to gradually gain experience in lesson planning and teaching different elements of a class. The institute HOD responsible for ESL is also involved in offering support and ongoing in-service training. Following a suitable period as a classroom assistant (for some it is as short as one term), many are employed as ESL part-time tutors. They may then go on to be sponsored to do the RSA CIT and in time do the RSA TESL (FACE) Diploma.

The courses are still in the process of evolution. However they employ a strict set of criteria aimed at highlighting the skills and strengths brought to ESL by black and bilingual teachers:

1.   The courses draw on the participants' own experience, both in Britain and abroad, whether discussing lesson planning, adults as learners, racism, teaching techniques or syllabus checklists.

2.   Discussions have a cross-cultural and comparative focus.

3.   The courses use as many experiential techniques as possible — observations, micro-teaching, role-play. etc.

4.   The trainers encourage bilingual discussion and evolve bilingual approaches, where appropriate to the group and to the subject under review (materials and teaching techniques in particular).

In consequence these courses have had a distinct approach and a style different from traditional models of induction training. Table 1 gives an outline of sessions included in the courses run by Lambeth and Wandsworth English Language Schemes.

Table 1

Topic for discussion	Activity	Aim of activity
Background to the course	Short input by trainers. OHP of route into training practice.	To put course in context of current thinking. Authority's Equal Opportunity Policy etc., opportunities after completing course.
Expectations/anxieties	Pair interviews.	To get to know each other. For trainers to begin to discover areas where students need confidence building, etc.
The need for black and bilingual ESL teachers and what attributes they bring	Pair work: discuss positive aspects of black bilingual ESL teachers. Plenary session. Tape recording of shop owners in Streatham High Road (Greek, Chinese, Caribbean, Irish, Spanish, Cockney, Midlands).	To reinforce positive aspects annd begin discussion of the elements students may feel less confident about.
Attitudes and expectations towards learning and teaching	Questionnaire regarding trainees' educational experience — in pairs Plenary on ESL students' expectations of education.	To elicit ideas/attitudes to education in other countries, methods and curriculum trainees have experience of. To discuss the 'baggage' adult learners bring in terms of prior learning experiences.
Race, class and gender	Lectures and discussions on the socio-political background to the teaching of ESL: immigration, institutional racism, racism and the education system.	To enable participants to focus on socio-political issues related to the practice of ESL. To foster a critical perspective on current ESL theory and practice.

Table 1 (continued)

Topic for discussion	Activity	Aim of activity
Adult learners	Pair work on the elements which support adult learners and those which inhibit.	To elicit important physical, emotional, psychological, cultural, environmental factors which affect adult learners.
		To think of ways in which advantages can easily become disadvantages and vice versa.
Negotiation	Trainers role-play a cookery tutor and a bilingual student 'negotiating' the curriculum unsuccessfully.	To show communication breakdown.
		Elicit analysis of communication and reasons for breakdown.
	In groups, trainees examine a range of first language and bilingual questionnaires, pictorial and English questionnaires.	Negotiation needs to be skilful and ongoing.
		Elicit ideas for negotiating with students.
		Use of bilingual approaches for negotiating curriculum.
Language needs	Case studies. Pairs discussion.	Analysis of real communication needs.
	Plenary and communications network.	Analysis of topic areas, raising awareness of the dangers of using this approach uncritically.
		Elicit a critical approach to the traditional topic-based syllabus.
Student and class profiles	Trainees to look at a class profile.	Analysis of how you decide what to teach, based on student's communication needs.
	Interview each other in pairs. Students to choose four main areas they want to cover on this course.	How to draw up a class profile.
	Group as a whole to fill up a 'class profile' for the course participants, based on the topic areas previously prioritized.	
Student profile	Plenary discussion.	How to get information about individual students gradually. What information is important or not.
		Use of bilingual approaches, e.g. questionnaires, interpreters, etc.
Micro teaching (repeated to allow each trainee the chance to teach)	In groups of 4–6. One trainee to teach for ten minutes. 3–5 trainees to learn. Anything (other than a language) can be taught, e.g. a card game, massage, mending a puncture, Indian music.	To build up confidence in teaching ability and expertise of the group.
		To give people a chance to look at and appreciate a range of teaching styles and approaches.
		To look at important elements in a lesson, e.g. introduction, explanation or demonstration, practice, revision etc.
Foreign language class	Participants receive a Hebrew lesson followed by discussion	Elicit what it feels like to be a student and learning strategies employed by students.
		To focus on teaching methods and materials.
		Use of bilingual approaches.
Teaching techniques and materials — elementary level classes	List techniques and materials which can be used, examples of materials for each technique.	To reinforce the use of basic techniques.
	Display of materials.	To analyse range of materials.
		To reinforce teaching terminology.
	Discussion in pairs of whether trainees have experience of these materials and techniques.	To have time to look at existing ESL materials, published and teacher- or student-produced.
	Bilingual approaches.	The use of specific bilingual approaches: grammatical comparisons, discussions in L1 and checking meaning and comprehension.

Table 1 (continued)

Topic for discussion	Activity	Aim of activity
Bilingual teaching materials	In pairs, trainees to look at a range of materials (all bilingual).	Discuss the use of and value of bilingual materials.
	Plenary.	
	In small groups to look at a range of non-bilingual materials and fill in questionnaires on adapting them for use with a multilingual group.	Discuss adapting non-bilingual materials.
		Where to go for bilingual resources.
	Plenary.	
Lesson planning — elementary level classes	In groups, discuss elements of a lesson.	Elicit the need for well-defined aims.
	Model lesson plan, 'the menu'.	To show broad planning areas.
	Model lesson plan broken down in terms of: time, activity (students and teacher), aim of activity, materials.	To show detailed planning process.
	Comparison of the two lesson plans and dovetailing.	
	In groups, plan a lesson (aim given) using a blank grid as in above exercise.	Practice the process of lesson planning.
Observations of two ESL classes	Discussion of observations. Participants have brought written observations (using a blank grid) of classes they have watched.	Analyse an ESL class in terms of aims, activities, materials.
		Elicit own experience as ESL students.
		Analyse and discuss pacing and 'shape' of class.
Deciding what to teach	Post Office game: 8 x 18p 3 x 13p written on OHP/board Participants to write down how they would ask for it.	Discussion on criteria for deciding which structures to teach, e.g. transferability etc.
		Comparison with traditional grammatical approach.
Functions/structures	Conversations in a shop. Participants to have previously written down a real conversation.	Analyse functions of language.
Deciding what to teach	Information session on how the situational/ structural/functional approach evolved in schools in the 60s/70s.	Develop awareness of different approaches to programming.
	Discussion on the advantages and disadvantages.	Develop a critical awareness of the dangers of 'phrase book' functionalism.
Grammar	Discussion of questions, in small groups, on grammar.	To look at the role of grammar in ESL.
	List of 12 important grammatical items for beginners.	Analysis of *lack* of ESL materials for grammar practice.
		Evolve criteria for grammar checklists.
	ESL grammar materials.	Familiarize oneself with ESL grammar materials.
Syllabus	In small groups look at a range of syllabuses.	To familiarize oneself with various syllabus approaches.
	Discussion on how various grammatical items can be developed from structures chosen in a functional syllabus or check-list.	To link the teaching of grammar to a structural/functional syllabus.

Table 1 (continued)

Topic for discussion	Activity	Aim of activity
Intonation, stress, rhythm	Short exercises to raise awareness of the importance of stress to convey meaning, e.g. rhythm, and take a sentence and stress different words on different occasions.	Raise awareness of the importance of non-linguistic features of communication.
	Exercises to look at the range of intonation, tone, pitch.	
	Discussion in two groups on the relative importance of intonation, stress and rhythm.	
Lesson linking and record-keeping	In small groups look at various examples of lesson linking plans. Discussion.	To look at different models.
	Overhead transparencies showing gradual build-up of lessons.	To analyse one way of building up a group of classes spread over two topic areas and the three skills.
	Record-keeping: some examples.	Analyse different ways of keeping records.
	Role-play: consequences of not keeping records.	Record-keeping in the teacher's own language.
Evaluation and what next	External, bilingual evaluator to help participants with the evaluation.	To assess effectiveness of course.
	Individual counselling sessions with each participant.	To assess areas that need further exploration in workshops, etc..
		To decide whether to go on or not.

Working with subject specialists in further education — two case studies

Pam Frame and Elizabeth Hoadley-Maidment

Introduction Recent developments in providing for bilingual students in further education mean that many more students are now enrolled directly on to mainstream courses and then provided with language support. (See McAllister and Robson, Section 3.) Bilingual students on mainstream courses spend most of their time in classes taught by subject specialists whose expertise is in teaching theoretical content or practical and vocational skills. The presence of bilingual students, often studying alongside monolingual English-speaking students, has led subject specialists to a realization that previously successful methods and techniques have to be adapted when used with a multilingual class. Consequently there is an increasing demand for training which is practical and which relates to both language and anti-racist aspects of teaching. (A similar situation is developing in adult education and demand for training is beginning to be felt from teachers of crafts, leisure subjects, etc.)

The two studies which follow describe two approaches to teacher training for subject specialists. They are presented as case studies since work in this area is new, and patterns of training are not fixed. The lecturers who receive training are all already qualified teachers and the methods used are therefore those appropriate to staff development, rather than courses in basic teaching techniques. The first case study describes work done at Harrow College for an FEU-sponsored project on Language Across the Curriculum (FEU Experimental College RP174). The second describes work undertaken by the ILEA through the Language and Literacy Unit. (See Evans, Section 6.)

An FE college

Although further education colleges vary enormously, it should be possible to identify a number of shared characteristics relevant to the difficulties inherent in developing suitable English language provision for bilingual students. Such institutions are large in size and offer a wide range of full-time, part-time and block release courses. The mix of courses will probably relate to traditional patterns of employment in a particular geographical location, or specialisms that have been developed and marketed effectively. Colleges have increasingly to be responsive to client-demand in terms of student-enrolment patterns: if insufficient students register for a particular course then that course will be closed, while others may be opened to meet additional demand for places. The college may operate across several main sites, geographically distant from each other, where neither staff nor students can easily develop any general sense of the college as a whole. Other boundaries exist through the administrative units, usually departments, to which full-time and part-time teaching staff are appointed. The extent and nature of contact between teaching staff will differ, even within the same department, or between those staff with similar teaching commitments. Problems are therefore likely to be experienced in initiating and developing college-wide perspectives, or in implementing policy. (See the second part of this article: The Inner London Education Authority.)

The context

Considerable curriculum change is currently being experienced in further education as a consequence of many interlinking features in the post-16 educational map (e.g. MSC requirements, changes to funding in NAFE, CPVE, GCSE etc.). Despite such influences many courses remain heavily dominated by the requirements of the public-examination system with a focus on mastering content rather than developing transferable skills, on product rather than process. To cover the requirements of a content-led syllabus within a relatively short teaching period it is hardly surprisingly that lecturers, many of whom are not teacher-trained, rely on lectures, demonstrations, and handouts to put information across to their students with little opportunity incorporated for active student participation in the learning process. The students themselves, fresh from the school system, come with expectations that lecturers will lecture, but are lacking vital study skills and strategies, not yet ready to learn from each other or to assume a greater degree of responsibility for their own learning.

On many courses class size is fairly large so that opportunities for more individualized tuition may be difficult to create. Students will be drawn from a wide ability range and include many 'second chance' students. Recent research (the Educational and Vocational Experience of 15–18 year-old Young People of Ethnic Minority Groups, October 1985 – commissioned by DES) has shown yet again that for many ethnic minority students further education is perceived as a key route to qualifications, training and employment. Thus for the majority of further education colleges cultural and linguistic diversity is a central feature of college life and should be a significant factor in planning and monitoring the curriculum offer. In a general climate of change there can be many opportunities for addressing the language needs of bilingual students and ensuring that these are incorporated into new curricula and organizational structures. (See McAllister and Robson, Section 3.)

Staffing issues

Within any one FE college the priority is to identify stable groupings of staff through which language policy can be implemented at course and classroom level. Staff may already work together as a course team to deliver an integrated course programme such as BTEC first or a CGLI foundation course. They may have regular course team meetings, and be engaged in developing assignments, profiling student progress, or a whole range of curriculum and staff development issues. Alternatively they may be overwhelmed by the administrative complexities of managing such programmes and find it difficult to move beyond the routine items on agendas. Other staff, typically those working on GCSE and 'A' level courses or on part-time classes, are involved in providing an à la carte curriculum, where the individual student selects his programme of study from available options. As a consequence staff groupings are likely to be based on subject areas, such as mathematics, biology, social sciences, literature and humanities, or on small administrative units of a manageable size. There is less likely to be a tradition here of working collectively on curriculum issues: since students are not shared across a common course team, the extent to which materials, teaching strategy, and assessment procedures are shared and discussed will vary. However, course teams, in one shape or another, appear to be the organizational structure currently favoured in the post-16 sector, and must therefore provide the base through which a greater responsiveness to language issues can be developed.

Once the stable groupings have been identified, the role of the language or ESL tutor, in relation to that of the subject tutor or tutors, needs to be carefully defined. It may be that subject tutors and ESL tutors are working together on joint courses which, although vocationally-based, recruit exclusively from those bilingual students who require English language support as an integral feature of their learning programme. A GCSE science course mounted by an ESL scheme for students who were relatively recent arrivals to the UK would be an example of such a course. The context within which collaboration takes place does shape the relationship between tutors. Where programmes are offered solely for bilingual students, the subject or skills tutors can find themselves in a servicing role, a mirror-image of the more usual mainstream context; these subjects tutors are also more likely to have demonstrated an interest in or commitment to this type of work and to have recognized it as an opportunity for professional development and change.

The role of the ESL specialist

For the ESL tutor employed to provide language support within the mainstream provision (on full-time courses recruiting a mix of black and white students, bilingual, multilingual and monolingual), there seem to be several current ways of working available, according to the role expected by the institution. The ESL tutor may be engaged in providing training for colleagues as part of an in-house staff development initiative; team-teaching with individual subject tutors to plan and implement lessons where language and content/skills are fully integrated; working as a full member of a course team with a particular development role; providing consultancy and support to a range of staff within a particular department or curriculum area; or putting on additional English language provision for students identified as being particularly weak.

It is essential, however, that such work be planned, managed and supported effectively at a senior level within the college management structure, so that the purposes and long-term objectives are fully understood by all staff engaged in these activities. Rather than individual ESL tutors trying themselves to find ways of getting in to working on mainstream courses, the college needs a collective response to the provision of language support and the sharing of responsibility across the institution. The specialist skills of ESL tutors, acquired through in-depth professional training, are an expensive resource to be utilized to maximum effect within an overall strategy for promoting access and equality of opportunity. One of the problems is a general lack of status accorded to language work; it is unlikely to be seen as a high institutional priority. Even where colleges have appointed staff with a specialist brief at senior grades, the task of working across the college organizational structure and across the curriculum remains very challenging. It is still all too easy to be marginalized, even when working on mainstream courses, if a proper environment and ethos for collaborative teaching has not been established. In the longer term it seems clear that it is the subject tutors themselves who need to play a key role in carrying out change, and that they need to be fully involved in staff development programmes and dissemination of issues, teaching strategies etc. amongst other subject tutors.

The role of ESL tutors in relation to English, communications and other language tutors may also need to be closely defined. Different colleges have their own traditional ways of providing English teaching across departments and types of courses. There may be a unit based in one part of the college servicing all English language work; alternatively each department may employ its own language-teaching staff on a full-time or part-time basis. It is unlikely to be easy to integrate ESL language support with other English and language teaching in the college in order to facilitate a coherent, consistent college-wide approach to language development. Again tutors from different disciplines bring different experiences, priorities and attitudes to their particular roles; such differences can easily become highlighted when organizational boundaries are crossed or areas of responsibility not clearly defined.

Language for learning: a case study

A language policy for a multiracial college can only operate effectively when it takes account of inter-cultural learning needs, recognizes and values the regular use of languages other than English, and gives positive recognition to skills and qualifications gained outside the UK. Language can no longer mean the English language, but all those languages in daily use within the college and its immediate community. The opportunity exists for a broad-based coalition of all staff who are already 'language aware', monolingual or multilingual, to carry through an integrated language programme across the curriculum.

Using the consultancy model, and basing our activities around existing course teams or groups of staff who had experience of working together, the project team established under the FEU Language Across the Curriculum Project set out to promote the 'active use of language for learning across the subject curriculum, to identify the nature and range of language demands made upon students, and to develop teaching strategies to support all students in meeting those demands more effectively'. (FEU Experimental College RP 174, 1985.) The work focused mainly on science and social studies GCE 'O' level courses, on BTEC General, and secretarial studies.

Whilst working with subject tutors in a variety of fairly informal groupings, it became clear that we were focusing on general issues of language awareness, the role of language in learning and teaching, and on teaching methodology. We became interested in strategies for teaching rather than the actual development of materials, since it seemed crucial that the subject tutors mastered the processes involved in structuring the learning to encourage active student involvement, and in anticipating language-based problems for themselves.

The project provided both the catalyst and the funding to enable tutors to work together on a series of related areas:
— how to move the emphasis, even on exam-based courses, away from testing and towards teaching.
— how to spend less time on simplifying materials or writing hand-outs, and more time on making learning more effective through, for example, structured use of textbooks or other learning resources.
— how to show students ways of improving their performance rather than relying on correction or exhortation.
— how to break content down into manageable learning chunks and find ways other than lectures to put information across.

— how to prioritize areas of the syllabus, so that more time could be allocated to learning strategies.

— how to involve students in assessing their own work or that of their colleagues.

— how to create opportunities for students to work collaboratively and learn from each other as well as teacher or textbook.

There was, therefore, a move towards a more student-centred approach, with the teacher structuring and monitoring group work and problem-solving, along with an increased use by teachers of strategies for eliciting, checking, and getting feedback to ensure student mastery of lecture or other input sessions.

What became most clear was the immense amount of time it takes to acquire different classroom skills, to experiment and put new approaches into practice, to jettison tried and trusted lessons, to evaluate one's own work as a teacher, to share that evaluation with colleagues, and to be prepared to continue in the face of failure or student resistance to the unfamiliar. In such collaborative activities the language tutor may well experience considerable stress in the consultant role, but for subject tutors the amount of risk-taking cannot be underestimated.

It also became clear that even where staff were used to working in course teams to deliver an integrated course 'package', this experience did not necessarily of itself affect actual teacher behaviour in the classroom, and that relatively traditional teaching methods co-exist quite happily with new developments in the curriculum.

Implications for FE colleges

The framework which is essential for such work to continue and become fully part of the college's way of operating requires both active support at senior management level, and an enthusiasm and interest from teaching staff. Opportunities for in-depth professional staff development should exist, with staff participation encouraged and recognized. Such in-depth development of individuals can then be supported and disseminated through course teams or similar group-ings, by subject tutors and ESL tutors working together. Language awareness is not, however, something one can pick up in the staffroom over a cup of coffee, but requires systematic long-term staff develop-ment initiatives. A college commitment begins rather than ends with the appointment of staff to specialist roles: Is the ESL tutor to work with staff or with students? How clear are the long-term objectives of any team-teaching arrangements? Are these the best ways to deploy scarce teaching resources? How can relatively junior staff have an impact across the curriculum and across the college? Are expectations unreal-istic? How can such changes in the curriculum or mode of delivery be incorporated into management practices, into the admission and coun-selling of students, course planning, staff timetabling, allocation of resources etc.? What should be the organizational response to the presence of bilingual students?

There is an essential ambiguity in providing English language support targeted at those bilingual students who require specific or additional tuition to reach an appropriate level of competence in English and to realize their potential for gaining qualifications, for access on to training courses, or for finding suitable employment.

Whilst facilitating access on to mainstream courses and providing integrated language support is crucial for equality of opportunity, there always remains the danger of labelling all bilingual students as being in need of support or help in order to achieve.

The benefits of tailor-made tutoring are unlikely to outweigh the advantages for a student of being firmly located within mainstream provision, among members of the same peer group, preparing for the same qualifications. Singling out individuals or groups of students for special or extra tuition has seldom carried with it high status and esteem from other staff or students. ESL tutors themselves can equally be affected by the low status accorded to their clientele. There is obviously an urgent need to focus on language potential rather than language poverty; to find ways of emphasizing the linguistic sophistication of many bilingual and multilingual students, to find ways of accrediting facility in languages other than English, and to look for vocational and academic relevance within a multiracial and multilingual society. For too long the concern has been with what such students cannot do, rather than with accreditation of existing levels of achievement and linguistic skills.

English language support alone is therefore too narrow as a main focus. An institution which is committed to providing genuine equality of opportunity and combating low teacher expectations, must be developing policy and strategy to counter all aspects of racism. Rather than operating in a policy vacuum, the work of an ESL team becomes part, but only a part, of a general anti-racist strategy located clearly within mainstream college provision.

The Inner London Education Authority

Language awareness training for subject specialists has developed from work done by Industrial Language Training (ILT) in the 1970s. When ILT was established as a national scheme in 1974, its brief was to improve communication in the multiracial workplace. One element of this was teaching ESL to ethnic minority workers, but the two-way nature of communication was recognized in the accompanying training for management, training staff and trades unionists. Initially this consisted largely of background information about the cultures and languages of the workers, together with exercises which enabled the managers to examine their own use of language. Since then the methodology has been greatly extended to reflect new developments in linguistic theory, new approaches in language teaching methodology and, most importantly, to respond to new pressures in the social and economic climate, particularly the growth of racism in Britain. (Roberts and Brookes, 1985.) Outside ILT, those who were working with bilingual students in general community and adult education also found that they were being asked to provide language awareness training for groups who had contact with their students, e.g. health workers, careers advisers, librarians, workers in advice agencies. Similar training methods were used and, with the publication of many of the ILT materials (Yates, Christmas and Wilson, 1981), these approaches became available to a wider range of trainers.

The growth of this type of training, however, has not been determined solely by the providers. ESL has been a particularly dynamic area of language teaching and one area of provision has always been for students who wish to continue their general education in this country or to take up training opportunities in MSC-funded schemes. The particular language and communication needs of these students were analysed by ESL teachers, drawing on a variety of theoretical and educational developments including the concept of 'language across the curriculum', sociolinguistic research on classroom interaction and the work done in the area of English for Specific Purposes. More recently it has been recognized that students will benefit more from the provision of good quality language support than from long periods spent learning English in ESL courses and this has led to a shift in resources towards the mainstream classroom. In the early 1980s linked-skills courses were established in which bilingual students studied vocational or recreational subjects with language back-up being provided by an ESL teacher who was present throughout the subject session. (See ILEA Linked-Skills Handbook, 1983.) The CET courses run by the Lancashire ILT unit and work done at Shipley College, West Yorkshire (McAllister and Robson, 1984) also developed models for team-working between subject and ESL specialists. All these initiatives meant that bilingual students were being taught by staff whose training was as specialists in vocational or academic areas. While many of them had developed techniques for checking understanding when teaching 'traditional' FE students, some of which were also useful when working with bilingual students, few of them had any professional training in the part that language plays in classroom learning. It has therefore become apparent that if language support for bilingual students is to succeed it must be accompanied by planned staff development for the subject specialists.

Language awareness training in the ILEA

The training to be described in the remainder of this paper is that which is currently being offered by the Inner London Education Authority. As the largest LEA in the country, the ILEA offers a wide range of provision for bilingual students wanting to continue their general or vocational education (see Hoadley-Maidment, Section 2) and is able to provide a variety of in-service staff development courses as part of this development.

The models of language awareness training described in Tables 1 and 2 have been developed in work with staff in further education colleges. Staff who have attended courses have included those teaching academic subjects such as maths and sciences, and vocational lecturers in engineering, business studies, hairdressing and clothing. Work has also been done with English and communications skills staff who have been offered separate introductory courses which build on their existing expertise in language analysis. Similar approaches are now also being used with tutors in adult education and with staff working in vocational training centres.

Many subject specialists have voiced concern about teaching bilingual students. This varies from a reluctance to enrol bilingual students on to courses on the grounds that their English is 'not good enough' through feelings of helplessness at not being able to 'get through' to bilingual students, to a wish to learn about approaches and materials that will enable these students to complete courses and pass examinations.

The demand for in-service training has grown enormously over the last three years in response to the following factors:

1.   The publication of authority policies on equal opportunity in the areas of race and sex. These have led colleges, departments and individual staff members to recognize the need to provide effectively for a multiracial and multilingual student body.

2.   The development of a range of provision for bilingual students with particular emphasis on providing language support for students on mainstream courses.

3.   Work being done in the area of Afro-Caribbean language, including the development of materials and methods to develop language aware-ness in both students and staff.

Planning training programmes

Tables 1 and 2 summarize the range of training models currently being offered in the ILEA.

The variety of models reflects the need to respond to the immediate needs of staff and to work within institutional and financial constraints. There is, however, an agreed approach underlying the different formats and the content and training methods used are very similar. The following steps are carried out at the planning stage:

1.   Analysis of the trainees' needs as they perceive them, and as they are perceived by ESL specialists working with them, by college management and by trainers with experience of this work.

2.   These needs are divided into three areas: skills, knowledge and attitudes. Realistic aims for each are chosen in relation to:

a) Participants' present knowledge about and experience of working with bilingual students.

b) The types of course on which they are working, for example, some staff are teaching groups composed entirely of bilingual students while others have small numbers of bilingual students in linguistically-mixed groups. The amount and nature of language support available to different courses also varies.

c) Participants' previous training, if any, in this area.

d) Practical and financial constraints. These will often determine the length of the course and the number of participants.

3.   The trainers are then chosen. Since there is at present only a small pool of people with experience in this area, the use of practitioners as trainers provides an element of 'training the trainers' in the course team. Courses are generally run by two ESL specialists, one of whom is an experienced trainer but who does not necessarily have classroom teaching experience in the subject area being addressed, while the second is chosen because they have worked in the subject area, usually as part of a language support team, but sometimes because they themselves have training and/or experience in the subject area. Where possible a subject specialist who has worked with an ESL tutor or team is also involved. This is almost essential for sessions which examine different forms of language support and team working.

4.   Course content is then agreed. All courses have an underlying philosophy that emphasizes the positive value of bilingualism,

recognizes the importance of anti-racist approaches to curriculum, materials and methods, acknowledges the role that students' other languages may play in learning, and draws attention to the fact that bilingual students may have already studied the subject in their own country and need to transfer the knowledge from one language and culture to the English context. Content and methodology are closely linked and both are decided at this stage in the planning.

Content and methodology

Most of the training currently being offered is at an introductory level. All these courses therefore aim to familiarize participants with a range of issues and to provide practical help for situations they face in their day-to-day teaching. A core of topics/issues now exists and trainers select from this, supplementing it with material that is directly relevant to the college or subject area. Second level courses, such as the nine-hour courses for subject and language specialists, are able to work more intensively on specific topics, e.g. analysing classroom language, choosing and developing materials.

The core

Introduction to cultural diversity. A brief introduction is given, usually through experiential exercises, e.g. filling in an application form in another language/script, stereotyping exercises. The aim is to help participants identify their own learning needs in this area and then to suggest ways in which they can increase their knowledge, for example, by providing a suitable book list on cultural background and immigrant experiences. In addition to this short formal session, issues related to culture and race are considered as they arise in other parts of the course.

Introduction to language. All participants need to acquire some knowledge of the main features of language before moving on to examine its use in the classroom. Some groups appreciate a formal input in lecture form but other methods may be used, e.g. asking participants to reflect on language they would need when holidaying or living in a country such as Greece or China, and then drawing out the theory from the discussion. Experiential methods are also used, for example, participants are given the chance to learn another language. Rather than using a traditional 'foreign language lesson' participants are often asked to learn a craft skill in another language. While this is sometimes taught in a language spoken by their students, e.g. Bengali, French is often chosen because it is the only language that most English people will have learnt at school. As most bilingual students studying subjects are not beginners in English this experience more truly reflects their situation than does a lesson in a totally new language. Exercises which have been used include pattern-cutting in French (with engineers), making beurre manié (with engineers), interpreting the general instructions on a French dressmaking pattern (with clothing staff) and dictation of a list of names from different languages and cultures (with business studies staff).

Student language use. As many bilingual students in further education appear to be fluent users of English and speak in local accents it is

Table 1 Models of training offered centrally

Format	Aims	Advantages	Disadvantages
One day conference for subject specialists and language teachers	1. Raise awareness of issues 2. Put over information to a large group quickly 3. Enable staff to meet, break down isolation	1. Can be aimed at key people 2. Attracts staff who would not want to participate in larger course 3. Can cover a broad range of issues, depending on format 4. Develops informal individual links 5. May lead to further training, e.g. working parties	1. May only attract staff who are already interested 2. Cannot do much real training 3. Dissemination – can be helped by publishing a conference report
10–18 hour introductory courses for subject staff	Introduction to skills and issues	1. Immediately applicable 2. Can focus on particular heads of the subject 3. Participants welcome chance to meet colleagues from other institutions	1. Numbers: only feasible in a large authority/area 2. Mixed interests/level of participants 3. Can only provide broad introduction
9-hour courses on particular language/classroom issues, for both subject and language staff	1. Aimed at those who have attended an introductory course 2. Develop skills and knowledge through more detailed study of particular topics/issues	1. Chance to work in-depth 2. Sharing of expertise between subject and language specialists	
Working parties	Intensive work on new areas	Result in products, e.g. reports, materials, training event	1. Dissemination 2. Logistics – timing meetings
Drop-in workshops	1. Support for individuals 2. Trouble-shooting	Immediate help on specific issues/problems	

Table 2 *Models of training offered within institutions*

Format	Aims	Advantages	Disadvantages
Whole team meetings/ training sessions	1. Consider language elements of each part of course 2. Analyse/modify/discuss syllabus, materials, assessment methods	1. Can focus on particular course 2. Can consider particular students 3. May broaden into consideration of language needs of all students	1. Limited time available 2. Not all courses have planned course meetings
Short courses (6–10 hours) for subject specialists from individual departments or faculties	Similar to central induction courses	1. Can be more specific than on a central course 2. Can reach more staff 3. Language specialists may also be able to attend	1. Cost/difficulty of releasing people (government funding, e.g. TRIST, may be available) 2. Sometimes done for very small numbers
Team-teaching on a particular course	Train the subject specialists through 'sitting by Nellie' methods, while providing language support for the students	1. Can really help subject specialists to think through the issues 2. Cross-fertilization between subject and language specialists	Only working with individual teachers, so expensive
Working parties	Develop curricula, materials for a particular course	1. Chance to work in-depth over a period of time 2. Pool expertise 3. Useful when new courses being developed, e.g. CPVE	Need to consider staff development in order to spread the findings
Externally-funded special project, e.g. FEU	To undertake a specific, pre-determined range of activities	1. Can draw in outside expertise 2. Solves resources problem and leads to more intensive development work 3. Disseminated through project report	1. Constraint of project framework 2. External funding may limit flexibility

important to alert participants to the fact that they use two or more languages regularly and operate in two cultures in their daily lives. This is done through exercises such as the study of a communications network and case studies. On longer courses participants may be asked to talk to one of their own students and then report back to the group on his/her pattern of language use.

An important part of the course is the examination of examples of students' use of English, both spoken and written. Participants analyse examples of student writing and speech and, after discussion of the reasons for errors of different types, the session considers strategies that they may use to help students overcome these. Group work is often used here.

Issues in classroom teaching

Teacher language. ESL specialists find that bilingual students often misunderstand subject teachers because they are unable to follow their methods of presenting information. These may include a lot of colloquial language and idiom, and few opportunities for checking understanding. Discussion of practical ways in which teachers may adapt their methodology when teaching bilingual students is done through exercises and often based on the analysis of video or audio tapes.

Study skills. Many bilingual students lack appropriate study skills and appear to take little responsibility for their own learning. This session provides an opportunity to learn about forms and styles of education in different cultures, to examine the relationship between developing study skills and general language learning and to make practical suggestions which will help students to develop skills that are needed for studying within the British educational system.

Teaching materials and assessment. Since much of the teaching material used in further education is written (textbooks, handouts, worksheets) and examinations have until recently been almost entirely written to time, examples of material are examined and participants work on adapting and writing supplementary materials for use with bilingual students. This session also provides an opportunity to look at cultural bias and racism in materials.

Working with ESL specialists in course teams

Work has recently been done on models of language support. Most courses use examples from this and other work as the basis for discussion of the nature of the partnership between language and subject specialists. Many subject specialists have questions and some understandable fears about this new way of working, so the session is normally run jointly by an ESL practitioner and a subject lecturer with experience of language support work. Issues covered include the following. Who controls the syllabus? How to liaise effectively outside the classroom. What can/should the ESL specialist do when giving language support within the subject class?

Conclusion   The work described in this paper is a recent development in in-service training and as such is still changing rapidly. It is hoped that readers will feel able to draw on the ideas presented to develop the work further and to apply it to a wider range of contexts. Greater prominence has been given to the role of language in recent government initiatives, including the Swann report, and in new curricular developments such as CPVE and GCSE, and this type of training will be required if classroom teachers are to implement their proposals.

References   FEU PROJECT NO. RP198: *Communications in a Multicultural Society* (in press)

ILEA LINKED-SKILLS WORKING PARTY (1984) *Linked Skills: a handbook for skills and ESL tutors*, National Extension College, Cambridge

McALLISTER, JEAN AND ROBSON, MARGARET (1984) *Building a Framework*, National Extension College, Cambridge

ROBERTS, CELIA AND BROOKES, THEO (1985) 'No Five Fingers Are All Alike' in *English as a Second Language in the United Kingdom*, ELT Documents 121, Pergamon Press

ROBSON, M. (1988) *Language, Learning and Race*, Longman for the FEU

YATES, VALERIE, CHRISTMAS, ELISA, AND WILSON, PETER (1981) *Cross-Cultural Training: Developing Skills and Awareness in Communication, A Manual for Trainers*, National Centre for Industrial Language Training, Southall, Middlesex

Appendix 1: Glossary of terms

Bilingual   People who regularly use more than one language are described as bilingual or, if they use more than two languages, multilingual. This definition does not assume any specified level of fluency in any of the person's languages.

Black   The term now generally used to describe British people who are of Afro-Caribbean and Asian origin and, by extension, other people and groups who are subject to racial and/or cultural discrimination.

Culture   This term is used in its anthropological sense to describe the complex pattern of beliefs, customs, traditions, ideas, social norms and values, family and social groupings, organization and activities which are shared by members of a community.

English as Second Language (ESL)   In Britain this term is used to refer to the philosophy, approaches and methodology used in teaching English to bilingual students who are, or expect to be, permanently resident in this country and who wish to participate in education, employment and the general life of British society. A distinction is made between ESL and English as a foreign language. The latter is offered to students who intend to live in their countries of origin but who wish to learn English for education, employment or leisure purposes.

Ethnicity   The cluster of beliefs, attitudes and behaviours which distinguishes one's own social, racial or cultural group from others. Such groups are not necessarily synonymous with race or racial identity.

Ethnic minority groups   Groups living in Britain who have a distinct racial and/or cultural identity.

Ethnocentric   The tendency to view events from the perspective of one's own culture. In educational writing the term is often used to describe approaches that are eurocentric, i.e. emphasize European values, achievements and approaches at the expense of others.

Equal opportunity   This concept maintains that all sections of the population should have equal chances to advance in terms of education, social mobility or career advancement. Equal opportunity issues may arise in relation to gender, race, religion, class, disability or sexual orientation.

Immigrant   The term is used by the government in defining eligibility for funding certain projects as well as in legislation relating to immigration and nationality. It can only be applied to people who have come to Britain and not to those who have been born here. As a descriptive term, however, it has pejorative overtones, and other terms such as black or ethnic minority are generally preferable.

Racism   A brief definition of this term is that racism equals prejudice plus power. In British education, much attention is paid to institutional racism. This occurs where institutions such as schools, colleges and LEAs maintain a set of rules, procedures and practices, perhaps unconsciously, which operate to deny equal opportunities to black people whether as students or staff.

Multi-ethnic education   There has been a range of responses to the recognition of the educational needs of multi-racial Britain. Multi-ethnic education was seen as a response in terms of acknowledging and reflecting racial and cultural diversity through interest in the culture of the areas of origin and the relations between this and British culture.

Anti-racist education   This approach differs from others in that it has been developed from a black perspective. It maintains that the main problem for black children is the result of racism within the education system and that equal opportunity will only be achieved when the various forms this takes have been identified and erradicated.

Abbreviations   **ALBSU**   Adult Literacy and Basic Skills Unit. National resource agency for adult basic education which also has a brief for ESL.

Access courses   Courses for mature students without formal qualifications to enable them to reach the standards required to enter higher education. Such courses are run by further education colleges and linked to polytechnics.

ACSET   Advisory Council for the Selection, Education and Training of Teachers. This body also credits a scheme of part-time in-service training for teachers of adults.

AE   Adult education

AEI   Adult education institute. Education for adults within the ILEA is provided through these institutions, which offer part-time tuition in a range of settings.

ALU   Adult Language Use Survey. Carried out by the Linguistic Minorities Project. (see Reid)

BTEC   Business and Technical Education Council: joint examination board providing a range of qualifications in vocational areas. (see Rosenberg)

CGLI   City and Guilds of London Institute: examining body providing a wide range of examinations in vocational subjects.

CPVE   Certificate of Prevocational Education. (see Rosenberg)

CRC   Community Relations Councils.

CRE   Commission for Racial Equality.

CSE   Certificate of Secondary Education: examinations formerly taken at age 16. Now subsumed into GCSE.

DES   Department of Education and Science.

DHSS   Department of Health and Social Security. This department is responsible for the operations of the Benefits system in the UK.

EAP   English for academic purposes. A branch of English as a Foreign Language. Teaches the English needed for studying in English at university and higher education levels.

EMT   English as a mother tongue. Term used to distinguish between ESL and the English taught to students who speak English as their first language.

ESF   European Social Fund.

ESP   English for special purposes. A branch of English as a foreign language.

FE   Further education. That part of the education system which exists to enable students to pursue studies of a technical, vocational or general academic nature beyond school-leaving age. Further education colleges cater for 16–19 year olds and for mature students.

FEU   Further Education Unit. National research and development unit for work related to further education. Linked with the DES.

GCE   General Certificate of Education. The examination is in two parts: Ordinary ('O') level taken at age 16 and Advanced ('A') level taken after a further two years' study. From 1988 'O' level is replaced by GCSE.

GCSE   General Certificate of Secondary Education. From 1988 this replaces GCE 'O' level and CSE as the main examination system in English secondary schools. (see Rosenberg)

HE   Higher education. The term usually used to describe education at the level of universities and polytechnics.

ILEA   Inner London Education Authority. The local education authority serving the twelve inner London boroughs.

ILT   Industrial Language Training. (see Cheetham)

JMB   Joint Matriculation Board: examination board which provides, inter alia, a test of English for overseas students wishing to enter HE. (see Rosenberg)

LEA   Local Education Authority. Education in England and Wales is organized and delivered through local government at the level of metropolitan boroughs or counties.

LMP   Linguistic Minorities Project. (see Reid)

MSC   Manpower Services Commission. Government training agency funding a variety of projects, including YTS. (see Cheetham)

NATESLA   National Association of Teachers of English as a Second Language to Adults. Professional association of ESL teachers.

NCILT   National Centre for Industrial Language Training. The national resource and training unit supporting ILT. (see Cheetham)

NCVQ   National Council for Vocational Qualifications. Umbrella organization for examination boards. (see Rosenberg)

NNEB   Nursery Nurses Examination Board.

NWRAC   North-West Regional Advisory Council. This organization provides a test of English for bilingual students. (see Rosenberg)

PICKUP   Professional, Industrial and Commercial Up-dating. An MSC-funded scheme to enable people to in employment to up-date their skills.

RAC   Regional Advisory Councils for further education. A major source of in-service training.

REPLAN   MSC-funded scheme for work with adult unemployed.

RSA CIT   Royal Society of Arts Certificate in Initial Teaching. A part-time in-service qualification for ESL teachers. (see Evans)

RSA Dip.   TESL FACE Royal Society of Arts Diploma in the Teaching of English as a Second Language (Further, Adult and Community Education). The main specialist professional in-service qualification for ESL teachers. (see Evans)

RSA ESL Profile   A system of accreditation for ESL students. (see Dunman)

Section 11   Funding provided by the Home Office for projects related to the needs of people from the New Commonwealth.

TEC   Technician Education Council.

TRIST   Training Related In-Service Training. The scheme has now been replaced by the LEA Training Grant Scheme (LEATGS).

TOPS   Training Opportunities Program. MSC-funded training programme for adult unemployed.

Urban Aid   Central government funding provided for work in inner cities.

WRNAFE   Work-Related Non-Advanced Further Education. 75 per cent of this work is now funded by central government through the MSC.

YTS   Youth Training Scheme. Two-year MSC-funded training scheme for school-leavers.

Appendix 2: Names and addresses of examining boards

Royal Society of Arts
8 John Adam Street
Adelphi
London WC2N 6EZ

City and Guilds London Institute
78 Portland Place
London W1N 4AA

Joint Board for Pre-Vocational Education
46 Britannia Street
London WC1X 9RG

Business and Technical Education Council (BTEC)
Central House
Upper Woburn Place
London WC1H 0HH

Institute of Linguists
Mangold House
24A Highbury Grove
London N5

Northwestern Regional Advisory Council for Further Education,
incorporating the Union of Lancashire and Cheshire Institutes
The Town Hall
Walkden Road
Worsley
Manchester M28 4QE

GCSE. Syllabuses available from the regional examining groups:

Southern Examining Group
Associated Examining Board
Stag Hill House
Guildford
Surrey GU2 5XJ

London and East Anglia Group
East Anglian Examinations Board
The Lindens
Lexden Road
Colchester CO3 3RL

Midland Examining Group
University of Cambridge Local Examinations Syndicate
Syndicate Buildings
1 Hills Road
Cambridge CN1 2EU

Northern Examining Association
Joint Matriculation Board
Manchester M15 6EU

Welsh Group
Welsh Joint Education Committee
245 Western Avenue
Cardiff CF5 2YX

Northern Ireland Examinations Council
Beechill House
42 Beechill Road
Belfast BT8 4RS

NCVQ (National Council for Vocational Qualifications)
222 Euston Road
London NW1 2BZ

Appendix 3: Other sources of information

The British Council
English Language Services Department
10 Spring Gardens
London SW1A 2BN

Commission for Racial Equality
Elliot House
10–12 Allington Street
London SW1
Tel: 01-828 7022

Centre for Multi-Cultural Education
Institute of Education
Bedford Way
London WC1
Tel: 01-636 1500

Runnymede Trust
178 North Gower Street
London NW1 2BN
Tel: 01-387 8943

British Refugee Council
Bondway House
3/9 Bondway
London SW8 1SJ
Tel: 01-582 6922

Centre for Information on Language Teaching & Research (CILT)
Regents College
Inner Circle
Regents Park
London NW1 4NS
Tel: 01-486 8221/2/3/4

Further Education Unit
Elizabeth House
York Road
London SE1 7BR
Tel: 01-934 9411

Adult Literacy & Basic Skills Unit (ALBSU)
Kingsbourne House
229–231 High Holborn
London WC1V 7DA
Tel: 01-405 4017

Department of Education and Science
Publications Despatch Centre
Honeypot Lane
Canons Park
Stanmore
Middlesex HA7 1AZ

Contributors

Yasmin Alibhai has worked as a trainer in equal opportunities and anti-racism, and has extensive experience of training in the Health Service, Civil Service, local authorities, education authorities and community groups. She was formerly a Senior Lecturer in English as a Second Language at the Industrial Training Unit, Southwark Institute, and is currently Race and Society Editor for the journal *New Society*.

Apu Bagchi was the multi-ethnic education coordinator at City and East London College before taking up his present post at Bilston Community College. He has extensive teaching experience in the further education sector. He was formerly a lecturer at Bedford College of Higher Education for eleven years. He has an MSc in social sciences and a Dip.Ed (University of London). Initially educated in Calcutta, India, he has been living in Britain for over 20 years.

Mike Baynham worked for a number of years as an ESL organizer in West London. He is currently a senior lecturer in adult basic education at the Lee Community Education Centre, Goldsmiths' College. He has published a number of articles on ESL and literacy work with bilingual students and is on the editorial groups of *Language Issues*, the journal of NATESLA, and the RaPAL (Research and Practice in Adult Literacy) Bulletin.

Rakesh Chander Bhanot was born in India and came to the UK in 1961. He has been involved in English language teaching and teacher training since 1972 and has taught in Spain, West Gemany and the UK. At present he is Senior Lecturer in the Department of English Studies at Hammersmith and West London College, as well as the multi-ethnic education coordinator. An examiner for the RSA and the Cambridge Syndicate boards, he has also contributed to various ELT journals and was the first editor of *Language Issues*. He is a member of the editorial boards of *Artrage* and *Multi-Ethnic Education Review*.

Brian Cheetham started his involvement with language teaching in the field of EFL, and for the last 12 years has been primarily concerned with ESL, both overseas (in Papua New Guinea) and in Britain, where he has worked in colleges, a vocational skills training centre, and for the Industrial Language Training Service.

Monica Collingham has worked in English language teaching and teacher training since 1972. She has taught in the UK and West Germany, and in Hong Kong, where she was an Assistant Director of Studies at the British Council. Until recently she was ESL Organizer at Tower Hamlets AEI (ILEA), and is currently a freelance lecturer and teacher trainer.

Sheila Dunman has worked for Coventry LEA since 1975 as organizer for the teaching of ESL to adults. Previous to that, her teaching experience included two years EFL work in Sweden and five years teaching ESL in a variety of schools in Birmingham. Before going to Coventry, she spent three years as a lecturer in the Education Department at Worcester College of Higher Education.

Elizabeth Evans has an MA in Twentieth Century American and English Literature. She has worked as an EFL/ESL teacher and teacher trainer at Waltham Forest College since 1972. In 1984 she was employed by NATESLA as the researcher on a one-year, DES-funded project into the training needs of teachers of ESL. She was the Chief Assessor of the RSA Certificate of Initial Training (ESL) scheme. Her current interests include the development of modular systems of teacher training.

Miriam Faine worked as an EFL teacher and teacher trainer in Rome and London for five years. She has taught ESL in London for six years, mostly to 15- to 19-year-olds in further education colleges. Her final post was as Senior Lecturer in English as a Second Language at Hackney College (ILEA). Since writing this article she has returned to her home city of Melbourne, Australia.

Pamela Frame is head of Faculty at Greenhill College, Harrow. She has extensive experience of ESL teaching and ESL teacher training in the adult/ further education fields and was Chief Assessor for the RSA Dip. TESL (FACE). She is a former chair of NATESLA and has recently completed a project on Language Across the Curriculum in FE, funded through the FEU.

Katherine Hallgarten was the coordinator of the ALBSU-funded Independent Learning Project at Morley College, London 1984–6. Before this she was a teacher and organizer with Neighbourhood English Classes and Head of the ESL Department, Islington Adult Education Institute. She is a former chair of NATESLA and is currently Vice Principal at Tower Hamlets Institute.

Elizabeth Hoadley-Maidment worked in the ILEA Language and Literacy Unit, where she was co-ordinator for work with bilingual students in further education. She was formerly Staff Development Officer at the National Centre for Industrial Language Training and Chief Examiner of the RSA Dip. TESL (FACE). She is now Community Education Development Officer for Oxford-shire Education Department.

Elizabeth Knight graduated in English Literature at Leicester University and has a doctorate in East African Literature (Universities of Sheffield and Nairobi). She completed a PGCE in TESL and TEFL in 1976 at Leicester University's School of Education and also has the RSA Dip. TESL. Since 1980 she has been teaching ESL in further education and adult education institutes in Inner London. Currently Head of the ESL Section at Haringey Community College, she is working on self access materials for bilingual students with the National Extension College.

Zorina Ishmail-Bibby comes from Guyana, South America. She has been involved in teaching English for a long time, having worked as a home tutor volunteer and part-time tutor in Northampton, where she now works full-time as English tutor, teacher trainer and volunteer home tutor organizer. Her main interests besides work are writing, dance and travel. Her short stories have been broadcast on Radio 4, the World Service, and published in the Arts Council's New Short Stories series. She also writes poetry and has given poetry readings.

Liz Lawson has taught EFL in Sweden and Spain, trained teachers in Poland for the British Council and taught English in further education in the North East. She is now teaching ESL at Islington Adult Education Institute in Inner London and is an assessor for the RSA ESL Profile Certificate. She is particularly interested in the development of counselling for students in the adult education sector.

Jean McAllister began ESL/EFL teaching in 1974 and, from 1976 to 1978, was involved in an Industrial Language Training Unit in West Yorkshire. In 1978 she was seconded to Shipley College to establish a special access to FE course for 16- 19-year-old second language learners. On the basis of this innovative work at the college, she and Margaret Robson co-wrote the book *Building a Framework* (NEC) in the early eighties. Since 1985, Jean McAllister has been Vice Principal at Shipley College.

Julia Naish worked until recently in the ILEA Language and Literacy Unit and had responsibility for developing ESL work in adult education. Previously she was Borough Language Coordinator in Camden and before that worked with Industrial Language Training in North London. Formerly Chair of NATESLA, she has experience of both ESL teacher training and materials writing. She is now a Vice Principal at the Central London Adult Education Institute. With Sandra Nicholls, she is co-author of *Teaching English as a Second Language* (BBC, 1980), and has contributed to a number of publications.

Sandra Nicholls has published widely in EFL and ESL, including two BBC radio series. She was chief examiner for the RSA Diploma in TEFL for five years, and she initiated and was chief examiner for the RSA Diploma in the Teaching of English as a Second Language to Adults in Further, Adult and Community Education, and the RSA Initial Certificate in Teaching English as a Second Language to Adults. She has contributed to seminars and conferences in Australia, Canada and Africa. She was Director of the Inner London Education Authority's Language and Literacy Unit from 1979–1985.

Krystyna Piasecka started to teach EFL in Poland in 1976. She returned to England in 1979 and has been teaching ESL since 1980. She now organizes ESL at Hammersmith and North Kensington AEI.

Euan Reid works in the Department of English for Speakers of Other Languages at the University of London Institute of Education, where he is currently engaged in teaching and research relating to initial teacher training. He was previously a research officer on the Linguistic Minorities Project, then Director of the Community Languages and Education Project, both based at the London Institute. With colleagues on the Linguistic Minorities Project he is a co-author of *The Other Languages of England* (R&KP, 1985).

Celia Roberts worked at the National Centre for Industrial Language Training for eight years. She has also taught in India, Spain and Hong Kong. She has published various reports and articles on ESLA and inter-ethnic communication and is author of *The Interview Game* (BBC, 1985). She is currently Reader in Language Studies at Ealing College of Higher Education.

Margaret Robson has worked as a teacher of language and communications for six years at Shipley College of Further Education and is co-author with Jean McAllister of *Building a Framework* — developing communication skills with ESL students (NEC, 1984). She has recently taken the work further in a two-year research project for the Further Education Unit, the outcome of which is a report, *Language, Learning and Race* (Longmans/FEU, 1988). She is currently working for the FEU as coordinator of the Curriculum Change aspect of the FEU project 'Staff Development for a Multicultural Society'.

Sheila Rosenberg moved from teaching English as a mother tongue to ESL in 1975 and has been teaching in and writing about the field ever since. She has had experience of the full range of provision for bilinguals, from home tuition to support for students on mainstream courses in further education. While Senior Lecturer for ESL at Southwark College, she was particularly interested in issues raised by testing and examinations. She has now joined the ILEA Inspectorate.

Marina Spiegel was born in Argentina and came to Britain at the age of eight. A graduate of London University, with an MA in Adult Education, she has been a teacher since 1974. She took up her current post with the ILEA as an ESL organizer in 1983.